FORMS
OF THE
MODERN
NOVELLA

FORMS
OF THE
MODERN
NOVELLA

MARY DOYLE SPRINGER

THE UNIVERSITY OF
CHICAGO PRESS
CHICAGO AND LONDON

For Norman
and for Mark and Joshua

MARY DOYLE SPRINGER received her
Ph.D. from the University of California
and is associate professor of English at
Saint Mary's College in Moraga,
California.

The University of Chicago Press,
Chicago 60637
The University of Chicago Press, Ltd.,
London

Library of Congress Cataloging in Publication Data

Springer, Mary Doyle.
    Forms of the modern novella.

Bibliography: p.
    Includes index.
    1. Fiction—20th century—History and criticism.
2. Literary form.   I. Title.
PN3503.S66   823'.02   75-9055
ISBN 0-226-76986-0

CONTENTS

FOREWARD   ix

1. APPROACH TO THE NOVELLA
THROUGH ITS FORMS   1
*The desert area of novella theory,
with pious hopes for a better
future*   2
*Length as essence, and how little
that helps*   7
*A beginning tour of novella
forms, and how much they
might help*   11
*Polemic on the value of formal
analysis and classification*   14

2. HOW DO I KNOW I'M LISTENING
TO A MESSAGE? or MODERN
APOLOGUE'S ANSWER TO
ALLEGORY   18
The degree of "caring" in The
Woman Who Rode Away   25
"Caring" in The Fox   31
Larger than life Spotted
Horses   32
Devices of Old Man   37

*A compendium of the signals
of apologue* 39
The magnitude of apologue 51

3. THE APOLOGUE THAT
PREACHES BY EXAMPLE   54
*The exemplary downfall of
Crane's Maggie* 57
*Atypicality in the making of a
typical "Day"* 65
*An unexemplary example in
James'* The Pupil 72

4. LOOSER AND TIGHTER PLOTS
AND THE POCKET OF GOOD IN
NOVELLA SATIRES   77
*Swiftian-Voltarian debts of
Vonnegut* 78
Parodic plot in Mann's
Tristan 81
Henry James, The Death of the
Lion, *and the plot question* 83
The positive heart of satire 87
*The good in social protest
novellas of Elliott, Orwell, and
Vonnegut* 92
*Miss Hurter and the positive
good in plotted novella
satires* 95
The satirist and the didact 97

5. DEGENERATIVE "TRAGEDY" IN
THE NOVELLA   100
Degeneration in Mann's
Death in Venice 102
*Struggle against degeneration in
Kafka's* The Metamorphosis 105
*Situational degeneration in three
James novellas* 109

*The pathos of degeneration
accompanied by
"education"* 116
*The art of degeneration
in* Melanctha 117
*Tragic action vs. "tragical"
apologue* 125

6. THE SINGLE CHARACTER
REVEALED TO US, WHO MAY BE
REVEALED TO HIMSELF, AND WHO
MAY OR MAY NOT PROFIT BY IT 128
Character revelation in Colette's
Julie de Carneilhan 132
*Questions with answers: The
learning plot in* Old Mortality *and*
The Virgin and the Gipsy 137
*The maturing of Tonio Kröger
and some others* 148

AFTERWORD 159
APPENDIX 161
NOTES 165
SELECTED BIBLIOGRAPHY 177
INDEX 185

FOREWORD

When I first began this generic study of the novella, it seemed to be largely an off-the-wall interest of my own, one very likely to be pursued in lonely magnificence, in notebooks which would be discovered Too Late, and then They would all be sorry.

As the study went on, I began to perceive that other readers love novellas as much as I do—they print and read so many of them—and that there was open to me not only an opportunity to define the novella but also to expand in various useful ways the whole "rhetoric of fiction" so brilliantly opened up by Percy Lubbock, Wayne C. Booth, Sheldon Sacks, and others. All that Booth taught us about the rhetoric of narrative modes could, I began to see, expand to include a rhetoric of character, of diction distinct from narration, of plot fulfillment, and ultimately a rhetoric of the form of the story as a whole. And novellas then became not only a delight in themselves but also, because of their relative purity of form, ideal examples for expanding prose fiction theory.

My good luck all along the way was to encounter friends and critics who prevented the solitariness of the pursuit by matching my excitement with unexpected fervor, and to these I have accumulated heavy debts, an accounting of which is due.

I wish I could bequeath to all aspiring literary theorists my first reader and sternest critic, Ralph W. Rader. He has read several revisions ever since the book began as an article which, like James's fiction, refused to confine itself. He saw the shape of the work almost before I did. Both his praise and complaints were in the finest tradition of literary midwifery. And he did that hardest thing of all, which was to relax his criticism once my ideas were brought to fruition, regardless whether they agreed with his. He knows how to treasure disagreements more than victory, so as to let the truth about stories thrive under the ongoing dialogue. To thank him is irrelevant, and is too little to express my affection.

The credit for setting the fire belongs to my first teacher of literary form, Sheldon Sacks, who opened up a brave new world of thought to an eager Miranda. That I have taken ideas I learned from him and reshaped them according to my lights is the tribute every student owes to his finest teachers.

My best friend, husband, and favorite literary antagonist, Norman Springer, has been my model for intense literary study. I watched in amazement while he spent a whole year on a line by line analysis of a single Melville novella, and learned from him that one might spill blood in arguments over literary details and come out with knowledge well worth having. Though he was teaching his own classes and working on his own book, he cooked all the breakfasts and half the dinners while I was writing and let me leech as always on his enormous energy, intelligence, and warmth.

For steady encouragement, and advice on stylistic points of novellas in German, I am indebted to Hilde Gerson. In her death I have lost a treasured friend, and also some extraordinary literary conversations.

Advice and consent of the most helpful kind has come to me from such sharp-eyed and kindly readers of the book as Robert Bloom, Thomas Sloan, Wayne C. Booth, Patricia Rogow, Rafael Alan Pollock, and my Sister-sister, Mary Ellen Doyle. Any flaws that remain are against their better judgments, but they can't say I didn't meet all their objections, either by accepting or rejecting them.

1
APPROACH
TO THE
NOVELLA
THROUGH
ITS FORMS

It must soon become apparent that a short
novel is something in itself, neither a lengthily
written short story nor the refurbished attempt
at a novel sent out into the world with its hat
clapped on at the eightieth page.

Howard Nemerov

"Kinds" are the very life of literature, and
truth and strength come from the complete
recognition of them, from abounding to the
utmost in their respective senses and sinking
deep into their consistency.... The confusion
of kinds is the inelegance of letters and the
stultification of values....

Henry James

We propose to consider poems as unique
existent things the structural principles of
which are to be discovered, rather than as
embodiments of general truths about the
structure of poetry already adequately known.

R. S. Crane

W hat is a novella? And how would an answer to that question enhance our understanding and appreciation of those works we call novellas, or "short novels"? It will be my purpose in this and succeeding chapters to respond to these two questions, and to show that the answers can reflect understanding on modern fictional works of all sizes.

The desert area of novella theory, with pious hopes for a better future

In recent years there has been a strong show of critical interest in developing a theory of prose fiction, especially of the novel. There now exist works of the first importance defining forms of the novel, considering closely its separate formal elements, and studying how some of these elements are related to its rhetorical or emotional effects.[1] The short story, too, has begun to receive extensive formal consideration.[2] Curiously, the serious study of the novella remains an almost desert area. Readers have long been pleased with whatever it is that this genre has especially to offer (witness the recent proliferation of paperback anthologies of novellas). Yet, except for occasional brief thematic treatment,[3] several historical and technical studies limited to the German *novelle*,[4] and the admirable historical work of Gerald Gillespie on terminology,[5] critics generally offer only introductory commentary which avoids the task of defining the novella in more than a few words, or else they ignore it altogether as a separate entity.

Theorists of the short story usually attend to the question of length and of magnitude as though no works existed to enlighten their comparisons except short stories at the one extreme and long novels at the other. But the novella does not, when it is ignored, fade away and refuse to make trouble. Ignoring it as a separate genre can lead to strange, if not insupportable, formal judgments about some of these longer works. Speaking of Conrad's *Heart of Darkness,* one critic accounts for length partly on grounds that Marlow is simply "given to commentary and speculation"; and he treats Tolstoy's novella, *The Death of Ivan Ilyich,* as a condensation down to a short story—"albeit a rather long one"—of a life too boring to be expanded into a long novel.[6] In the case of short stories, the necessity of trying to incorporate into the discussion only a few of what I would separate out as novellas helps tempt the critic into niceties of classification which are sometimes helpful, sometimes overelaborate (the most ardent lover of formal distinctions may tire under such classifications as "painful" lined up against "tragedy" and "pathos," with subclasses of "romantic pathos" and "caustic pathos").[7]

Yet, when analysis does not serve to gather in longer works, there results a kind of gap in nature. Elizabeth Bowen speaks of the short story as "free from the *longueurs* of the novel and also exempt from the novel's conclusiveness—too often forced and false."[8] Where does this leave the novella: free as the short story, or stricken with conclusiveness like the novel?

That the novella has some existence of its own, more palpable than a phantom occupying shadowy space between a short story and a novel, is recognized mainly by the two groups who bump up against the question most conspicuously: writers of novellas, and editors of both novella anthologies and short-story anthologies.

Martha Foley, perhaps the best-known anthologist of American short stories, claims to have sat down with her predecessor, Edward O'Brien, who founded the *Best American Short Stories* annual series, and made a considered decision to "be responsible for the introduction of the word novella into the English language," mainly because she detested the term "novelette," which was "used in the sense of a condensed novel, a digest." O'Brien, it developed, had a handy acquaintance with an editor of the *Oxford English Dictionary*, whom he persuaded to include the word "novella." The story turns out somewhat unhappily: Martha Foley admits that the meaning of the word is still "often distorted" in dictionaries. The degree of clarity that she herself supplies can be left to my reader's judgment of the following imaginary dialogue she conducts with herself about definitions of the genres of prose fiction. When she asks herself "What *is* a short story?" the answer is: "I wish I knew.... A short story is a story that is not too long." And "if it is very long and interesting, I suppose it could be called a novel." Next question: "What about the novella?" Her answer:

> It is a beautiful form of writing, longer than a short story, shorter than a novel, which authors love. Many editors, including myself, have to forego it because of space limitations.[9]

Editors of novella anthologies seem to depend mainly on practice, or on custom, to define their choices. Thus, neither reader nor editor is surprised when he finds collected together such long-accepted "short novels" as Mann's *Death in Venice,* Dostoevsky's *Notes From Underground,* James's *Daisy Miller,* Joyce's *The Dead,* Kafka's *The Metamorphosis,* Melville's *Bartleby the Scrivener, Benito Cerano,* and *Billy Budd.* The difficulty arises when the editor necessarily departs from previous anthologies to make some choices not ordinarily encountered. At that point he seems to feel an implicit question which he does not wish to answer simply in terms of length or taste: "What definition of the novella accounts for the choice of these works as belonging under that title?" Under the relatively safe shelter of an "introduction" (which by custom can raise questions without providing full answers), the problem is taken up with minimal seriousness, and never with any scope which would begin to match the attention that has enlightened the study of the short story and of the novel.[10]

I should like to pause here at the outset of my discussion to agree with Foley and O'Brien that the term "novella" is the most useful one. My reasons are two: (1) I wish to stress both the dignity and separate identity of the novella—my whole purpose will be to help describe that identity; (2) the term is increasingly appearing as common currency—one sees it in film credits, in indexes of critical articles such as those provided by the Modern Language Association, and one hears it used among teachers and students of literature. As Percy Lubbock long ago pointed out, we are in need of a common language for discussing literature. One contradiction that must be faced is, that despite the above evidence favoring a public choice of the term novella, an overwhelming number of anthologies are titled with the term "short novels." I am convinced that this is because, in the absence of a concentrated empirical study of what factors define the novella as a distinct genre, the easiest way is to fall back more or less unconsciously into an assumption that Martha Foley recognized to be false, namely, that these works are condensations or digests of what might have been long novels if they had not ended as "short novels."

That there exist in literature such condensations of what should have been long novels is undoubted. But I believe that the key to understanding genre is to understand that such works are, in the relation of their size to their formal purposes, flawed. They are works whose architecture as a whole (though some of its parts may have beauty) has failed. There is a need to recognize that each genre is defined by its own special powers, and that these are not simply a matter of degree—that is, of the same powers expanded or contracted. If I am right in this, Vladimir Nabokov is treating the matter too casually when he says that the writer of novellas operates by "diminishing large things and enlarging small ones." As Mark Schorer puts it:

> The "possible" for the novel is different from the "possible" for the short story. The distinction is relative, and does not help very much to define either *genre*. Is it not necessary to look further, to ask whether the difference in unity between a short story and a novel is not rather one of kind than of degree? Do we not all the time read novels that we feel should have been short stories, and short stories that should have been novelettes, at least? Is it not that the unity of a novel can encompass one kind of thing and the unity of a short story another kind?[11]

The answer to these questions is clearly "yes," except that the "kind" in each of these genres is so various that I would use the plural and speak of "kinds" or "forms" that each of these genres can encompass.

John Galsworthy, though he does not think the matter through to an answer as Schorer does, produces a vivid metaphor to elucidate the problem:

> What dictates the size of the bottle into which we pour our wine—or vinegar? Certainly not deliberate resolution, for then one would have written nothing but stories of from ten to thirty thousand words.... The whole thing is a puzzle. Why should one have to write a novel when a certain figure, incident or idea takes possession of the imagination; a short story about a second incident or figure; and a tale of medium length around a third? I cannot answer; but I am convinced that he is in luck to whom the unseen hander-out of bottles offers the pint.[12]

A genre called, increasingly often, the "novella" does exist in terms, not simply of length, but of some kinds of things it does and in terms of some kinds of beauties which only the "pint" size contains—all of this intuited, when not clearly expressed, by both critics and authors.

Henry James, in his preface to *The Lesson of the Master,* clarifies the connection that exists between the length of fiction and its "organic form." He gives an obviously delighted account of what happened to him at the foundation of "the small square lemon-coloured quarterly" called "The Yellow Book":

> I was invited, and all urgently, to contribute to the first number, and was regaled with the golden truth that my composition might absolutely assume, might shamelessly parade in, its own organic form. It was disclosed to me, wonderfully, that—so golden the air pervading the enterprise—any projected contribution might conform, not only unchallenged but by this circumstance itself the more esteemed, to its true intelligible nature. For any idea I might wish to express I might have space, in other words, elegantly to express it—an offered license that, on the spot, opened up the millennium to the "short story." One had so often known this product to struggle, in one's hands, under the rude prescription of brevity at any cost, with the opposition so offered to its really becoming a story, that my friend's emphasized indifference to the arbitrary limit of length struck me, I remember, as the fruit of the finest artistic intelligence. [13]

James makes it quite clear that by opening up "the millennium to the 'short story'" he does not simply mean enlarging the short story and giving it a chance to breathe but rather that a distinct other genre which he calls the "nouvelle" is being given a new chance at separate existence and formal identity. He goes on to say:

> We had been at one—that we already knew—on the truth that the forms of wrought things, in this order, *were,* all exquisitely and effectively, the things; so that, for the delight of mankind, form might compete with form and might correspond to fitness; might, that is, in the given case, have an inevitability, a marked felicity. Among forms, moreover, we had had, on the dimensional ground—for length and breadth—our ideal, the beautiful and blest *nouvelle;* the generous, the enlightened hour for which

appeared thus at last to shine. It was under the star of
the *nouvelle* that, in other languages, a hundred interesting
and charming results ... had been, all economically, arrived
at.... It had taken the blank misery of our Anglo-Saxon
sense of such matters to organise, as might be said, the
general indifference to this fine type of composition. In
that dull view a "short story" was a "short story," and
that was the end of it. Shades and differences, varieties
and styles, the value above all of the idea happily *developed*,
languished, to extinction, under the hard-and-fast rule of
the "from six to eight thousand words"—when, for one's
benefit, the rigour was a little relaxed. For myself, I delighted
in the shapely *nouvelle*.

We have not yet really recovered from "the dull view that a 'short
story' was a 'short story,' and that was the end of it." We seem to
have missed a kind of turning point in genre. To escape our still
blank Anglo-Saxon sensibility, it seems useful to re-read James
employing such words for the novella as "blest and beautiful," and
also "shapely"—as though, if we were only to look, we might see
what shapes it had, and thus appreciate its blessedness and beauty.

In a *Paris Review* interview another master of the genre,
Katherine Anne Porter, seems to intuit some comparative definition
of the "short novel" when she says, "A novel is really like a
symphony, you know, where instrument after instrument has to
come in at its own time, and no other. I tried to write it [*Ship of
Fools*] as a short novel ... but it just wouldn't confine itself."[14]
Thomas Mann, in the preface to his "short stories" describes the
same kind of difficulty when he says, *"Death in Venice* proved
persistent well beyond the terminus which I had fixed for it."

*Length as essence, and
how little that helps*

In the notebooks of Henry James it is suggested that he may have
excluded a story from the collected edition of his works because it
"did not justify its length of twenty-five thousand words."[15] Another
time, what James called an "awfully good possibility" in a story idea
grew to an "unwieldy thirty-six thousand word tale." The question is
again very like the one of confinement or persistence raised by Porter
and Mann. How do works go about justifying their length or,

conversely, show themselves unwieldy? It is clear in all these cases that an author cannot safely choose length arbitrarily, since there are some things which a novella does better than a short story and better than a novel.

The length of the novella ought, in my view, simply to be accepted empirically: a count of any anthology of novellas (except, of course, anthologies that make no distinction that excludes short stories) will attest to a common length between 15,000 and 50,000 words. The kinds of works which are now recognized as novellas began to arise in the nineteenth century, with its publication habits as described in the quote from James above, and novella length has been as arbitrary as a magazine editor's rejection slip based on space; that is, authors have sometimes proceeded under the necessity of doing what *can* be done once length is enforced. Editors and publishers are probably as responsible as authors for the common count that causes E. M. Forster (in *Aspects of the Novel*) to say that literary works "when they contain 50,000 words or more, are called novels" —once again an empirical statement of fact which does not begin the discussion of novel forms but does carry some seeds of that discussion within it. A significant story is told of Howells (as editor) proposing a story idea to Henry James, which James refused because he "had quickly seen that he couldn't manage what he wanted within the limit of fifty thousand words."[16] Howells's limit is nothing but a fact of space—James's refusal, and its bases, are the subject of our real interest.

I would, if I could, avoid strict length limits, for they suggest something we are bound to feel is ridiculous, namely, that five hundred words over a certain length causes a short story to become a novella, and five hundred words less than a certain length causes a novel to become a novella—thus once more connecting all three as though they were merely extensions or reductions of each other.

My preference, in discussing word limits, would be to speak of "a fiction of a certain length" with no more, and no less, mystery than when one speaks of "a woman of a certain age": one knows she must have certain qualities unavailable either to youth or to old age, and we do not have to specify the exact number of pages in her book of life in order to know that. What the defining *qualities* of such a woman are, becomes the matter of much greater interest if one wants truly to know and appreciate her. And I wish to call sharp attention to the plural, "qualities," for it suggests what I shall hold to be centrally true of the novella: that it is not itself a single form, in the sense of being capable of realizing only one kind of affective power. As Gerald Gillespie concludes from his historical study, "The theorist dealing with the *novella* should always remember that, ultimately, *novellas* exist in the plural. This caution prevents blind concentration of attention on some specific example, some 'model' *novella* in the singular." [17] Let us assume as demonstrable, then, that *the novella is a prose fiction of a certain length (usually 15,000 to 50,000 words), a length equipped to realize several distinct formal functions better than any other length.*

The achievement I hope for will be a definition of the novella less by what it is (I have just said that what it *is* is simply a length of prose fiction), than by describing what it does: a series of formal functions which can best be achieved at that length, functions which cause authors intuitively or consciously to choose that length.

Stated another way, my central problem has by now defined itself rather clearly as a question of what Aristotle called "magnitude," and it is a problem susceptible of solution by formal theoretical modes that derive from Aristotle's thought on poetry. In the *Poetics* he calls that work beautiful which has "as much magnitude as is in accordance with what is likely or necessary." [18] Though his discussion is limited to the length of tragic plots, we can take for granted that "likely or necessary" can be extended to a discussion of that length which would be suitable, or "necessary," to the realization of *any* affective power, be that power tragic, comic, serious, didactic, satiric, or some subclass of these.

Authors must, then, discover the length appropriate to their formal purpose; if not, they risk failure of that purpose. In the aesthetics of short fiction, as in that of all the other arts, the right size for a work is not necessarily its actual size—it is possible to say that a statue is too tall, or a story too short. This is, of course, what James meant when he spoke, in the preface cited above, of stories having "languished, to extinction, under the hard-and-fast rule of the 'from six to eight thousand words'." To say that editors, for their own publication needs, have forced modern authors to operate at certain lengths, often arbitrary and precise, is not to credit editors with defining the genres of prose fiction. It says, rather, that editors have either caused authors' formal purposes to languish fatally, or forced them to formal purposes particular to a certain length. It points to the converse of the argument I have been making:—an author restrained by a short-story length will tend to restrict himself to certain kinds of formal purposes which can be most effectively realized at that length. Because James's formal purposes were very often understood by him to be appropriate to the novella length, he felt squeezed.

When I turn to the discussion of formal purposes, I enter an area of indebtedness too great to be covered in a footnote, to theorists of prose fiction whose concepts and method also derive from, and are logical extensions of, Aristotle's *Poetics,* chief among them Sheldon Sacks, R. S. Crane, Wayne Booth, and Elder Olson. All careful readers intuitively perceive that fictional works depend for their coherence on certain general, as well as particular, formal principles (it is a remarkable experience to watch students apprehend this unaided), but Sheldon Sacks has brought this intuition into conscious theory and method in the seminal first chapter of his book *Fiction and the Shape of Belief.* There Sacks delineates three major informing principles discoverable in prose fictions: *actions, apologues,* and *satires.* Since I expect to show that subforms of these are some of the forms which define the novella, it seems important to describe them.

All fiction consists in setting characters into some kind of motion, conflict, or action, but Sacks reserves the term *"Action"* for the kind of "unstable relations" between characters that are tightly plotted in order to be resolved into either a tragic, comic, or serious effect. *"Apologue"* makes use of the characters and what happens to them to maximize "the truth of a statement or statements," a principle which other critics variously call "allegory," "parable," or sometimes "fable." *"Satire"* takes its usual meaning: that informing principle whereby all parts of the fiction cohere in the purpose of ridiculing objects in the world outside the story.

As principles of wholeness, Sacks insists, these forms are "mutually exclusive," so that if we wish to understand, for example, a story which is formally an apologue, we must not confuse it with the kind of stories which formally are actions—thus whose ends are not primarily didactic—or the appreciation of the whole may be lost.

Everywhere that I employ the word "form" in my discussion I shall understand the term as Kenneth Burke, in *The Philosophy of*

Literary Form, minimally defines it: "The functioning of a structure to achieve a certain purpose," be that purpose ridicule, the centering on the truth of a statement, or the realization of a tragic, comic, or serious resolution of an action where the characters themselves are our chief concern. And I would enlarge upon Burke's definition by adding the stress that R. S. Crane lays on form as tightly connected in every case to potential feeling (*dynamis*), whether a feeling of ridiculousness (satire), a feeling that a statement is true (apologue), or a feeling for the fate of characters (action):

> Form as we conceive it is simply that which gives definite shape, emotional power, and beauty to the materials of man's experience out of which the writer has composed his work. [19]

In no case will I employ the word "form" to mean merely structure without that final "emotional power" of which the structure is only one cause: the power of a story being comparable to the "capacity to cut" in W. K. Wimsatt's metaphor of the poem as a carpenter's saw: "The goodness of a saw, its capacity to cut, is determined by the steel fashioned in a certain shape." [20]

And, just as form does not mean structure alone, neither will I employ it to mean weights and measures of parts separate from their formal power. In a discussion of Katherine Anne Porter's *Noon Wine* as it relates to genre, one critic describes the novella as "more ambitious than the short story. It introduces more characters, more fictional time, more motifs, more settings, and more revelatory moments." [21] What distinguishes it from the long novel, in this view, is simply compression of novelistic elements—a court trial is "recollected, not dramatized," and one gets "a sense of the passage of time without the drama of an extended action" that would be offered in a novel. Once more, the novella is reduced to definition that is too single (general) and relative: "more" items than a short story, less drama than a novel.

*A beginning tour of novella forms,
and how much they might help*

The novella is its own genre by means of taking its own forms. Chapter by chapter, I plan to discuss each of several formal

functions for which that "certain" novella word-limit seems necessary, together with a discussion of the devices that fulfill these
functions, so that we may recognize and enjoy them appropriately
when we come upon them again in other novellas than the ones I
shall choose to analyze. Lest my reader feel he is constantly waiting
for late guests to arrive at the party so that he can see what the whole
congregation looks like, it seems proper to begin by briefly listing
some of those functions which the novella seems definitively to
achieve.

1. *The serious "plot of character,"* [22] wherein the action is
resolved to serious effect in three variations of this plot: (a) simply
revealing the character (Colette's *Julie de Carneilhan*); (b) showing
the character in the process of learning (Porter's *Old Mortality*); and
(c) the character not only learning but beginning to profit from what
he learns (Mann's *Tonio Kröger*). In long novels, characters not only
learn but complete their process of change in a complexity of
interaction with other characters (James's *Portrait of a Lady*). When
the focus is on a single character revelation, or on a single isolated
learner, the novella is an appropriate length for that function.

2. *The degenerative or pathetic tragedy,* of which Mann's *Death
in Venice* is a prime example. It consists in the relentless, relatively
simple (in plot), and swift degeneration of a central character into
unrelieved misery or death. Its relentlessness and the depth of the
misery expand it beyond the single episode which often characterizes
the short story.

3. *Satire* which, whether loosely plotted (James's *The Death of the
Lion*) or an episodic structure of the Gulliver kind (Vonnegut's *Cat's
Cradle*), chooses the novella length because the object of ridicule is a
single one rather than a compendium of the follies of mankind.

4. *Apologue.* In order to demonstrate that apologues are a
prominent form in novellas (authors seem to undertake very long
prose apologues only at the risk of failure, for reasons I shall try to
suggest), I plan to undertake a description of the literary signals that
help distinguish modern prose fiction apologues from actions. Here
the ordinary reader's intuition can often be trusted better than the
judgment of the practical critic who has trained himself to find a
"theme" in every action, thus tending to turn his discussion away
from centrally absorbing characters, and by this ignoring the form
he is really dealing with. What a pity if such initial preconceptions
should cause us to talk about *Death in Venice* as an example of civic

corruption rather than attend to the unhappy fate of Aschenbach. In order to maintain the examination of theme where it is truly useful, namely, in those works whose organic unity depends on a theme or statement, we need to know how to recognize such works. The problem is a real one for modern literature; Aesop's fables presented themselves with their moral statements tacked on clearly at the end, and old allegories revealed themselves with characters who were personified abstractions (when Christian ploughs through the Slough of Despond, we know what he is formally about, as distinct from Aschenbach), but modern apologues "look like" other stories at first glance.

5. *The Example,* a subclass of apologue often dealing with a single character in incidents which are not plotted to aim at our feelings for the particular character but instead to make use of our feelings for didactic ends, for exposing this character through his actions, as one example of a large human type. Thus, the implicit statement of this type of apologue always begins in the same way: "It is like this to be . . ." (Crane's *Maggie, A Girl of the Streets*). As in the action plot of character, the concentration on a single character accounts in part for the novella length.

Once I have suggested, in the examination of a number of novellas, that the novella functions most often to achieve these several particular kinds of forms, perhaps I shall automatically have answered the question of what makes a novella short-but-not-so-short-as-a-short-story yet much less lengthy than a novel, and a genre independent of those other two. And, if the generalizations of this chapter should prove valid in the actual examination of the multitudes of novellas, they may lead to still another generalization. Apologues and plots of character are thought-provoking, serious forms; and novellas exist also in the realm of limited tragedy. If these predominate as the major types of the novella, they may be asking us to pay attention to the possibility that the novella lends itself especially to the serious or restrainedly tragic, seldom or never to the comic, though parts are often comic*al* in the service of satire and other forms. A remark by one anthology editor, that the novella is a "literary genre which specializes in themes that remind men of their own frailty," [23] led me to take a count of several other collections. None contained a novella whose principle of coherence could be called comedy.

Comedy is, of course, slippery of definition in modern criticism.

Ten years after *Wise Blood* first appeared, Flannery O'Connor prefaced it with an introduction calling it a "comic novel about a Christian *malgré lui,* and as such, very serious." Indeed, once one accepts the Christian assumptions of this novella, even Hazel Motes' death is a "happy" ending. So also *The Violent Bear It Away* is comedy, its comic expectations built "with a certainty sunk in despair" around a boy protagonist who is "trudging into the distance in the bleeding stinking mad shadow of Jesus." If this is comedy in some intellectual formal sense, it feels like something much harsher. The expense (given our dour expectations in real life) of making plausible a truly joyful ending is probably reserved by its necessities to the long novel—and perhaps to novels of an earlier era which was still hopeful enough to represent life not as it is but more as it might be.

Polemic on the value of
formal analysis and classification

Formalists who undertake these kinds of generalizations are often viewed as forcing stories into Procrustean beds, or engaging in the nefarious activity of pulling the wings off butterflies. And indeed the apprehension of form does determine limits and inhibit flights. I would argue, however, that they are the kind of limits which not only give us new knowledge but very likely new pleasure—the butterfly not only left intact, but its wings more visibly beautiful and functional than ever. Limits keep us from fruitless wandering and misreading, and there is no more reason to eschew an illuminating "science" of prose fiction than there is reason to refuse a biological classification of *homo sapiens*, though we know well that it does not fully account for all those richly different human beings. It does, however, keep us from mixing men with apes and expecting them to have the same powers. And, pursuing the analogy inside a classification, it keeps us from mixing tall men with short men, or long novels with novellas, as though their powers were the same.

Thus, formal criticism can be a freeing critical activity to the extent that it causes us to ask the right questions about a novella. While recognizing the value of other critical modes for solving other literary problems, I have chosen the modes of close textual analysis together with formal classification as the ones most capable of solving the problem I have set up shop to try to solve. For there are no enlightening differences to be discovered between novellas as against short stories and novels if we concentrate on parts in isolation (plot, character, diction) without reference to how they "work" in the kind of whole in which they appear and relative to the magnitude of that whole. For example, in a discussion of *Benito Cereno* I might suggest that no negative criticism of Captain Delano as an American stereotype, or of certain scenes as overly stylized and unreal, can be valid if those choices of Melville's are just what are needed for apologue, though they would be inappropriate to tragedy, where appealingly "real" characters and situations increase tragic intensity. Similarly, the criticism would be invalid if these choices are seen to be appropriate at one length of fiction though they might turn dull at another. The study of form gives us language for describing, and therefore understanding and appreciating, the wholeness of our reading experiences. And comparisons of works which we have discovered to be of like form will serve not only to validate our sense of which forms predominate in and define the novella but also to validate our judgments of beauty and worth. Without some hope of enhancing my reader's feeling of the beauty and worth of a number of novellas, I could not justify this present study as other than an academic exercise.

My proposal to undertake the task of defining the novella through its formal functions thus clearly arises because I think it has no other way of being defined. And I undertake definition not for sterile generalization as an end in itself but to demonstrate that close readings of works of any length, undertaken with some sense of the form to which the particular work belongs, may produce a reading that is truer to the story's own intention than is a partial or impressionistic reading. I propose not a formal distance but a formal closeness, and a formal richness that borrows from other theoretical modes wherever they prove helpful in the formal discussion of character, narrative manner, diction, and so on. Knowledge is ever a good thing, but it is not so much for the sake of theory as an end as for the story's own sake that I shall try, as I have already suggested, to see details always in the context of the whole effect within which they function as integral parts. And try after that to discuss at length the kinds of wholes that predominate in the novella as a genre. Surely it was for the story's own sake that James said " 'Kinds' are the very life of literature, and truth and strength come from the complete recognition of them, from abounding to the utmost in their respective senses and sinking deep into their consistency." [24]

Yet perhaps one should lend only one ear to James, lest one sink too deep into that tempting consistency. For the story's sake I shall want also to face whatever analytic difficulties formal perception brings, and lend the second ear to Konrad Lorenz, who warns in *On Aggression* that "Analysis may call our attention to irregularities which perception has overlooked. Perception has the function of discovering laws and it always sees things as rather more beautiful and well regulated than they really are." The warning is a salutary one for analysts and critics, but it has more to do with life than with art, which is in fact "more beautiful and well regulated" than life. At the point where literary analysis arises by dialectic to some perception or concept of the whole, there arises the meditation on beauty which Ortega y Gasset saw as the fitting occupation of the critic. In his *Meditations on Quixote* he calls the meditation "an erotic exercise; the concept, an amorous rite." Empirical classification and definition are then no more, and no less, than one of these "amorous rites," one of the labors of love we perform, in return for which we receive the full measure of joy available to us from literary works of high quality. Because I agree with James that novellas are often works of extraordinary shapeliness, blessedness, and beauty, it seems to me especially appropriate to designate as an "amorous rite" an extended study of them.

My plan will be to analyze rather closely the forms of a few novellas typical of general forms that seem to recur within the novella genre, with references to as many others as it may take to make my case convincing. The study is based in a canon of about a hundred novellas which I have read sufficiently carefully to feel that I may be "right" enough about them to convince most of their other interested readers. For the sake of economy, I shall often make declarative statements about the given novella without reiterating each time the basic humility that must attend such labors. Let me at least suggest at the start that I recognize the need for both caution and humility in the face of the disagreements that inevitably arise between equally careful readers, including those who are ardent enough about literary form to pursue in great detail the relation of individual parts to the whole in which they appear. Not only have other readers disagreed with my interpretations, but later interpretations of my own have sometimes disagreed with earlier ones, however carefully arrived at. One must even hope that this will occur as a happy sign that one's reading abilities do not remain at the same level but improve with experience. This is not to lean perilously in the opposite direction from where I am going and to suggest that literary form is simply a matter of opinion. It is rather to agree with Socrates in the *Phaedrus,* that an ongoing dialogue is a better way to reach the truth than to write down as final the approximate truth one has at a given stage of one's understanding. Nevertheless, the approximate truth is my written tribute to the interest and beauty of the stories I am reading, and my provocation to others to continue the dialogue.

In exposing my general plan, I should say also that the nature of my study will cause me to take only minimal account of what Wellek and Warren call "extrinsic" factors—for example, the history of short fiction. I shall take as a given Jules Romain's statement that the type of literary work we now recognize as novella, "in its maturity, is a product of the nineteenth century" (a fact well documented in Gillespie's history of novella terminology cited above) and that it is carrying on through the twentieth without diminution of its "blest" qualities. Gillespie's work confirms that one cannot draw any but the most tenuous connections—connections much too thin to help my problem of definition—between the original "novelle" or short tales of, for example, Boccaccio, and the modern works that begin around the 1800s on the Continent, in England, and in America. It is works written in the nineteenth and twentieth centuries that we are accustomed to call novellas or "short novels," and it is that period to which my selections belong.

2
HOW DO I KNOW I'M LISTENING TO A MESSAGE?
or
THE MODERN APOLOGUE'S ANSWER TO ALLEGORY

If an author wishes to take me on a long quest for the truth and finally present it to me, I will feel the quest as a boring triviality unless he gives me unambiguous signs of what quest I am on and of the fact that I have found my goal when I get there...

Wayne Booth

The action of an allegory is quite different from a plot. Its characters and incidents are determined like those of a thesis-novel, by the doctrine to be urged; the only difference is that they are metaphorical, whereas the thesis-characters and incidents are literal and instantial.

Elder Olson

Using new techniques for representing characters, for revealing subtle states of awareness, for achieving complex emotional effects—techniques developed during two hundred years of experimenting with novels that are unique realizations of principles common to represented actions—our new novelists have created new apologues.

Sheldon Sacks

As one reads novellas, evidence increases that apologue is so frequent and appropriate a form in the novella as to be one of its defining functions. It is probably not without significance that Samuel Johnson's *Rasselas,* a forerunner of the modern prose apologue, is a work of only about 40,000 words. If pressed to name a long didactic prose work of fiction, one would have to cite a work more strictly allegorical, like *Pilgrim's Progress,* and be hard put to name another. Moving for a moment into the psychology of form: readers and writers both seem intuitively to know that a fictional sermon or statement should be short, for it is not likely to hold our interest as long as representations of our complex, sinful selves, which make a more direct approach to our feelings. (And it may be that part of the explanation for the pleasures of *Pilgrim's Progress* is that, in dramatic manner and lyrical resources, it departs from prose fiction and approaches instead the mode of the famous verse allegories.)

Clearer reasons why apologues take to the novella length will, I believe, arise in the close study in this chapter of several individual novellas by Lawrence and Faulkner. In the course of that study it seems necessary that I should also try for some answers to a central and difficult question: How do we recognize apologue in modern fiction? What are its signals, and how do they relate to the novella length?

A general primary function of all fiction is to interest the reader imaginatively in What Happens to Whom, and this is true for apologue as well as other forms; were this not our interest, it would make sense for us to turn to the more forthright statements of essays or sermons, and let fiction alone. Characters and a story line, then, are the immediate attraction. Yet if apologue, as a particular form of fiction, intends as its unifying—thus dominant—principle the "maximizing" of the truth of a statement or statements,[1] then that statement must be caused to become the dominant affective concern of the reader. If this end is to be successfully achieved, What Happens, and To Whom, and the artistic means for presenting these, must bend to the requirements of the message the story wishes, before all else, to leave with us.

"Before all else" and "unifying principle" are the key ideas propelling us now, in addition to Sacks's previously cited warning that, *as principles of wholeness,* the forms of fiction are "mutually exclusive." If we view literary devices as parts only, or as individual devices which authors incorporate into their literary style, they will be seen to operate at all lengths of fiction, and to move from one novella form to another; and in such a discussion there can be no talk of mutual exclusion. But parts separate from their wholes will not finally be enough for us, for as Ernest Hemingway once said: "Prose is architecture, not interior decoration." Devices do group together and change roles according to the form they subserve, some devices serving one form better than another. And the grouped devices of apologue can be seen to serve best at the novella length.

Medieval allegory had its devices for clueing the reader very handily (too handily, it appears, to suit the modern reader's taste for realism in fiction). When a character in a black hood, named Death, begins by accosting a character named Everyman, their encounter can be emotionally compelling in certain ways, but it is instantly clear that the nature of the compulsion is to interest ourselves in generalizations and abstractions rather than individuals or an ordinary human complexity. And when Death issues his first command, "Everyman stande still! Whider arte thou goinge/Thus gaily? Hast thou thy maker forgete?" there is no doubt in us that the large expectations set up about where Everyman is "going" will have a rhetorical end beyond, and different from, the rhetoric of plot fulfillment in works we call "actions."

Much later on in the history of didactic literature Samuel Johnson, in *Rasselas,* is still employing rather bare-boned literary devices to clue the reader to his formal purpose. Though he does not solve his problem by means of one-dimensional characters who are personified abstractions, he offers no more than the thin dimensions of Prince Rasselas, who sets forth to find happiness so that *we* may learn the truth that essentially happiness does not exist in this world. The statement is reinforced by episodes along the journey, and they are structured, at their most connected, as a story line merely, distinct from a plot. Because our concentration and strong feelings are, by these traditional devices, released from character and plot and from demands of realism, the bare bones of the statement shine through without difficulty. Indeed, the didactic bones are left so bare as to prod the modern reader painfully, and cause him to protest with the narrator of *Bleak House* that allegory exists to make the head ache.

In the novella since Johnson, the bare bones tend increasingly to disappear. We seem to want our didacticism embodied in real, and yet more real, life, and there's the rub. Beginning perhaps as early as Melville, and no later than Henry James and some of his European contemporaries, we have come to live in a literary era where it seems not quite nice to be violated by an obvious idea; in an era of critics like Jorge Luis Borges, who pronounces that "For all of us, allegory is an aesthetic error." [2]

This does not mean we are losing our interest, either emotional or aesthetic, in the making of statements through fiction. Isaac Bashevis Singer was quoted in a recent interview as saying "Storytelling is a forgotten and neglected art. We have broadened the definition of literature too much. Everyone has to write with the message and there are no stories being told." I shall argue that Singer's dichotomy is not a necessary one, but I agree that there appears to be a strong current need for "answers" which has caused the didactic emphasis of some twentieth-century art, especially the drama. D. W. Robertson is, then, probably going too far when he says that "To the modern mind, a work of art which implies an explicit answer to a problem raised seems in bad taste." [3] The truth is, we want *implied* answers in fiction as much as readers ever did, and the question for Robertson is how those answers can be at once "implied" and "explicit"—"im-" and "ex-" being direct opposites which express rather precisely the difference between apologue and overt allegory.

Part of the point about "the modern mind," however, remains: the mode of fictional representation from which we infer our "answers" (as an empirical study of apologue novellas more and more reveals) is the drawing of human beings of such human complexity as to make them seem borrowed from actions. As Wayne Booth has pointed out, there are many respects in which all of "modern fiction has tried to move closer to life itself than was ever attempted by earlier fiction" (*Rhetoric of Fiction*, p. 293). As early as 1914 Henry James, in "The New Novel," was already noting "an appetite for a closer notation, a sharper specification of the signs of life, of consciousness, of the human scene and the human subject in general, than the three or four generations before us had been at all moved to insist on." [4] He sees himself and his colleagues refusing to turn "the sentimental key" on every fictional situation, preferring instead "the possibility of hugging the shore of the real as it had not, among us, been hugged."

If this is the general taste and habit of modern fiction (and surely the taste has only strengthened between the time of James's statement and the time of Booth's), apologue need not expect to exempt itself; but neither can it exempt itself from its own nature, which is to subordinate all of its fictional devices to the making of a statement. Thus, in my view, Sacks is even closer to describing the problem of modern apologue than he is to *Rasselas* when he says:

> It is clear that within any one of the exemplary episodes Johnson's task was to *increase our interest in the agents of apologue to the greatest degree possible short of obscuring the relation of the episodes to the controlling theme.* To the extent that he failed to do this, his fictional example would be unconvincing; to the extent that he went one step over the line and made our interest in the relationship of characters in the episodes stronger than our interest in what the episode exemplifies, then no matter how convincing the episode was artistically, it could no longer convince us of the truth of the now-obscured statement.
>
> [*Fiction*, p. 77—emphasis added]

An excellent statement of the formal necessities of apologue. But the movement toward making fiction "convincing" and "closer to life itself" became, in the nineteenth century and at least the first half of the twentieth, a general taste which extends to all forms of fiction and is no longer a formal sign of actions alone. It has strongly affected apologues written after *Rasselas,* causing some critics to lose part of whatever faith they had in the formal necessities of modern fiction. What is at stake, however, is not faith in literary form as such, but faith in (and enjoyment of) new methods and devices by which a given form fulfills its necessities. Booth, at the crucial point of concluding *The Rhetoric of Fiction,* warns that "what is needed is not any simple restoration of previous models, but a repudiation of all arbitrary distinctions among 'pure form,' 'moral content,' and the rhetorical means of realizing for the reader the union of form and matter" (p. 397). The key word here is, I think, "arbitrary," and the warning seems to be addressed to that reader who might say: "I can't recognize my 'previous model' of apologue, so therefore I cannot be reading apologue."

Booth goes on to judge that when one finds oneself among those works (and they include all of the forms I have spoken of among novellas) wherein "human actions are formed to make an art work," then "the form that is made can never be divorced from the human meanings." Booth is precisely *not* saying that human meanings cloud over the form, or melt it into an indefinable mix, so that it is hopeless to try to distinguish fictional forms—actions, apologues, satires, or others that may appear—as "mutually exclusive" kinds. He is, rather, facing directly the problem increasingly presented by new variations of old forms ever since the rise of the realistic novel—variations which we can nevertheless analyze with relative clarity as we study form in the "shapely" novella.

And it is a fact that critics still recognize the beast. Either intuitively or consciously, with or without strict faith in form, reviewers of new books and fiction theorists of all persuasions continue to employ terms like "fable," "moral tale," "thematic emphasis," and even "allegory," suggesting that such distinctions continue to crop up in our minds as we read, and enlighten our reading. Possibly because these critics suspect that their terms derive from old "arbitrary distinctions" which no longer sound quite right for modern fiction, they often employ them more loosely than formally (looked at one way, every story has a "theme," which does not mean all stories are apologues in their wholeness), apply them to parts only, and would probably resist if pressed to justify their terms in any firm relation of parts as contributory to the cohesion of a whole. Yet the terms do have their modern applicability because, as I have said, their formal universality transcends time. There are profound unexamined assumptions, essentially formal, in the use of a term like "fable" or "moral tale," which can exist without their user's knowledge (but derive from their user's experience with fiction) which can help us if we do examine them closely. The close look does not often take place simply because "To achieve an insight is infinitely more poetical than to examine an assumption."[5] Not only is it more poetical, it is much easier. This we will surely discover when we try to discuss novellas by such diverse authors as Lawrence and Faulkner which are formally of apparent perfection, which something in our experience (let us try to describe it) tells us are apologues, but which contain enough attributes of actions that it is difficult to say what caused us to decide.

Scholes and Kellogg have noted that there are "some narrative works which gain many of their effects precisely by straddling this precipitous border between the illustrative and the representational.... Obviously, both critical approaches depend on an assumption about the nature of the work, an assumption which ought itself to be examined closely in the context of each narrative." [6] If I understand the idea of "straddling" correctly, they by no means speak of a mixed form but rather of an increasingly urgent need to decide whether the "nature of the work" is, in principle, "illustrative" (apologue) or "representational" (action).

Later in their book Scholes and Kellogg make clear their belief that "A great part of the pleasure of allegory is doubtless to be accounted for by the ingenuity of an artist who can actually sustain both a fiction and a complex idea." [7] Our trouble remains real, however, when we confront the problem of the formal "nature of the work." These authors are speaking of a form they call "allegory" (I hold with the term "apologue" as a more distinct and modern word for what they mean). But "sustaining both a fiction and a complex idea" also seems to apply when R. S. Crane speaks of setting an *action* "in a larger context of ideas or analogies so that it may come to seem, in its universal implications for human beings, not simply the particular and untypical action it might otherwise be taken to be." [8] E. M. Forster, too, spoke of what he called "prophetic" actions, and the bloodiest possible theoretical question is thus raised: how many "ideas," "analogies," "universal implications," and "prophecies" can an action sustain and still be recognized in its wholeness as an action, not an apologue? Or conversely, when a story contains a large measure of "representational" human complexity, how can we formally identify it as apologue?

Sheldon Sacks has tentatively suggested that apprehension of generic differences may always arise intuitively, which ought to lead to more perfection in formal criticism than one often notices. [9] Perhaps, however, we do intuit the disappointment that arises from our generic errors, errors that may drive us consciously to hypothesize anew, pushing toward a better accounting of the parts that refused to "fit." Hypotheses of this kind are, I believe, based on literary acculturation and sometimes are aided by conscious recognition of the signals of forms, for example, of apologue, such as I shall try to deduce in this chapter.

After one has read a great deal, part of the disappointment must also be based in experience, but I think we must grant some innate hunger of the audience for unity in art, a hunger which has caused the coherence of artworks throughout human history (even in our time, which demands that closeness to "life itself"), so that it takes a conscious act of will on the part of a Virginia Woolf or an E. M. Forster to demand that fiction become plotless, more like life. There is an adult defiance of human nature in such a theoretical demand. If the action of a bedtime story contained three wicked witches and only two were dead when the "happy" ending arrived, no normal child would go to sleep without insisting on the destruction of the third witch. Is the child the victim of plot, "constrained, not by his own free will but by some powerful and unscrupulous tyrant who has him in thrall" (Woolf) to finish the story? If so, the tyrant would seem to lie buried in the child's human nature.[10]

In any case, since fictional works all proceed feelingly, wanting before all to cause an emotional response, possessing that general *dynamis*, in the resolution of our problem it is fitting to look first into the "rag-and-bone shop of the heart." We must trust, as far as it can take us, our "gut" reaction. Sometimes that initial reaction will simply be a provocative disappointment: "I don't understand why this story proceeds in this way—I can't even tell who the main character is." The problem could be a badly made story. But before we make that leap in judgment we owe the work, and the forms that works can take, a more intellectual accounting. We can look and see what the signals are that are demanding this response and not that; and we can observe them all the more accurately when they appear in the "pint-size" bottle of the novella.

The degree of "caring" in THE WOMAN WHO RODE AWAY

How, for example, shall I resolve the disappointment and puzzlement of my initial reaction to a particularly difficult novella, Lawrence's *The Woman Who Rode Away*? The woman is an appealing character: brave enough to resist frustration, and braver yet when she suffers first the minor fears of her journey forth, and then the major fear of her own death. Fearful expectations, then, are set up; as in actions (but with differences to be noted), we are made to "care" about her and her fate, and Lawrence freely takes the risk of keeping us more or less close to her. There is something like a plot instability: how dare this woman ride off alone away from home and family to satisfy her curiosity about strange Indians? Why does she know she is to die, and how dreadful will be that death at the hand of these "mysterious, marvelous" primitives when it comes? And why *must* she die?

In the answer to that last question, I believe, lies the key to the puzzle and the resolution of our dissatisfaction. She must die, and we must feel the fearfulness of it, not for the sake of tragic fulfillment, but for the sake of the message: that female restlessness must be overwhelmed (must "die") by that shaft of sunlight which is the phallic principle (a profoundly different matter, it is made clear, from mechanistic male domination)—"The mastery that man must hold, and that passes from race to race" (p. 581).[11] It then becomes a matter of great formal interest to observe that Lawrence, at the ultimate moment, articulates that statement instead of fulfilling what would seem to have been his artistic obligation in a tragic action, namely, to subject us to the actual pain of the woman's death which the whole story has led us toward (though the leading, as we shall see, is of a special kind).

Three pages before the end, we are coolly and finally removed both from the woman's feelings (the last we know of them is, "She felt little sensation, though she knew all that was happening") and from our own feelings for her. We become absorbed instead in a ritual pageant composed of repetitively selected colors—"copper-dark men," "copper-pale tree trunks," "pale, flaked copper," "dark, red-bronze," "dark, painted faces" becoming gradually, in the ceremonial intensity, "black," "black eyes," "black mirrors," the "black, empty concentration" of the long wait, the knife poised in the Indian priest's hand, for the final strike of the "red sun." There is an accompanying ritualistic use of movement: "swaying," "winding," "lurid dancing priests," "the long thread of the dance, shaking slowly and sumptuously," accompanied by the steady upward movement of "her swaying litter" to the place of sacrifice. The intention is clearly a mesmerizing of the reader toward the acceptance of the event whose human agony we are spared, with the aesthetic purpose of causing us to accept that final statement.

An occasional reader, out of his or her preconceptions, willfully refuses to be spared. Kate Millett calls this "a death which is astounding in the sadism and malice with which it is conceived" and advises that the story be compared to the "commercial hard core" of

The Story of O. She complains that Leavis and Tindall "fudge the meaning of this story by mumbling vaguely that it is all allegorical symbolic." [12] She asserts that it is "symbolic" only "in the same sense as a head exposed on London Bridge." Yet she herself calls the woman's Indian captors the "embodiment of an idea." Certainly it is perfectly possible, in the light of an extrinsic position on "sexual politics" to look upon the governing statement of Lawrence's story as wicked. That is a different matter from noting how much more likely thematic criticism is to impose an intrinsic misreading than formal criticism, which is willing, at the least, to look at what is actually there in the story and to refuse to ignore the aesthetic details that quite simply forbid us (if we hold language in common at all) to take this death scene as sadistic and malicious.

In the end we can look back and see that character and plot, diction, scene, and all other aesthetic details have been systematically subordinated to the making of the reader's apprehension of the story's final statement, whether he personally likes the statement or not. We apprehend the didactic significance of the one willful act of the woman (she is never named)—the riding forth in quest of "something wonderful" which we are to discover along with her—and survive to understand. (I find myself instinctively using terms from medieval literature such as "riding forth" and "quest" for, stepped up in realism, it is still these conventions from a strongly moral earlier literature which Lawrence employs to such effect.)

Specifically, we can review our fear of "the woman's" death and see that it was not the kind of instability suited to a tragic action. In a sense, Lawrence never allowed fear of her oncoming death to become an instability at all. We are only a few pages into the story when she is already "feeling like a woman who has died and passed beyond. She was not sure that she had not heard, during the night, a great crash at the centre of herself, which was the crash of her own death. *Or else, it was a crash at the centre of the earth, and meant something big and mysterious*" (p. 552).

From that point on her will-lessness is stressed, and her "wonder," and her "feeling once more as if she had died." She becomes increasingly powerless, and it is with "a slight thrill of exultation" that "she knew she was dead." By the end of the very first chapter, nothing is really left for the reader in the way of ordinary suspense or fear. In a "deathly" atmosphere, "She slept and woke and slept in a semiconscious numbness of cold and fatigue. A long, long night, *icy and eternal*, and she was aware that she had died" (p. 557).

I have italicized those elements in both the above longer quotations which formally lift this death out of its individual attachment to this woman (who is at the start as "real" to us as any other "rather dazzling Californian girl from Berkeley") into the realm of the meaningful "centre of the earth," into "something big," into the realm of the "icy and eternal." What it is that is "wonderful," "wild," and "eternal" has been caused to become our focus of concern—in the very midst of her fearful adventure.

It is well worth noting that, in this very midst of realistic human passion and complexity, the great writers of modern apologue habitually, with considerable skill and daring, articulate their statement. Lawrence does it not only in the last sentence but in the middle of *The Woman Who Rode Away*:

> She seemed at last to feel her own death; her own obliteration. As if she were to be obliterated from the field of life again. In the *strange towering symbols on the heads of the changeless, absorbed women she seemed to read once more the Mene Mene Tekel Upharsin*. Her *kind* of womanhood, intensely personal and individual, was to be obliterated again, and the *great primeval symbols* were to tower once more over the fallen individual independence of *woman*. The sharpness and the quivering nervous consciousness of the highly-bred white woman was to be destroyed again, *womanhood* was to be cast once more into the great stream of impersonal sex and impersonal passion. *Strangely, as if clairvoyant, she saw* the immense sacrifice prepared. And she went back to her little house in a trance of agony.
>
> [P. 569—emphasis added]

Note how brilliantly the statement is framed at either end by her agony, and filtered through her consciousness, at the same time as the narrator does not seem to lose his statement-making hold on us (are we certain it is *she* who is fully aware of "the quivering nervous consciousness of the highly-bred white woman," or is she still its victim whom *we* are made aware of?). In this case I have once more italicized the diction which signals the statement-making to the reader—that which is changeless, that which is to be seen, that which is openly symbolic by affirmation of the author, that which was individual now become generalized ("kind," "womanhood").

If the statement is already made, why does the story continue? Millett fluffs off this formal question with a bitter judgment: "Now that the sermon has been delivered, the [sadistic] proceedings may continue" (*Sexual Politics,* p. 289). My answer is that this is a fictional unity, not an essay, and its rhetoric is the "rhetoric of fiction." The fiction, the What Happens and To Whom, must continue until the apologue statement has been worked out—fictionally (thus, emotionally) completed for the reader. This requires further struggle on the woman's part, an extended ritual which makes clear that the statement does not refer simplistically to "sexual politics" but to the triumph of primitive nature over *all* "civilized," mechanized unnaturalness, and a completion of the journey that must end with the flash of the sun on the fatal knife.

What is remarkable is that, by the end, not only are there no questions left about what statement the story intends to make, there are also no fictional expectations left over. The reader has been caused to surrender all his right to ask "What happened to the jealous husband and the children she left behind?" It is the glory of modern apologue, and the skill of Lawrence in this story, that here the reader's surrender is much more richly and subtly achieved than our surrender to Samuel Johnson when (out of formal necessity) we decline to ask Prince Rasselas, "Why aren't you much more vigorous about rescuing Pekuah from the Arabs?" (instead of leaving her there for seven months to be theorized about). The husband in the Lawrence story is, for the first few paragraphs, much more real to us than Pekuah is. He has a physical presence, a personal history, an age of fifty-three, accidents, accomplishments; he feels lust, loves company, hates pigs, possesses and overprotects his wife. Then, with consummate skill, Lawrence enmeshes him in "the nakedness of the works," "the machinery of the extracting plant," reduces his marriage to the "last and most intimate bit of his own works," abandons him among "deserted works," and a "bunch of half-deserted miners' dwellings," then causes his "departure" on "business." "Deadness within deadness," and he is gone. By what seems legerdemain in retrospect, he has become the mere signification of the civilized, mechanistic male world; then, he and "the child, like the servant, shrank into silence" and never again were any of our business. Thus does the apologue writer use what Philip Rahv calls "techniques of planned derangement," employing them for "cracking open the certified structure of reality" and loosening its hold on us.[13]

"Caring" in THE FOX

Formal consideration of Lawrence's novellas is especially helpful in solving the problems of apologue because he obviously wishes to make use of all forms of fiction to embody messages which will shine forth prominently. Actions can, and generally do, embody morals without being centrally organized, as apologues are, to promote a statement as their main fictional purpose. *The Fox* carries within it a message very similar to that of *The Woman Who Rode Away*; but in the case of *The Fox* the statement is formally subordinate to the making of a serious action. Here the human complexity of March, who must cure her restlessness by "going to sleep" in her lover (as the woman in the other story must die) dominates the story and our feelings. In *The Fox* something daringly akin to another killing takes place when the lover coolly allows the tree to fall on Jill, March's woman friend, and there is no ritualistic aspect or mesmeric diction that allows us to accept what ought to be morally untenable. In this case we accept it because of a rhetoric of character appropriate to action, which centers on character: Jill has been demeaned in Henry's view of her as a kind of "chicken" whom the "fox" must get out of the way in a manner of extinction which the animal world takes for granted (the animal world being analogous to March's own deeper nature, into which she must gradually sink).

These situations, though they are fraught with metaphorical overtones, are represented directly and humanly, and "the moral of the story" (which is by no means as clearly formulable as in *The Woman Who Rode Away*) comes to us by the way of an action which centers our attention and feelings first and always on character and outcome. As must be the case if we are to call this a unified action, all plot expectations are fulfilled credibly. The hopes that have been built in the reader for March's successful submission appear close to fruition by the end but are not yet possible because the richly complex character of March's independence, we are made to feel, does not yet permit it.

If the apologue statement of *The Woman Who Rode Away* were to be fulfilled in *The Fox*, March would *have* to give in, and would then be behaving "out of character." *The Fox* ends, as it must, with the man's loving impatience, and with March's not-yet-resolved struggle (though we are led to hope it will be resolved) between submission and the pain such submission *must* cost her because that is the kind of human being Lawrence has made for us and caused us to care about.

This kind of fulfillment of all plot and character expectations does not make *The Fox* necessarily a better story than *The Woman Who Rode Away* (though I think it is). The two novellas are of different fictional forms, and in each case the devices of the artist are employed as they need to be: plot and character are appropriately subordinate in the apologue; in the action they are central, of the formal essence.

The question for modern apologue, we begin to see, is partly one of very complex and subtle distance-making. Given the modern taste (nay, absolute affection) for a direct encounter with internal feelings and states of soul, plus the modern inclination to didacticism in literature, how is the artist to reveal the statement of his apologue clearly without putting us at too great a distance from character, from human "caring"?

It is already clear that we cannot distinguish apologue by absence of plot and character. Nor can we define action by its lack of didactic emphasis. But we must distinguish, or take the risk of misapprehension. When we are disappointed in a story, it is usually either because we see obvious aesthetic failures and moral trivialities, or because we misapprehended the story form, thus misclassifying it so that it appeared as an ugly maverick among the flock we placed it in. It has disappointed the expectations we imposed on it, because they were the wrong expectations. Intuition, feeling, and intellect all belong to the apprehension of stories as much as they belong to the production of them.

Let us allow these novellas to lead us, then, to apprehend them within the categories to which they really belong. Classification at its best is an activity which releases the individual work to reveal all its excellences because it is seen in the context of other works of its kind and is not chained either to an incomprehensible individuality or bogged down in the vagueness or largeness of all-encompassing terms like "theme" or " fiction" (the real imposition). Lump them both simply as works of "fiction," and *The Fox* will win, while the skills employed in *The Woman Who Rode Away* will be lost: that stylized ending must seem inhumane, and the author will seem demoniacally to have suppressed the woman's pain and to have coldly forbidden the fear and pain we should be feeling at this barbarous killing. Or again, lump the two works together as examples of the theme of redemption by the phallic principle, and the excellences of *The Fox* must be lost, because March's redemption is at the end incomplete. Either way, we have reduced the stories by treating them deductively, rather than discovering their principles of organization by induction and hypothesis.

That principles bind us in literature is only a constricting idea until we think more about it. Percy Lubbock has said: "The only law that binds the novelist throughout, whatever course he is pursuing, is the need to be consistent on some plan, to follow the principle he has adopted." What follows from this is that we, in turn, are bound to discover that principle or be confused, thus displeased.[14] So that it is in the name not only of intellectual curiosity but of the pleasure appropriate to each of two different kinds of works, each of them successful of their kind, that I appeal for us to continue to try to find the distinguishing signals of apologue as they arise in the study of actual novellas.

Larger than life SPOTTED HORSES

The statement evolving from William Faulkner's novella, *Spotted Horses* is something like: *There is no appeal to economy and order from the random violence of nature, including the nature of men. Children and women avoid the worst of the violence to the extent they remain close to their own natures.* The tone is not solemn, but one of humorous despair, summed up in the old justice who tries to apply law and order to "that spotted corruption of frantic and uncatchable horses" and cries at the end: "This court's adjourned! Adjourned!"[15]

In the ordered making of our sense of disorder, it becomes appropriate that there be a flux of characters, without a center on any. Flem Snopes may or may not have owned the spotted horses—he has too much animal cunning to be caught in the unnatural bind that results from claiming ownership; like the horses themselves, he can never be "brought to court." He is only at rare times a center of conversation, never a center for the action (though his amoral nature hovers over it). Men, women, and children come and go in a flux ordered only by the thesis of the novella. They are extremely "real," visible characters, yet even as we look at them they are enlarged and frozen in meaning by means of repetition. Mrs. Littlejohn seems to exist for "watching the lot" where the horses are shakily confined and, from her veranda, "watching the lot again," until we are caused to watch with her and to judge the significance of what happens there. Her role is restricted to "looking into the lot" (there are more than a dozen variations on this repetition) and to heavily stressed earth-mother functions such as washing (her washboard is a weapon against the horses)—first clothes, then dishes. She sounds the dinner bell, holds high the lamp, and like other women is associated mysteriously with the pear tree, the mockingbird, and especially the moon. These elements recur in cyclic fashion, apprehended only vaguely and superstitiously by the men in the story:

> A moon like this is good for every growing thing outen earth.... So there was a old woman told my mammy once that if a woman showed her belly to the full moon after she had done caught, it would be a gal.... You get enough women showing their nekid bellies to the moon or the sun either or even just to your hand fumbling around often enough and more than likely after a while there will be something in it you can lay your ear and listen to.
>
> [P. 46]

As the elements recur, they do almost nothing to advance the story line but do everything to make a separation between the enduring nature of women and the violent ephemeral nature of what Mrs. Littlejohn calls "You men." Mrs. Littlejohn has her watchful, nurturing nature, and there is the "patient, insensate, timeless" nature of the "gray and shapeless" Mrs. Armstid, whose passivity is attached to mules as her husband's foolish activity is to the horses (who would, however, naturally refuse to be attached to *him*).[16] When the wild horses stampede, they divide their rush in two, moving to either side of the center where Mrs. Armstid sits, as they had lept, without harm to him, over the head of the little boy.

The children are closer in nature to the women than the men but are caught uncertainly in between. There is the twelve-year-old girl who takes an axe to bed with her because "what with this country still more or less full of them uncaught horses that never belonged to Flem Snopes, likely she feels maybe she can't swing a mere washboard like Mrs. Littlejohn can—and then come back and wash up the supper dishes" (p. 54). And there is Eck's little boy, who seems to exist in the story for his repeated untouchability in the midst of the wild horses, yet also for the repeated threat that he will grow up to be like the other men. He wears "diminutive overalls—a miniature replica of the men themselves"; he is the "little boy pressing close to his father." They squat "against the wall, side by side and, save for the difference in size, identical, eating" (p. 49).[17]

Once again, as in Lawrence, the devices of apologue show forth artificially in the midst of the reality of the scene. Unnatural repetitions build significance, but they do not build many-sided characters. The epic, larger-than-life devices of epithet and simile come once more into play. Mrs. Armstid, as she does in other Faulkner stories, lives the epithet of "gray and shapeless." The horses are frighteningly literal, but they attach themselves increasingly to a quality of natural violence. The horses are attached by simile to much smaller animals lest they seem too fleshly: "larger than rabbits and gaudy as parrots" (p. 4), "deadly as rattlesnakes, quiet as doves" (p. 4), "like partridges flushing" (p. 8), "like dizzy fish in a bowl" (p. 8). They are unavailable to human management (though they are uneasy allies to the animal cunning of a Flem Snopes who never tries to claim ownership of them) because, "phantom and inextricable" (p. 39), they are in the world of men but not of it, seeming "not to gallop, but to flow, bodiless, without dimension" (p. 10). They are "like phantom fish, suspended apparently without legs now in the brilliant treachery of the moon" (p. 38).

The more one quotes, the more one perceives the diction of extreme artifice. The "straddling" of Faulkner between the real and the artificial is yet twice as certain of itself as in the Lawrence novella. In *Spotted Horses* we imagined we had fixed ourselves in a southern rural setting among earthy poor whites, only to find ourselves sailing to Byzantium. There is a horrendous and hilarious realism in the invasion of the horse into the house, but its larger significance is achieved by the artificiality of the narration:

> A lamp sat on a table just inside the door. In its mellow
> light they saw the horse fill the long hallway like a pinwheel,

> gaudy, furious, and thunderous. A little further down the
> hall there was a varnished yellow melodeon. The horse
> crashed into it; it produced a single note, almost a chord,
> in bass, resonant and grave, of deep and sober astonishment;
> the horse with its monstrous and antic shadow whirled
> again and vanished through another door.
>
> [P. 41]

It is both a shocking and wildly funny event in the real world and
(send not to ask for whom that "resonant" and "grave" chord
sounds) a metaphorical invasion of human order by wild nature,
which can be apprehended only in the most unreal terms.

Paul Berchner has said of the allegorical interpretation of medieval works that "Not every lion in a story represents either
Christ, or St. Mark the Evangelist, or the devil, or a vice; some lions
represent only themselves." [18] The same warning obviously applies to
an apologue reading of *Spotted Horses,* or an apologue reading of
any piece of modern literature, often merely an all-too-reductive
habit which clouds the apprehension of works that are formally
actions. It is true to say (as Berchner does), but not enough to say,
that "the reader will still have to use his good judgment and
determine from the context whether or not an allegorical sense of
symbolic value is to be attached." The task of judgment becomes
more difficult in modern apologue where there is a smaller and less
rigorous set of traditional symbols comparable to the lion of St.
Mark, and rarely any overt personified abstractions like Death and
Everyman.

What judgments and determinations, then, must we make about
the context in order to be certain that the spotted horses are both
literal and metaphorical—and at the service of apologue? In
response, I wish to repeat my suggestion that the reader depend on
his intuition of the story as a whole, and check his initial hypothesis
against those signals of apologue which, when several or all of them
appear in the same story, give us not only permission but direction to
"read in" significance beyond the literal. In addition to the already-
described apologue rhetoric of diffuse and one-sided characters,
repetition, and epithet, Faulkner employs here a diction which could
only be ridiculous if we were intended to apprehend these horses as
primarily real-world piebald ponies corralled amid the sights,
sound, and smells of a naturalistic barnyard. Here the horses are

"monstrous and antic," elsewhere they have "cerulean eyes," "harlequin rumps" which move in "calico rushes"; and their guardian (though, as he munches his gingersnaps, he scarcely seems to us a Bible scholar) perceives them bitterly as "transmogrified hallucinations of Job and Jezebel" (pp. 6 and 7).

I am aware that Faulkner has come under criticism for stylistic excess carried on for its own sake. I wish to take my stand on the question with Warren Beck, who says that "while Faulkner does not avoid elaboration, neither is he its slave. . . . Faulkner's diction, charged and proliferate though it may be, usually displays a nice precision." [19] I agree with Beck especially on the point that "Definition of his story as a whole and the enhancement of its immediate appeals to the imagination are his constant aims." I would add that any reader who continues to imagine Faulkner uncertain of his form, or in love with elaborate language merely for its own sake, owes it to himself to reexamine the realistic simplicity of diction in a short action such as "That Evening Sun," which depends for its effect on a maximum of direct speech and a minimum of narrative comment, and is composed largely of simple, factual sentences.

Once again in *Spotted Horses,* as in the Lawrence apologue, the statement has its moment of being articulated almost directly. Once the "lot" has become enlarged for us into a symbol for the weak human attempt to confine the unconfinable "fury and motion" of nature (including some kinds of human nature) which the horses stand for, the following statement translates readily into the major statement around which all parts of the story cohere:

> It had seemed like a big lot until now, but now the very
> idea that all that fury and motion should be transpiring
> inside any one fence was something to be repudiated with
> contempt, like a mirror trick.
>
> [P. 8]

This statement occurs early, and all the rest of the story seems to exist to bear it out. The "mirror trick" of the lot becomes not only contemptible but ridiculous when the lot is replaced by that other order-making futility called a court, with its "actions," "litigants," "change of venue," "baffled and helpless bailiff," its dependence on the word of the "Bible," "almanac," and a "copy of Mississippi Reports dated 1881," its "caricature" of the "Justice of the Peace" who cannot cope with the absent defendant Snopes any better than the lot could cope with the "phantom" horses—and we smile at all our futile selves as he adjourns his court in despair and frustration.

Devices of OLD MAN

In *Old Man,* the statement is again brought close to overt articulation through the words of the story. *Driven by "outrage" against "the old primal faithless Manipulator" who has cast him as a "toy and pawn" on "a vicious and inflammable geography," on a "flood" of difficulties ("deliberate and irresistible and monstrously disturbed water"), Man's natural connection to ongoing life forces him to heroic acts of survival even with his foot lodged only on "a muddy slope, slipping back." When he is most afloat and fighting, given "permission to endure" by the "cosmic joker," he is yet better off than in a surrender to the "Farm" and "prison" of conniving civilization.* (It seems to me worth pausing to observe how different is the activity of abstracting a complex statement, which takes into account all the parts of the story, from the activity of abstracting a two- or three-word "theme" which could apply with equal ease to a hundred other stories.)

Once again, the apologue is busy with devices for placing a large distance on the immediate situation. Like Lawrence's "woman," the "tall convict" and "the woman" he rescues are unnamed. Animal similes see men "shackled in braces like field dogs" and "their backs turned to the rain as sheep and cattle do." That the flooded river is to achieve the same symbolic weight of uncontrollable nature as the spotted horses is made clear in a simile where the river is seen to "turn without warning and rush back upon him with furious and deadly intent like a frenzied stallion in a lane."

Additional devices (not singular to apologue but very appropriate to it) make their appearance: *biblical imagery* ("that earthen ark out of Genesis"), *biblical suggestion* (the Flood, the parodied Holy Family, the innocent snakes who share "paradise" with the ship-wrecked humans), and *biblical simile* ("like a translation out of Isaiah"; "she too had stemmed at some point from the same dim hill-bred Abraham"); *universality* achieved by probing backward into history ("a lightwood club the size and weight and shape of a Thuringian mace") and into myth (Helen, Hercules); *universality of diction* ("Money ain't got but one language"; "That first startled glance had been ample to reveal to him all the generations of her life and background, who could have been his sister if he had a sister, his wife...."; "And who to say what Helen, what living Garbo, he had dreamed of rescuing from what craggy pinnacle or dragoned keep"; the convict's wish to surrender become "an indictment of all breath and its folly and suffering, its infinite capacity for folly and pain, which seems to be its only immortality"); an ancient enlarging human magic attached to *the repeated use of the number seven* (the crime committed at age seventeen has called forth seven years of punishment, and the current ordeal takes seven weeks, man's reduction, or enlargement, of the seven days God took to make the world).

In both these novellas Faulkner takes the risk of a great deal more dialogue than is often the case in apologue (there is minimal conversation in *The Woman Who Rode Away*). In *Spotted Horses* the risk is mitigated by the diffusion of attention among many characters (as a similar diffusion mitigates the risk in the dramatic exchange of Crane's *The Open Boat*). In *Old Man* there is both conversation and center on a single character. In this case distance on the character is achieved by all the above devices and by another frequent device of apologue, the intrusive narrator.

The "Now look here, dear reader" type of narrator who occurred in eighteenth-century, and some of nineteenth-century, fiction of whatever form, has largely disappeared with the increase of realism in actions, precisely because he interferes with realistic closeness. He can, however, reappear when needed for didactic fiction such as *Old Man*. There are several intrusions, designed precisely to set the reader at a distance from the unnamed convict. The narrator openly conjectures among several possibilities accounting for the behavior he observes: "Perhaps ... or perhaps...." Other times he is overtly superior to the characters he is observing: "A deep faint subaquean rumble which (*though none in the truck could have made the comparison*) sounded like a subway train" (emphasis added). Note that the reader is being asked to make the enlarging comparison which allies poor rural convicts with similarly trapped city folk.

(A remarkably similar conjectural and superior tone appears in the narration of Stephen Crane's *The Open Boat*, which is significantly subtitled "A Tale Intended To Be After the Fact": "In the wan light, the faces of the men must have been grey. Their eyes must have glinted in strange ways as they gazed steadily astern. Viewed from a balcony, the whole thing would doubtless have been weirdly picturesque. But the men in the boat had no time to see it" (p. 25).[20] The tone appears again in the opening of the second chapter: "It was probably splendid. It was probably glorious, this play of the free sea.")

Several such intrusions in the first ten pages of *Old Man* subtly establish an overt quality to the narrative which keeps us at two removes from what is going on, and which steadily haloes with light the truth we are to apprehend as a result of our distance on what is happening. For example, the word "outrage" first appears in the narrator's voice, enlarging the outrage we will be made to feel through the sufferings of the particular convict to an implicit statement about the outrage suffered by Man in general, which is part of the apologue statement as a whole. Even when he is directly describing the convict's past, the diction of the narrator is so clearly his own—elevated, contemplative—that he causes us to think as *he* wishes about the events, rather than enter into direct sympathy with the convict's much more limited point of view. We are caused to watch as God watches.

A compendium of the signals of apologue

Having examined several apologues in some detail, I should now like to gather together, from these and other novellas which I shall simply assume are apologues, some of the signals of modern apologue. I shall engage in what R. S. Crane called "reasoning back from the nature of an achieved result to its necessary or desirable conditions" (*Languages*, p. 45). The "achieved result" in this case is any novella which, in its own individual way but with some techniques in common with other stories of the same form, embodies a statement or message as its principle of coherence.

At the back of all I have said, and will say, I hear another critic's voice sounding the warning: "Deep Readers of the World, Beware!" I know without being warned—I affirm—that a hundred symbols or a hundred instances of universalized diction do not an apologue make. Great stories *all* have a tendency to enlarge upon their immediate human content. Let me simply reiterate that when the human content is systematically disabused of its immediacy—of its emotional center on the resolution of relations between characters—by heavy use of some or all of the signals discussed below, we should look for apologue. Some of these same signals can and do appear in actions and especially in satires. My claim limits itself to a strong suggestion that when several of these signals appear together in the same story—that is, appear conspicuously or repetitively—the possibility of apologue as the unifying principle should be examined. The suspicion will be confirmed when the statement is expressed as one would express the juice from an orange, the flavor of the juice confirming the nature of the fruit. (As I have suggested in the discussion of *The Fox*, it is very hard to do this with actions; the "lifeliness" of the situations, the demands of plot, interfere.) The reward is certain to be increased enjoyment, arising from contentment that one has fully understood, that parts of the story no longer dangle puzzlingly, that we have given beauty its due. Beauty of the work as a whole, intrinsically, can in fact become apparent in no other way, for an apologue can never be a fully satisfying action.[21]

Distance on character

I cite distance on character first because it is the one indispensable sign of apologue. We may come close to "real" characters—they may even be central characters, as in *The Woman Who Rode Away*—but they may never be the all-in-all of our concern. By definition, the statement and its fictional elaboration have that status. (The reverse is true of actions, wherein any statement-making would be fully subordinated to our concern for the central characters and their fates.) There is, in fact, a sense in which all the other signals of apologue are bent to this one indispensable requirement of producing distance between the reader and the fictional characters (distance being in its turn a requirement for giving the message room to shine through), and I shall try to show this as I discuss the other signals. Specifically, in the area of character delineation itself, distance is maintained by such devices as the following.

    1. Not naming the character (*The Woman Who Rode Away*, the narrator of Kafka's *The Burrow*, the "taller convict" of *Old Man*); or naming him in some generic epithet ("our islander" in Lawrence's *The Man Who Loved Islands*, "the American" and "the

Spaniard" in *Benito Cereno*, "the Swede" and "the Easterner" in Crane's *The Blue Hotel*). Ian Watt quotes the remark of Hobbes that "Proper names bring to mind one thing only; universals recall any one of many." Another variation on not-naming is the fictional device of significant proper names for people and places, a practice which keeps our attention fixed on the significance of the person or place at the expense of individualizing them. Though this device has been employed in the past in various forms of prose fiction (Mr. Allworthy in the comic action, *Tom Jones*) it is employed in modern fiction mostly in apologue (Castle Keep in *The Burrow*; Bookwright, Mink Snopes, Quick, and the ironic "Justice of the Peace" in *Spotted Horses*; Doom in *Red Leaves*, Bolton Lovehart and Rusty-Butt Hill in Robert Penn Warren's *The Circus in the Attic*).

2. Dispersal of attention among two or more characters (in *Benito Cereno*, Andreyev's *The Seven Who Were Hanged*, *Spotted Horses*, Crane's *The Open Boat*, Warren's *The Circus in the Attic*).

3. Killing off the character before the story opens. (In Tolstoy's *The Death of Ivan Ilyich* the opening scene of Ivan's funeral is employed to cast immediate emphasis on the style of life rather than the particular life of the one man who will serve as an example. Miss Emily is also dead at the start of that shorter apologue, *A Rose For Emily*).

4. Making the characters seem less than human, or actually animal (the narrator in Kafka's *The Burrow*, the blacks in *Benito Cereno*). I realize that I have suggested that Lawrence reduces Jill to a kind of chicken in the action of *The Fox*. It is crucial that he never states this on his own authority but only in the consciousness of Henry, just as Henry's association with the fox is a very delicately suggestive one. In both cases the characters remain acutely human to the reader. (An even more interesting case of an animal in an action is Gregor in Kafka's *The Metamorphosis*. He never loses his human nature until he dies—his turning into a dung beetle is a tragic event which happens to a human.) Lawrence never takes the risk of overt animal simile or of the kind of technique Kafka uses (very different from that in *The Metamorphosis*) when he places small animal carcasses around "the burrow," presumed to have been the food and the prey of the narrator, himself animalistic. One critic has pointed out the moral effectiveness that accrues to an animal narrator who "is, of necessity, outside morality" so that his

moral judgments reflect the more strongly on the moral inadequacy of humans.[22]

5. Reducing characters to two dimensions (Mrs. Littlejohn, who exists mainly to "watch the lot" and comment in *Spotted Horses*), or to one dimension by means of an epithet or label—the "grey and shapeless" Mrs. Armstid. These are close to what Sheldon Sacks calls "species characters," and he points out that they provide a shortcut to evaluation of the thought the story is provoking (*Fiction,* chapter 4). They derive from (though with much more realism and subtlety) the technique of personifying abstractions in allegory, or from the technique of Homeric epithet. Long novel actions like those of Dickens employ such characters for other kinds of shortcutting, but in contemporary novellas they usually suggest apologue. Perhaps even more conspicuous examples are the "burrowing" narrator of *The Burrow,* Eck's boy in *Spotted Horses,* who exists only to show that the child is father to the man, and the "woman of brilliance and audacity" whom we shall find in Crane's *Maggie.*

Relative plotlessness

Plot, in the sense of the necessary resolution of expectations which have been set up regarding conflict between characters—that Aristotelian "beginning, middle, and end"—is not typical of apologue. As I suggested earlier, What Happens is very likely to be what I would call a story line, as distinct from a plot. Things happen sequentially, step by step, incident after incident, bound together not by plot necessity but in time sequence. The boundaries can be the beginning and end of a journey, as in *The Woman Who Rode Away,* the beginning and the end of a voyage, as in *Old Man* or Crane's *The Open Boat,* the first to last steps of solving a mystery, as in *Benito Cereno*—structures from allegory that go back beyond *Pilgrim's Progress* to Dante but work for prose fiction apologue with the most satisfying economy at novella length.

A story line is bound to have less sheer excitement than a plot, but it has plenty of interest of its own kind. As Angus Fletcher points out, "One thing at a time does not imply that as an organization of agents the fable fails to have interest. The sum of all single steps may be extremely complex, as in a mosaic."[23] When the pieces of the mosaic are all fitted together, the interest and satisfaction will not be the same as the satisfaction of plot fulfillment in the death of the third witch (in my earlier instance of the bedtime story) but will lie instead in the fulfillment of the apologue statement. "The dramatic personnae," Fletcher suggests, "will not have to interact plausibly according to probability as long as they interact with a certain logical necessity" (*Allegory*, p. 182). Interest and satisfaction sometimes derive from conscious awareness that an apologue story line is not to be attacked as a poor plot when, just as it is, it is right for the job the story needs done. Stephen Crane, surely a master of the novella apologue, sets up in *The Blue Hotel* a tense action which is confined to the hotel itself and which would seem to have an "ending" when the Swede beats up young Scully. But the apologue statement requires for its fulfillment a whole new episode set in the bar, and a new set of characters.

Manipulation of our sense of time

1. *Present tense.* A story which employs present tense (Norman Mailer's *The Man Who Studied Yoga*, Kafka's *The Burrow*, the opening paragraphs of Carson McCullers' *The Ballad of the Sad Café*) is clearly suggesting not a particular action which occurred in a fictional past but is saying "It is always like this," thus suggesting an immediate quality of universality and timelessness, as against the particularity of actions.

2. *Uncertainty of time.* Warren's *The Circus in the Attic* makes use of many times—thus no certain time—by beginning with the present, moving back to cover several characters in several different wars, chooses one modern character to summarize and exemplify the "circus" of failed heroes, reverts to present tense, and concludes (with the authority of the whole novella backing up what lies ahead) in future tense.

3. *Large gaps in time.* In *Old Man* time is not only connected to the number seven and its uses but is also employed in leaps which disturb the immediacy of what is going on, in order to enlarge the reader's sense of significance: "Even when he tried to tell it, even after the seven weeks and he safe, secure, riveted warranted and doubly guaranteed by the ten years they had added to his sentence for attempted escape, something of the old hysteric incredulous outrage came back into his face" (p. 119). In Tolstoy's *The Death of Ivan Ilyich* and Flaubert's *A Simple Heart* (both of which I shall later call "example apologues") leaps of time enlarge the ongoing

quality of which the given life is an example. Years passing in a
single leap carry both the suggestion that years can be skipped
because all years have the same quality and that the author is
selecting out of the sameness those years or incidents which most
expose the quality the story wishes to expose. As Ivan looks back, he
can see "that deadly official life and those preoccupations about
money a year of it, then two, and ten, and twenty, and always the
same thing." It is worth noting that what is being built by this device
is reiteration at the expense of plot excitement, almost the reverse of
the suspenseful expectation which is the lifeblood of actions. "Now
time must pass" says the narrator of *The Ballad of the Sad Café.*
"For the next four years are much alike." The story is being
interrupted, rather than advanced, while the matter of the story is
having its significance stressed.

Ritualistic and improbable effects

I have called attention to the portentous, didactic quality of
ritualistic scene-making in *The Woman Who Rode Away.* A kind of
balance is maintained between "reality" and unnaturalness, as is the
case in Carson McCullers' *The Ballad of the Sad Café,* whose
characters are painfully real at the same time as they are hemmed in
by the ritual numbers seven and three, the magic of kidney stones,
and so on. But it is notable that Lawrence and McCullers, as
twentieth-century writers in the grip of the taste for "real life,"
weight the balance in that direction. Melville in *Benito Cereno,* like
Conrad in *Heart of Darkness,* makes no attempt to "explain"
by links to the real world his unlikely items: Babo's Spanish flag in
the barbering scene is as unexplained as the three women in black in
Heart of Darkness, or the harlequin man, or the man who puts out
the fire with a water pail which has a hole in it.

   As we move backward in time, the tendency is stronger to force
the reader away from his natural bent in order to press the apologue
statement. One stunning example is the stag in Flaubert's novella
The Legend of St. Julian Hospitator:

> The huge beast stopped; and with blazing eyes, solemn as a
> patriarch or judge, and to the accompaniment of a bell
> tolling in the distance, it said three times: "Accursed,
> accursed, accursed...."

Rarely has one sentence been asked to carry so many out-of-nature and ritual elements: the talking beast (in this case the simile attaches him to man), the portentous blazing eyes, the ritual of the tolling bell and of the magic number three. It is no real surprise to learn at the very end of it that the story is "depicted on a stained-glass window in a church in my part of the world" and thus is lifted altogether out of the natural world. The extreme devices of this story, brilliant in their extremity, are worth careful study for an appreciation of the skill with which realistic authors like Faulkner have modified such devices in the service of more modern apologue. The resonant chord of the melodeon in the scene quoted from Faulkner's *Spotted Horses* is in the natural world of that scene at the same time as it is fraught with as much apologue significance as the thrice-tolling bell in Flaubert.

Repetition of words and images

Repetition has various functions in various novella forms, but the numerous examples of repetition already cited in the discussion of individual apologue novellas will have convinced my reader that it exists extraordinarily often in the service of apologue, and the effect it produces of reiterating a truth is fairly obvious—though it is important to point out that repetition is sometimes employed to stress what might not otherwise be obvious in the message itself. Fletcher says that "the enigmatic surfaces [of didactic works] are known not to be random and accidental by virtue of their periodic repetitions" (*Allegory,* p. 172).

I would add that the repetition of a word may often not be as imaginatively effective as a repeated image—the pear tree or the "grey and shapeless" woman in *Spotted Horses* may carry more weight than tolling the word "outrage" two dozen times in *Old Man*. The words "a proper café," repeated by McCullers, are not so effective as the image of the closed café which frames the story by appearing at the beginning and again at the end. Stephen Crane, in *The Open Boat,* makes maximum use of the repeated word *for* the repeated image: "Then the oiler took both oars; then the correspondent took both oars; then the oiler; then the correspondent. They rowed and they rowed" (p. 28). By comparison, the single word "outrage" in the Faulkner story makes only a beginning theme which will have to be fleshed out by scene-making into the complete apologue statement. Crane, however, presents the *image* of outraged frustration directly for the reader's emotional response, then doubles the response by repeating the image. The image *is* the message, affectively, in a way no single repeated word could ever be. The scene is not only rendering a theme of "outraged frustration"; it is already fleshing out that theme emotionally as part of the larger apologue statement *The Open Boat* wishes to make: *Man may be thrust under at the very point when his repeated labors should have allowed him to "nibble the sacred cheese of life."*

I am at pains here not merely to discuss a variation in repetitive skill in two particular novellas (in my view Faulkner, in *Spotted Horses*, is at least the equal of Crane in image-making). Rather, I wish especially to stress that apologue novellas *make* for us, as distinct from stating to us, the apologue statement. Apologue is not the same thing as a parable, where first the affective story is rendered and then the analogous "moral" is stated. Although as I have suggested earlier, a nearly overt statement is often situated somewhere within the apologue story, it is not separable or independent from the story itself. As Sacks puts it: "In the apologue, the most poignant experience, the most subtly created character, the most eloquent prose, become integral parts of a complete work only as they move us to some realization—implicit or formulated—about the world external to the literary creation itself." [24]

Traditionally symbolic settings

Without much discussion on my part, it will be clear to most readers that we are often drawn into a fictional truth about Mankind by a setting of the activity of the story in one of those places where mankind gathers and is most on display—*The Blue Hotel,* the "sad café," the prison in *Old Man,* the ships of Conrad's *Youth* and *The Heart of Darkness,* the theater of Mann's *Mario and the Magician,* the house parties of *The Great Gatsby.*

Heavy-handed narrative, or authorial commentary

When intrusive narrators, such as those of *Tom Jones* and *Middlemarch*, gradually disappeared from the fiction scene in general, they did so because of the pressure of writers like James, who both reflected and increased the reader's taste for the "dramatic," the "real." It began to be apprehended by writers that, when characters were well drawn and their actions suspenseful, commentary need not come between them and the reader. By just this same token, however, the intrusive narrator can and does crop up again when he can serve a formal purpose—for example, when distance between reader and character is needed for the apprehension of a statement to which the character and action must be subordinate. The intrusive narrator (sometimes identifiable as the author), in the period of the novella, is often a signal of apologue. As Booth points out, for such purposes "a direct authorial comment, destroying the illusion that the story is telling itself, may be what will serve his desired effect rather than kill it. . . . There is pleasure from learning the simple truth" (*Rhetoric of Fiction*, p. 136).

That direct voice sounds out on the first page of *Benito Cereno* to condemn Captain Delano before we can get close to him. The narrator sounds his possessive note—his control over character—when he speaks of "our islander" in *The Man Who Loved Islands*. He "tells" instead of "shows," he reiterates, he generalizes, he tells us how to think and read, as in *The Ballad of the Sad Café*: "So for the moment regard these years from random and disjointed views" (p. 23). [25] In the same story, when "the time has come to speak about love" (p. 23), *he* speaks about it, in a dissertation on the nature of love which frankly disrupts the story line but advances its general statement. [26] He kills immediacy to suit the needs of the apologue: "Remember that it all happened long ago" (p. 25). He summarizes the large scene: "Yes, the town is dreary" (p. 65).

Often this narrator supplies the cement that the reader needs to hold the story together when plot does not. In a story pervaded by deliberate unclarity of focus, Lawrence's *The Man Who Loved Islands,* he moves in brazenly to solve the problem: "This story will show. . . ." He speaks sometimes—as here—in the first person, not to bring us close to himself as character, but to make his control of the apologue complete. For, where plot and character are not the center of control, we must still have coherence in order to apprehend the whole. As James says in *The Art of the Novel*: "I understand no breaking-up of the register, no sacrifice of the recording consistency, that doesn't rather scatter and weaken." If there is already a deliberate diffuseness of plot and character, the "recording consistency" of a conspicuous narrator may be crucial to that coherence which cannot depend on plot and character.

And it may be worth noting that the "recording consistency" of the conspicuous narrator is not only a unifying device but a psychological one which points up the positiveness of apologue as a form, positiveness which is one of the pleasures of that form. It bears comparison with the formally different but equally positive voice of the narrator in comedies like *Tom Jones*, where the hero can fall into disasters while the reader keeps some distance and preserves his hopefulness, often by command of the narrator. The statements made by apologues are often painful ones (for example, the statement I have attributed to *The Open Boat*), but the very willingness of a story to say something, to provide an answer, to generalize and wind up a case in a hundred pages or less, is a more positive and hopeful thing than, for example, the naturalistic novels which tend to be lengthy, unwilling to finish describing the horrors of the world. When one has not only a statement-making novella, but one presided over by a statement-making narrator, it gives us, as Lionel Trilling suggests, "the opportunity to identify ourselves with a mind that willingly admits that it is a mind ... a mind thinking and planning—possibly planning our escape." [27]

Relative lack of dialogue

While the narrator is speaking, the characters obviously can not. To the extent that they do not speak, they can act out the apologue without the interference that might arise if we were to come too close to their consciousness. *The Legend of St. Julian* gets through its first eleven pages with only one short break for direct speech. In *The Ballad of the Sad Café* there are rare one-line exchanges, no real conversations. The entire last nine pages, including the horrifying battle between Marvin Macy and Miss Amelia, are rendered ritualistically without a single word from any of those present. The reader is half in control of assessing the events for himself, half under the control of the narrator, but out of the emotional sway of directly represented characters and events. Similarly, the last six pages of the ritual death of *The Woman Who Rode Away* are rendered without direct speech. As R. S. Crane has pointed out, speech imitates "primarily actions, passions, and the manifestations of character" (*Languages,* p. 51), and these are not the primary business of apologue.

Generalization and overt statement

What *is* the business of apologue is to enlarge on What Happens and To Whom until its significance can be emotively gathered into a general but precise statement. Thus it becomes natural to employ the generalization, often in conjunction with an intrusive narrator, as in *The Ballad of the Sad Café*:

"The hearts of small children are delicate organs" (p. 27).

"A groom is in a sorry fix when he is unable to bring his well-beloved bride to bed with him, and when the whole town knows it" (p. 29).

"People are never so free with themselves and so recklessly glad as when there is some possibility of commotion or calamity ahead" (p. 37).

All these statements bear their part-to-whole relation to the statement which governs the whole story, but they also contribute to the general didactic tone which sets the reader's frame of mind for apologue.[28] They can also serve the purpose of closing off considerations usually appropriate to actions, such as our relative closeness to a suffering first-person narrator. Hermann Weigand quotes several aphorisms uttered by the speaker in Kafka's *The Burrow* and points out that the effect is to make us feel that the speaker "knows the concept of tragic irony without feeling the shudder of his own tragic involvement."[29] I would make the further point that the character's noninvolvement helps to bar the reader, too, from the shudder of tragic involvement, forcing us also to generalize on the creature before us.

And of course once the reader's frame of mind has been "set" for apologue, it becomes natural for the story to want to make its statement overt. In the examples already discussed I have suggested that apologues (which are inductive) exercise more or less indirection about this, but the statement seems usually to be discoverable in relatively complete articulation at some point in the story. Stephen Crane, in *The Open Boat*, feeling perhaps that his obligations as a realist are well fulfilled in the dramatic events of the story, brazenly repeats the apologue statement not once but several times. No less than three times he presents it more or less dramatically as the collective "reflections of the men" which "might be formulated thus":

> "If I am going to be drowned—if I am going to be drowned—
> if I am going to be drowned, why, in the name of the seven

> mad gods who rule the sea, was I allowed to come thus far
> and contemplate sand and trees? Was I brought here merely
> to have my nose dragged away as I was about to nibble the
> sacred cheese of Life?"
>
> [P. 41]

At another point the narrator takes back the statement (which, as
here, is sometimes a rhetorical question) from its conjectural
appearance in the minds of the suffering voyagers and "tells" it
rather than "shows" it:

> When it occurs to a man that nature does not regard him
> as important, and that she feels she would not maim the
> universe by disposing of him, he at first wishes to throw
> bricks at the temple, and he hates deeply the fact that there
> are no bricks and no temples. Any visible expressions of
> nature would surely be pelleted with his jeers.
>
> [Pp. 45–46]

(My attentive reader will not have overlooked the number seven in
the first of the above quotes. A rereading of *The Open Boat* in the
light of Crane's use of all the apologue devices is recommended for
sheer delight. In my mind it epitomizes the excellences of modern
apologue, achieving ideally a moving story which illuminates the
dominant statement.)

One peculiar variation on the generalization exists in some of the
titles of apologues—Norman Mailer's *The Man Who Studied Yoga*,
Richard Wright's *The Man Who Lived Underground*, Lawrence's
The Man Who Loved Islands, *The Man Who Died*, and *The Woman
Who Rode Away*, Mark Twain's *The Man Who Corrupted Hadleyburg*, Kipling's *The Man Who Would Be King*. In each case the title
seems to lead into a story of an individual, and indeed it does. But
there is some psychological quality to the generic terms "Man" and
"Woman" which serves as an advance signal of apologue. And so it
proves out in all the named cases.

Heavily stylized prose

Enough instances have already been cited from Lawrence and
Faulkner to show that artificiality of diction plays its role in
apologue. R. S. Crane speaks, without explanation, of the "moder-
ately stylized prose of actions"; but perhaps the explanation has
become self-evident—in an action we seem to want few barriers

between us and the characters about whom we must be made to care. The Byzantine complexity of the diction quoted from *Spotted Horses* functions to lift us out of the real rural scene and our concern for characters into the world where ideas can predominate. Aristotle (*Poetics*, 1460b) warns that "Diction that is overbrilliant obscures character," a price that actions cannot afford to pay but apologues often choose to pay deliberately, precisely to bar some of our concern for character.

Robert Penn Warren, in his novella *The Circus in the Attic,* works with simple, realistic narration, then lifts us out of the real into the ideational by sudden passages:

> She took her school course, got her job, and after a while married an insurance salesman, a widower, in the office where she worked. She had left Bardsville, and she never came back....
>
> Once done, it seemed like something which had always had its existence, waiting not for her doing but for her recognition. It was done, but it had always existed, even before her doing, an expiation *or* a vengeance, or an expiation *and* a vengeance, inextricably interfused, the violent act caught like the very face of life between two mirrors, to be reflected, mirror within answering mirror, expiation and vengeance, vengeance and expiation forever in opposite directions, forever toward the inwardness of self and forever toward the outwardness of the world, into twin infinities.[30]
>
> [P. 105]

The act committed is simply and directly told: "She had left Bardsville." What is not simple is the didactic significance of the act and the far from simple language that elevates its significance. Mixed styles purposely mixed.

The magnitude of apologue

While I have not been directly relating the devices of apologue to the novella length in the foregoing discussion, I hope that the necessity of a certain length will by now seem implicit in all that I have said about the procedure of apologue in general and the procedure of the individual novella apologues I have discussed. Given the human desire (not only of our age but of all ages) for the imitation of life, we cannot accept pleasurably a work which at great length allows the didactic to dominate the mimetic (except, as I have suggested, when

the mode is poetry, not prose). I do not, by the way, wish to accept
"didactic" and "mimetic" as mutually exclusive narrative procedures. In apologue it is still the imitation of life which enchants
us. Something Happens to Someone, and it is that, as I suggested at
the start, which causes us to read apologue as against sermon or
essay.

Apologue has its own artistic (pleasurable) devices for narrating
that Something, and a tasteful length is one of them. As Scholes and
Kellogg put it: "The human intellect being what it is, fable tends
toward brevity in narrative" (*Narrative,* p. 14). We cannot too long
sustain the distance from characters that is created when they are
nameless, compete with each other for our attention, exist and act in
reaches and leaps of time (or for all time), are dead before they are
alive, are relatively silent, are reduced to animal likeness or to lack
of complexity. We cannot sustain an excess of generalization or
abstraction. We cannot sustain an effusion of artificial language.
We cannot sustain repetition beyond a point where it is working too
obviously. We (at least we moderns) cannot sustain for too long a
controlling voice telling us what to think.[31]

But we must and do sustain all these pleasurably up to that point
where the apologue has come clear, is enlarged in some perfection
and realized by us. Overdo it, and you have the turgidity of *Ship of
Fools*, rendering inevitable a protest like Wayne Booth's: "Why, why
did Miss Porter feel that she should try to get everything in? Did she
really think that it would be more powerful to give forty instances of
depravity than twenty, or five?"[32] Underdo it, and you appear to
have a trivialized action rather than a roundly achieved apologue.

Short-story apologues do exist because apologue, for the above
reasons, is more amenable to brevity than length. Hawthorne
succeeded in his task (and is little in vogue among modern readers)
because he wrote conspicuous allegory. Joyce's "Counterparts"
succeeds, in my view, because its brevity is attuned to the simplicity
of its statement. But this is rare. Shirley Jackson's "The Lottery"
and Faulkner's "A Rose For Emily" are, in my reading, intended as
apologues but, because they do not sustain and enlarge their
statements at an appropriate length, the fictions tend to carry only
themselves, and many readers are reduced to treating them as mere
horror stories, extracting dime-novel thrills from the stoning in the

one case and the telltale [sic] grey hair on the pillow that betrays murder and necrophilia in the other.[33] How relatively poor it seems if we apprehend the murder of Homer Barron as a sick thrill, when the intention seems to have been to enlarge the horror to a statement about the murder of the whole Northern adventure (robber barons?), strangled in the bony dying clutches of the old South.

3
THE APOLOGUE
THAT PREACHES
BY EXAMPLE

First you hear it, then you meet it in the flesh.

Wright Morris,
Love Among the Cannibals

Soon we shall contrive to be born somehow
from an idea.

Dostoevsky, Notes From Underground

Un genre qui n'est pas un monde, et qui
coincide non avec un élargissement et une
découverte du monde, mais avec une réduc-
tion, un classement et une utilisation du
monde.

Albert Thibaudet

When a part so ptee does duty for the holos we
soon grow to use of an allforabit.

James Joyce, Finnegans Wake

To speak of a modern taste for "reality" in fiction, as I have been doing in the last chapter, seems to speak of what I had offered not to, namely, factors extrinsic to the novellas themselves—the desires of the reader, the pressure of the times. While pressure for realism has indeed affected prose fiction writing in general,[1] a fact remarked by many more authors and critics than I have cited, it is important to observe also that, in well-made stories, the realistic details do not function merely as decoration applied at the behest of readers or critics but function organically in the formal achievement of each work. Modern apologues, unlike medieval allegories, do not often make statements about abstract morality, and for that very reason they do not ordinarily represent character and event abstractly; though, as we have seen, within their own frame of realism they provide their own kinds of distancing.

Accordingly, Lawrence's "woman who rode away" is as alive and real to us as she needs to be to develop our sense of precisely how humanly difficult is the surrender to the principle for which this apologue wishes to press. Conversely, when it becomes necessary that the apologue statement not be blurred by involving the reader too closely in the pain of her death, Lawrence departs into the relatively unreal color patterns and ritual already described; for the form of the story demands that he do this. To speak of these intrinsic necessities does not obviate the extrinsic possibility that the *kind* of statement that Lawrence felt moved to make was a result of his life and times.

Writing in an earlier time, Hawthorne may have fulfilled a personal and social need to write deductive allegories which would furnish with moral ideas what James dared to call the "unfurnished" souls of New Englanders, to whom realism might be unattractive (certainly Melville, writing more realistic works of the novella length in the same era, was relatively less popularly accepted). That is history speaking. Formally speaking, I have already suggested that, whatever the context that pushed Hawthorne to his general bent toward allegory, the short-story length works only because he sacrifices reality to the needs of his allegorizing. The historical period can govern the taste for allegory in prose fiction but, in the production of the given story, the artistic requirements of allegory govern the length and the degree of realism.

To say that realism functions organically in each apologue does not, then, cross off the possibility that a general taste for realism in fiction has determined the *kinds* of didactic stories we read now, which are not often allegories. The Example Apologue, with which this chapter will concern itself, seems to me a phenomenon that might naturally have been expected to appear in the era of realistic fiction. Let us imagine an author in the last half of the nineteenth century, or in the twentieth century. As an artist, he undertakes the task of art—to give form to the unruly stuff of life. As a man in touch with his times, he wishes to accept and represent life realistically. Not only does he wish to represent it but, responding to another signal from a pressured and difficult era, he wishes to articulate some truths about it. One way to resolve these needs fictionally is to represent life realistically but with extraordinary selectivity of focus, so that the apologue will be expressed by a particular example of a general situation, and the statement will always begin: "It is like this ..."

- —to be forced by slum life into prostitution; Stephen Crane's *Maggie, A Girl of the Streets*;
- —to be imprisoned in a Soviet labor camp; Alexander Solzhenitsyn's *One Day in the Life of Ivan Denisovich;*
- —to live blindly as an upper middle-class bureaucrat; Tolstoy's *The Death of Ivan Ilyich*;
- —to have that kind of simple religious fervor which elevates a narrow life; Flaubert's *A Simple Heart*;
- —to be a rationalistic "man of acute consciousness"; Dostoevsky's *Notes From Underground*.

Many of the devices I have already described as recurring in apologue inevitably recur in the example apologues. The most conspicuous difference that marks this subclass of inductive apologues is its ability to focus closely on what happens to a single central character and still cause its statement to dominate the fiction.[2] The character exists not, as in actions, for his own sake and the production of our emotional response to him personally as a result of what happens to him. Instead, we are made to respond emotionally to the character in ways that cause us to apprehend him as a representative of an exampled way of life—which may appear to come close to a contradiction.

The exemplary downfall of Crane's MAGGIE

Resolving this contradiction was clearly a challenge and a difficulty for some nineteenth-century authors like Stephen Crane who were bridging the gap between allegory and modern apologue and finding themselves caught between the techniques of overt didacticism and the developing techniques of dramatic realism in prose, which were now moving across formal boundaries. As I shall try later to show, technical brilliance results from this struggle in twentieth-century works like Solzhenitsyn's *One Day in the Life of Ivan Denisovich*, a work not necessarily more moving than Crane's *Maggie*, but in a few respects more skillful. (Let me make it clear that I am *never* saying that literary works are better or more moving simply by reason of coming from our time rather than earlier times—and, in my view, the modern dislike of allegory is simply a fashion based in what I hope is a temporary moral uncertainty, and which Dante, Spenser, and even Langland, will continue to surmount. What can and does improve is the growing store of technical knowledge which modern authors develop out of their experience with earlier ones.)

Crane had an understanding, nearly unmatched in modern fiction except by Faulkner, of how to burden exciting and realistic events with an apologue (let all readers renew for themselves the excellences of *The Open Boat*, *The Monster*, and *The Blue Hotel*). What he seems not to have perfected were the skills needed for an example apologue like *Maggie*, skills necessary to bring his audience movingly close to a single realistic character who would subserve the apologue purpose of exemplifying the results of a way of life.

Not that he did not work at it—close observation will reveal *Maggie* to be as elaborately "worked" as a fine tapestry. Crane himself appears not to have lost faith in *Maggie;* he is reported to have spent in 1893 the (then) staggering sum of $869 to publish it himself. This seems, when we read the novella, to have been partly a matter of placing value on sheer labor, which produced some remarkable effects at the expense of some others that were needed.

Maggie's descent into prostitution must be made to seem, before all, a result of slum life. Thus Crane puts distance between us and character by leaving her to one side, or totally out, of chapters whose chief aim is to present that life, including such crucial chapters as the first and the last. It is certainly arguable that we will not be able to understand innocent Maggie's descent from grace without being shown the slum context, a hell in which grace is impossible despite Maggie's real and pathetic efforts; but some authors (Flaubert, Dostoevsky, and, later, Solzhenitsyn) have managed to keep focus both on the way of life and the exemplary character.

The opening chapter is a realistic bloody battle between gangs of slum urchins who reveal their didactic function promptly by coming from "Rum Alley" and "Devil's Row." We believe in the battle full of stones, blood, oaths, and sobs, but it also is enlarged with mock-epic elements: the epithet of "the boy with the chronic sneer" (who will grow up to seduce Maggie); the similes that enlarge the battle—"notes of joy like songs of triumphant savagery" and "fighting in the modes of four thousand years ago." Maggie's little brother aims to be, like Ajax, "a man of blood with a sort of sublime license" (p. 34).[3]

In chapter 2, when father and son return home and we at last meet Maggie, she is the most natural and pathetic small girl imaginable, but her setting is presented in a self-consciously artificial diction:

> Eventually they entered a dark region where, from a careening building, a dozen gruesome doorways gave up loads of babies to the street and the gutter. A wind of early autumn raised yellow dust from cobbles and swirled it against a hundred windows. Long streamers of garments fluttered from fire-escapes. In all unhandy places there were buckets, brooms, rags, and bottles. In the street infants played or fought with other infants or sat stupidly in the way of vehicles. Formidable women, with uncombed hair and disordered dress, gossiped while leaning on railings, or screamed in frantic quarrels. Withered persons, in curious postures of submission to something, sat smoking pipes in obscure corners. A thousand odours of cooking food came forth to the street. The building quivered and creaked from the weight of humanity stamping about in its bowels.
>
> [Pp. 34–35]

The scene is a painting by Bosch, absolutely general at the same time as it is detailed and absolutely real. Maggie, as she emerges from it into the forefront of the novella, is at once totally real and only one of the details. Though Crane did not manage to keep her steadily in the forefront of events, this technique works surprisingly well to make her various appearances in the story seem to us realistic and consistent. She is the illuminating example both of the slum scene itself and of what can happen to one of its members, in fact to *all* of its members who, like Maggie, are initially innocent and hopeful.

There is a similar, though more awkward, surfacing of Jimmie, Maggie's brother, of Pete, the lover who abandons her, and of Mary, her mother—each of them has at least one chapter which seems reserved to him or her alone. Upon reflection (and here one wishes that Crane could depend on emotional effects rather than reflection) we can see that these chapters both exemplify aspects of slum life which Maggie by herself cannot and elaborate the attitudes of those close to her which contribute to the downfall of Maggie and of girls like her. There are numerous other characters who justify their existence by their exemplification of slum life, and to this formal end they are kept carefully at a distance by a technique which we will observe again in the Solzhenitsyn novella—the reductive epithet. In chapter 11, the violent saloon confrontation between Jimmie and Pete (Jimmie's fruitless protest against the deflowering of Maggie), the event is framed and distanced by the gradual retreat of a bar character named, solely and repeatedly, "the quiet stranger" (p. 70). In the scene of Maggie's despair at meeting Pete's other woman friend, the woman's activities and conversation are painfully real to us as they are to Maggie, but she and her escort are kept at an appropriate distance by a striking technique: characters inside the scene naturally call them by name, but the narrator refers to them only by repeated epithet: "the woman of brilliance and audacity" and "the mere boy" (repeated thirteen times in the very short chapter 14).

The final chapter, reserved to the mother's reception of the news of Maggie's death, employs almost ritualistically an alternation of epithets between a strange "woman in black" and "the mourner," who is the mother. It has been observed that this novella is an ironic reworking of the biblical story of Magdalen;[4] the elevated feeling of the ritual of that last chapter thus brings us appropriately to the ironically Christ-like forgiveness of the last words in the story, in which Maggie's only "mourner" screams "Oh, yes, I'll fergive her! I'll fergive her!"

The ironic nature of "the mourner" and of all the previously described epithets in our other apologues suggests that irony is a feature of all the classes of apologue. Rosemond Tuve points out that irony, like its "neighboring trope" of metaphor, "implies what it can not overtly state without losing the formal character which defines it as a figure; both figures are, as it were, open at one end, allowing interpretations which can be supported by proper evidence but not proven."[5] Apologue itself can be seen as a large metaphor, often fraught as in this case with irony, and Tuve's statement about interpretation cannot be too much stressed. Except where the author, as I have shown, briefly states his message, the fiction does its work *feelingly*—it "implies," it gives "proper evidence," but it cannot be "proven." The statement of *Maggie*, like that of all apologues, is capable of formulation, but it strikes the reader as a *felt* statement arising in the gap between the literal and the ironic or metaphoric borders of the trope.

I should not like to leave *Maggie* without some comment on its extraordinary narrative movement and texture. Solzhenitsyn (rising perhaps on the shoulders of earlier Russians such as Tolstoy and Dostoevsky) will be seen to understand more than Crane about how to maintain closeness to his central character without defeating the apologue form. Crane, however, produces his own kind of rhetorical unity, dependent on structure rather than character. Though by definition the apologue lacks a tragic hero and plot, the story line of events in *Maggie* still moves sequentially (as against necessarily— Maggie's death is appropriate but not necessary) toward a predictable unhappy ending. Three of the chapters are set in cabarets and open with place descriptions which, each by each, are progressively more threatening. So great is the authorial skill that I wish to quote the descriptions in sequence to illumine their apologue effectiveness:

> An orchestra of yellow silk women and bald-headed men, on an elevated stage near the centre of a great green-hued hall, played a popular waltz. The place was crowded with people grouped about little tables. A battalion of waiters slid among the throng, carrying trays of beer-glasses, and making change from the inexhaustible vaults of their trousers pockets. Little boys, in the costumes of French chefs, paraded up and down the irregular aisles vending fancy cakes. There was a low rumble of conversation and

a subdued clinking of glasses. Clouds of tobacco smoke
rolled and wavered high in air above the dull gilt of
the chandeliers.

[P. 54]

Maggie has never seen anything like this. Its charm for her is
unmitigated, though it is slightly mitigated for the reader by small
storm warnings such as "irregular," "low rumble," and "clouds."
The word "irregular" is picked up thematically in the second
description:

In a hall of irregular shape sat Pete and Maggie drinking
beer. A submissive orchestra dictated to by a spectacled man
with frowsy hair and in soiled evening dress, industriously
followed the bobs of his head and the waves of his baton. A
ballad-singer, in a gown of flaming scarlet, sang in the
inevitable voice of brass. When she vanished, men seated at
the tables near the front applauded loudly, pounding the
polished wood with their beer-glasses. She returned, attired
in less gown, and sang again. She received another
enthusiastic encore. She reappeared in still less gown and
danced. The deafening rumble of glasses and clapping of
hands that followed her exit indicated an overwhelming
desire to have her come on for the fourth time.

[P. 76]

The "low rumble" has now become a "deafening rumble" and in
the next cabaret it will be "replaced by a roar":

In a hilarious hall there were twenty-eight tables and
twenty-eight women and a crowd of smoking men. Valiant
noise was made on a stage at the end of the hall by an
orchestra composed of men who looked as if they had just
happened in. Soiled waiters ran to and fro, swooping down
like hawks on the unwary in the throng; clattering along the
aisles with trays covered with glasses; stumbling over
women's skirts and charging two prices for everything but
beer. . . .
    The usual smoke-cloud was present, but so dense that
heads and arms seemed entangled in it. The rumble of
conversation was replaced by a roar. Plenteous oaths heaved
through the air. The room rang with the shrill voices of
women bubbling over with drink-laughter. The chief element

in the music of the orchestra was speed. The musicians
played in intent fury. A woman was singing and smiling upon
the stage, but no one took notice of her. The rate at which
the piano, cornet, and violins were going seemed to impart
wildness to the half-drunken crowd. Beer-glasses were
emptied at a gulp and conversation became a rapid chatter.
The smoke eddied and swirled like a shadowy river hurrying
toward some unseen falls. Pete and Maggie entered the
hall and took chairs at a table near the door. The woman who
was seated there made an attempt to occupy Pete's attention
and, failing, went away.

[Pp. 81-82]

Not only is the quality of the cabarets steadily worse (note how
repetition functions in this case to drive home the *change*), but their
association with prostitution becomes steadily more relentless. In the
first cabaret the description ends entirely pleasantly, giving way to
action among the characters. But several paragraphs (unquoted)
later, like the reiteration of a musical theme, it begins again with
repetition of the original opening: "The orchestra of yellow silk
women and bald-headed men gave vent to a few bars of anticipatory
music..." (p. 55). Then a dancer in a pink dress "gallop[s]" upon
the stage. She sings, leaves, then reappears to divulge "the fact that
she was attired in some half-dozen skirts. It was patent that any one
of them would have proved adequate for the purpose for which
skirts are intended" (p. 56). The tone is factual, the charm of the
scene remains intact, but a very slight suggestion of soiled female
virtue has been introduced.

In the second cabaret what was pink has turned to "flaming
scarlet," the word "soiled" has been introduced overtly (it is
repeated often throughout the novella), and by the end of chapter 12
Maggie, on her way out, brushes against a "painted" woman and
"with a shrinking movement, drew back her skirts."

In the third cabaret all has become speeded up, the atmosphere is
both noisy and noisome, the pattern is one lady-of-the-evening for
each table, and the implied whore is linked this time not to the exit
but to the entry of Maggie and Pete.

Of course I am aware that I have remarked on only a few of the
elements at work in these descriptions. Even the smoke has a
didactic life of its own (slum life at its worst gets dirtier, more

airless, more confusing), while incorporated in an entirely realistic scene upon which the author moves Maggie like a pawn.

A narrative progression is again carefully employed to formal effect—this time from symbolic light to symbolic darkness—in the chapter (17) which gives us the scene of Maggie's final degradation (we understand her to be Maggie, but she is referred to throughout the scene simply as "the girl"). At first she tries to ply her trade where "electric lights, whirring softly, shed a blurred radiance." We remove to the "mingled light and gloom of an adjacent park." Next Maggie is seen to bypass "more glittering avenues" and goes into "darker blocks." Her potential customers range from the rich in the cheerful "places of forgetfulness" to a moneyless drunk. Then: "The girl went into gloomy districts near the river, where the tall black factories shut in the street and only occasional broad beams of light fell across the sidewalks from saloons" (p. 96). (Only the sound of a violin comes from one of these saloons—the end of the road which began at the cabarets with their orchestras—and this time Maggie is entirely on the outside, and is herself the whore.) The fearfulness increases when "farther on in the darkness she met a ragged being with shifting, bloodshot eyes and grimy hands," after which "she went into the blackness of the final block," and—

> Afar off the lights of the avenues glittered as if from an impossible distance. Street-car bells jingled with a sound of merriment.
> At the feet of the tall buildings appeared the deathly black hue of the river. Some hidden factory sent up a yellow glare, that lit for a moment the waters lapping oilily against the timbers. The varied sounds of life, made joyous by distance and seeming unapproachableness, came faintly and died away to silence.

The progression is not only from light to dark but from life to death. The chapter is a microcosm of the whole novella, which substitutes for plot a unifying time-line, the life of Maggie from childhood to death. But not all of that life; only such scenes from it as will serve to stress it as exemplary, scenes which mark off slum life as death-dealing, scenes which show how "her fate is representative of a society" (Booth, *Rhetoric of Fiction*, p. 136).

In the context of our study of the magnitude of such novellas, it is worth noting that narrative progressions like the above (especially the three cabarets) are too large and elaborate for a short story, and their effect would very likely go unnoticed if they were to be spaced out in a full-length novel.

Some of the highly conscious and artificial effects which I have described in *Maggie* are adversely commented upon by one of Crane's critics, Arthur Edelstein, who calls the "Bowery novels" (*Maggie* and *George's Mother*) "somewhat clumsy." [6] Quoting F. R. Leavis on a device he calls "adjectival insistence," Edelstein notes that "Crane exhibits a related tendency in his constant editorial modifiers" (I have previously termed them epithets) "which deprive the facts of their own voice by announcing to the reader his obligatory responses." Edelstein complains also about repetition: "In the opening chapter of *Maggie*, there are four physical assaults. And they proliferate relentlessly, hardly a chapter passing without an assault or the threat of one. Brutality, these events compulsively declare, is a pervading condition of life in the slums" (p. 18). He goes on to speak of Crane's "tic of insistence," of his "straining after emphasis," of the "fervent presence of an author arranging as total a contrast as possible between event and perception. The irony, in brief, visits itself on Crane as well as upon his characters, by exposing his interference" (p. 19).

The irony, in my view, visits itself on the critic by working so effectively in the novella. It is irresistible to quote Edelstein because he is so truly an example of a good reader who intuitively responds correctly, is open to the effects of the story each by each, but whose failure to follow his intuition to an apprehension of apologue form causes him disappointment, causes him to dispraise precisely those literary devices which work so well to Crane's purpose. What else should apologue do but announce to the reader—make him feel certain of—his "obligatory response"? How appropriate it is to employ repetition, as one could not in a realistic action, to "compulsively declare" that "brutality . . . is a pervading condition of life in the slums." By means precisely of repetition, one of the most important concepts the novella wishes imaginatively to convey has been successfully conveyed to Edelstein. Inevitably, because he consciously appreciates only the artistic modes more suitable to actions, Edelstein is forced to conclude that *Maggie* is unsatisfactory from a point of view it never intended to satisfy. Thus do our literary disappointments often accrue from our formal literary misapprehensions.

*Atypicality in the
making of a typical "Day"*

The problem of the example apologue is just this: never to lose the excitement and suspense of What Happens to Whom, which in every story is unlike in any other story, and at the same time cause the individual fiction to reveal itself as a general mold. So that Tolstoy is able to say of the dead Ivan Ilyich: "Ivan Ilyich's life had been most simple and most ordinary and therefore most terrible." So that Solzhenitsyn—and once again we can note the habit of apologue to choose a point in the story where its statement becomes overt—can end *One Day in the Life of Ivan Denisovich* by saying: "Of such days from gong to gong in his term there were three thousand six hundred and fifty three.... Three days extra due to leap year."[7]

We are intensely aware of Shukhov (Ivan) as a breathing, suffering, resourceful personality—much more so than was the case with Crane's Maggie. Most of the story is revealed so intimately from Shukhov's point of view that it seems at times to border on stream of consciousness. Even that final sentence of the novella could come from his consciousness—it has the stamp of his ability to face facts unblinkingly. Yet the story is clearly not centered on Shukhov for his own sake but for Shukhov's day as an example of all days any prisoner might spend in a Soviet labor camp. He is made to seem an individual for the sake of reminding us that *all* human beings are individual even under the intensely uniform pressures of such a life. The resource open to the author of such a work (and Crane did not yet know how to fully exploit it) is to represent an individual and what happens to him with great realism but simultaneously to confine, focus, and restrain the individual, make *use* of the individual to exemplify the general style of life or the general kind of person.

A comparison may help elucidate the problem. There is only one Hamlet in the world. He is melancholy, and the play doubtless sought some of its effect by playing on the Renaissance fear of melancholia as a general humor; but Hamlet's melancholy is, before all, particular to Hamlet personally, is there to be part of his personal tragedy. There is likewise only one Shukhov in the world— but the reader is constrained to experience his pain of one day *only* so that he can sample the extended pain of all such prisoners. We are close to him for the sake of his reactions *as a prisoner in this kind of place.* Quite unlike Hamlet, (or, for a closer contrast, Camus' Meursault in prison), Shukhov's background and human relations are suppressed except for the minimal indications which help us to understand how *anyone* might be condemned to such a life, and strive to survive it.

Perhaps the difference that makes the one character a particular tragic protagonist, the other exemplary, seems fragile at first glance, but it becomes a solid difference as one examines the artistic devices by which *One Day* differentiates its form from that of *Hamlet*. Both works happen to begin with early-morning confrontations. But consider the difference that diction immediately makes in the novella:

> At five, as always, reveille was sounded....
> For some reason they hadn't come to open the barracks yet. And Shukhov didn't hear the usual noises of the orderlies lifting the latrine barrel....
> Shukhov never slept past the rising gong. He always got up when he heard it. Until lineup there was an hour and a half of one's own time, not the government's. Anyone who knew camp life could always earn a bit then.
>
> [Pp. 544-45]

We are only seventeen lines into the story at this point. We are already moving into the consciousness of Shukhov, but our reaction to his thoughts is being steadily manipulated. The particular morning with its minor surprises is being presented so as to cause our appreciation of the likeness of this morning to all others in the camp. That they hadn't come to open the barracks "yet" is surprising because on all other days they will have done so by this time. We have had three uses of the word "always," one "usual," one "never." Finding out what *always* happens, the noises that are *usual*, what Shukhov *never* does because the nature of camp life does not permit it, has already led us a long way toward that conclusion 115 pages later that there are "three thousand six hundred and fifty three" of "such days" to be expected—an ending worth comparing with Dostoevsky's more subtle parenthesis at the close of *Notes From Underground*:

> (The notes of this paradoxalist do not end here, however. He could not refrain from going on with them, but it seems to us that we may stop here.)

Examples cannot end, as plots do. They go on forever.

Solzhenitsyn, on his opening page, moves in with some other indications of apologue. There are large generalizations and broad categorization: "Anyone who knew camp life could always earn a bit then" (p. 545), and "the men who die in camp are the ones who lick bowls" (p. 545), and "that kind took good care of themselves, though it cost the blood of others" (p. 545). Later these generalizations take on the enlarged quality of aphorism: "Six ounces of bread rules life" (p. 585).

Repetition serves its usual reiterative function. One paragraph begins "Shukhov never slept past the rising gong"; two paragraphs later: "Shukhov always got up at the rising gong" (p. 545). So do they all, "always," or pay the penalty.

Another repeated element is the use of hypothesis and future tense, both based on knowledge of what is usual (knowledge, of course, intended for the reader). Hypothesis: "A guard might be looking for someone for some work, or he might be looking for someone on whom to vent his meanness" (p. 555). How does Shukhov know? Because these are the habits of guards. "Working like hell would be the only salvation" (p. 546). Why? Because it has customarily been the only salvation, day after day, year after year.

Direct predictions in future tense are based also on what happens habitually: "Some of them were going to be missing part of their bread that evening" (p. 547). Why? Because they are fulfilling once more some conditions that caused them to miss bread on other evenings.

Example apologue can and does make good use of rhetorical questions, an intriguing way to state what the author wishes the reader to hold as obvious:

"In the mornings, what was there to look for on a zek [prisoner]?" (Nothing.)

"What else was there to do?" (Nothing.)

"What protection would it be?" (None.)

If the question is exaggerated (a natural inclination arising from Shukhov's long desperation, which keeps us close to him while helping to exemplify his situation), the answer can be specified:

"What has Shukhov been eating for eight-years-going-on-nine?" Answer: "Nothing."

The novella makes unusually interesting use of epithet, in some cases combined with the reduction of men to animals. Der is "the swine," and there are also "Fetyukov, the jackal," "Panteleyev, the dog," as well as "Alyesha, the Baptist." This serves more than the usual apologue purpose of distancing characters so that the reader is caused to think in narrow but general terms. In this case (as in some cases described in *Maggie*) epithet serves to fade the other characters into the background so that Shukhov can stand out as *the* live exemplar of life in the camp. We are removed from these other characters, close in some respects to the "body and soul" of Shukhov. But observe the total effect of the manner of representation that brings us close to Shukhov: "Everything on Shukhov was government issue. Here I am, so to speak, feel me over body and soul" (p. 566). We are in his intimate consciousness here precisely so that we may appreciate the extent to which he exemplifies men reduced to "government issue."

The skill of such devices cannot be too much admired. Solzhenitsyn has gathered to his use not only the traditional stylistic devices for keeping us at a distance from character but, in the case of Shukhov, has managed (but carefully, *selectively*) to keep us close to his consciousness and physical feelings by devices—for example, by presenting interior states of mind—once employed only in actions. Simultaneously, he has produced that degree of selectivity and generality of tone that make the character function primarily as a type.

More than that, he has managed, by means of his example apologue, to produce commentary on Soviet life in general (very clearly a subsidiary aim of this novella), while making it serve, part-to-whole, the coherence of his example of the labor camp. Thus, it is perfectly in keeping with the usual expectations of camp life that Shukhov's brigade should be afraid to be shifted to a new project, significantly named "Socialist Life Town." Even while the new project is described naturalistically—as real a place as the construction zone where the brigade is finally sent to work—its name causes the reader to think symbolically:

> The Socialist Life Town was now just a bare open field, all snow ridges and drifts. But before anything could be built there, the prisoners would have to dig holes, set in posts, and put up barbed wire—fencing themselves in so they couldn't escape. Only when that was done could they start to build.
>
> [P. 546]

Elsewhere, there are discussions among the prisoners (whose main comfort is naturally conversation) of elements in the larger Soviet life outside the camp—discussions which, like the above quotation, enlarge the reader's sense of all of Soviet life as a labor camp. Consider the following exchange which occurs quite without warning or preparation:

> "No, old fellow," Tsezar said softly, casually. "Objectivity demands you recognize that Eisenstein is a genius. *Ivan the Terrible*—isn't that a work of genius? The dance of the *oprichniks*! The scene in the cathedral!"
>
> "Affectation!" Kh-123 grew angry, holding his spoon in front of his mouth. "So much art it isn't art any longer. Pepper and poppy seed instead of our daily bread! And then, too, it's the most repulsive political idea—justification of one-man tyranny. Mockery at the memory of three generations of the Russian intelligentsia."
>
> Eating his kasha absentmindedly—losing all the good of it.
>
> "But what other treatment would they have passed?"
>
> "Ah, *passed*? Then don't talk about genius! Say simply that he's a bootlicker, that he executed a dog's order. Genius doesn't fit its treatment to the taste of tyrants."
>
> "Hmm, hmm," coughed Shukhov, too shy to break into the intellectual conversation.
>
> [P. 599]

I quote a large portion of this passage because of the remarkable variety of elements working together in it. The conversation begins without warning, in the middle, suggesting that the regimented life in camp causes conversations habitually to be interrupted. The discussion of the function of art under Stalin's rule serves to remind the reader that the day before us exemplifies not just a single camp but a system within the context of a larger punitive system, where there are rules about what will "pass," analogous to the smaller (but also life-and-death) rules about what will pass in camp. That one speaker has a name and the other a number is an inconsistency which would be intolerable in an action but serves here to illuminate the fact that whether named or merely numbered, these prisoners are digits in a system.

And finally, Shukhov's shyness connects the scene to the central character at the same time as it makes the general point that the camp contains not only unfortunate POW's from World War II like

Shukhov, but also dissident intellectuals. Even the kasha has its apologue function: here there is so little food that one must eat it slowly and appreciatively. The point of view from which the prisoner is "losing all the good of it" is Shukhov's, thus keeping the incident within the unity of the day's incidents by means of a unifying consciousness—much as I have described the intrusive narrator functioning in other apologues.

One can even employ a narrator—someone more intellectually aware than Shukhov—to speak in the first person and do, himself, the job of presenting himself as an example. In *Notes From Underground* the narrator says: "I am convinced that we underground folk ought to be kept in check. Though we may sit forty years underground without speaking, when we do come out into the light of day and break out we talk and talk *and* talk...." (The final ellipsis is part of the text, and works in the same fashion as the final sentences of both *Notes* and *One Day*: to suggest that what has gone before is just an example of how "underground folk" always behave.)

The focus in *One Day* has been, then, on a central character, has been unified by his consciousness quite as an action might be—and the story line has been bounded by one day in *his* life. Yet these devices, so often devices of actions, have been subsumed in the requirements of apologue. As Sacks has pointed out: "Using new techniques for representing characters, for revealing subtle states of awareness, for achieving complex emotional effects—techniques developed during two hundred years of experimenting with novels that are unique realizations of principles common to represented actions—our new novelists have created new apologues" ("Golden Birds," p. 291).

All I have described in this and other apologues documents this statement, and it is in keeping with Sacks's historical emphasis to note that the Faulkner and Solzhenitsyn works document his statement best. Faulkner, however, keeps at the command of his apologues one resource of actions which, almost by definition, might seem to be unavailable to example apologue. I refer to suspense. In the case of *Spotted Horses*, Faulkner can round out the apologue statement by resolving the problem of the horses into no resolution at all ("This court's adjourned!"), though we were certainly waiting eagerly to see what would happen. In *Old Man* the danger presented by the flood works directly to make us feel a truth about the world in general: that the worst danger is better—that is, summons up a higher humanity—than the safety of confinement by authority. In the case of the example apologue, however, if it is trying to make us feel the truth of a statement that begins "It is *always* like this ... ," what suspense, what unknown, can be introduced to keep the reader intrigued about What Happens?

In fact, there are two answers.

First, the whole situation exemplified may be one we know little about—most of us are not in touch with either the slum life of nineteenth-century America, or the inside of Soviet labor camps of this century. It is in fact rather obviously the aim of example apologues to inform us of the truth of a condition previously unknown to us. If it happens that we are already in touch with what is being exemplified, the nature of our pleasure (and suspense) is the gradual production of the "shock of recognition" of the way of life being displayed.

Secondly, "One day" (or one life, or one series of selected events) can never be a perfect example, because the details change even though the large situation is an ongoing truth which the details exemplify. Right before the concluding statement of *One Day*—that one day which we will be specifically told exemplifies thousands of others—the narrator spells out the surprises in Shukhov's day about which we were suspenseful:

> Shukhov went to sleep, quite content. He had had many successes that day. They hadn't put him in solitary, the brigade had not been driven to the Socialist Life Town, at lunch he had made off with an extra kasha, the foremen had surpassed their quota, Shukhov had had a damn good time laying that wall, he hadn't been caught with that piece of blade at body inspection, he had earned something from Tsezar at evening, and bought himself some tobacco. And he hadn't become really sick.
>
> [P. 660]

The summary reminds us that the day's events have indeed been suspenseful for the reader (though it is important to note that the kind of suspense is item-by-item, episodic, quite unlike plotted suspense in actions). There is also, of course, a fine irony in listing the kinds of problems whose resolution can bring happiness to such a prisoner.

The main point to be made is that these *kinds*, and only these limited kinds, of problems could arise, singly or together in various combinations limited by the truth of camp life. In the rhetoric of example apologue, the force that drives the reader is not so much What Happens—the limits on that are much more fixed even than the "likely and necessary" limits of a tightly plotted action—but, given what kinds of things must happen in such a situation (a slum, a labor camp) When and How will they happen?

Once again, the novella length shows itself appropriate. If there is a limit on the quality of suspense, and if there is a strict limit on the variety of events that can define the truth of the exemplified situation, one must limit also one's length or risk sameness. If the boundaries of the example are a day, one must end when one has exploited the limited possibilities of that day (there can be no such richly eventful day for Shukhov as for Leopold Bloom). If the boundaries are a lifetime (as in *The Death of Ivan Ilyich* or *Maggie*) the risk of sameness if one continues on is implicit in the very notion of exemplification. What is wrong with Ivan Ilyich's kind of life, that we must be aware of, is precisely that one can take a sickening leap over seventeen years because the intervening ones were all alike. What is wrong with Maggie's life is that, to go on about it at novel length would be simply to repeat the incidents of degradation and brutality that set the apologue in motion in the first place (four such incidents in a row have already wearied one critic!). Blessed be the shapely novella, once again.

An unexemplary example in James's THE PUPIL

Critical disagreements have proliferated around *The Pupil,* by Henry James, as they sometimes do around stories which lack perfectly achieved form, leaving room for critics to build reputations on "far out" interpretations. (As indicated by its critical bibliography, Faulkner's *A Rose For Emily* is a notable honeypot of this kind, perhaps for the formal reason of its length, as I have suggested earlier.) I am choosing to discuss the James story briefly because I think the perception of imperfect form contains enlightenment which derives from the study of form, and is one avenue to contentment with a clearly moving story which nevertheless arouses puzzlement that is unresolved by any formal classification. I doubt that any author in fact sits down to produce a work of a given class, with conscious intent to make an apologue in one case, an action in another. Partly he intuits the form he needs as his material develops, partly he may work from his preconceptions about what is universally good in art, and mistakes can enter into such products.

James was a highly conscious artist, who not only worked with advance plans but was able to discuss his products in his famous prefaces. Yet preconceptions could override his plans. His notes make it clear that he had a strong customary taste both for the novella length and for the "dramatic" as against the ideational. In his preface to *The Pupil* it becomes clear that, for once, his interest was split among formal approaches such as the tragedy facing the boy Morgan, the learning process of the tutor, and a strong desire to exemplify a type of American abroad. Thus he mentions a friend who spoke to him of "a wonderful American family, an odd adventurous, extravagant band, of high but rather unauthenticated pretensions, the most interesting member of which was a small boy." [8] He says that the novella "worked itself out with confidence" as "little Morgan's troubled vision" of the group, though in fact the novella events are very rarely filtered through Morgan's point of view. At the same time James speaks of himself as "the social chronicler," a "student in especial of the copious 'cosmopolite' legend, a boundless and tangled but highly explorable garden." He goes on to ask:

> Why, somehow—these were the intensifying questions—
> did one see the Moreens, whom I place at Nice, at Venice, in Paris, as of the special essence of the little old miscellaneous cosmopolite Florence, the Florence of other, of irrecoverable years, the restless yet withal so convenient scene of a society that has passed away for ever with all its faded ghosts and fragile relics.
>
> [*Art*, p. 152]

He speaks of his fear that

> We were to lose ... a vast body of precious anecdotes, a long gallery of wonderful portraits, an array of the oddest possible figures in the oddest possible attitudes. The Moreens were *of the family* then of the great unstudied precursors—poor and shabby members, no doubt; dim and superseded *types*.
>
> [*Art*, p. 153—emphasis added]

It was this fear of losing the record of a type, he admits, that caused

him to take, "too greedily, perhaps . . . as many things as possible by
the way." The result of such greed he saw as inevitable: "It is after this
fashion that he [the author] incurs the stigma of labouring uncannily
for a certain fulness of truth—truth diffused, distributed and, as it
were, atmospheric" (*Art*, p. 154). Laboring after truth in a story
is a "stigma" to James, and in *The Pupil* he seems to have seen himself
(as indeed we see him) close to being violated by an idea. And so it
proves upon reading: the novella gives generous space to lengthy
passages which stress the "type" of the Moreens, with such summary
remarks as "It was a houseful of Bohemians who wanted tremen-
dously to be Philistines" [9] (p. 417); and these passages are overdone if
they are there to subserve the tragedy of young Morgan simply as
authentic background. Conversely, there are the many dramatic
conversations and hints of a tragic outcome (Morgan's bad heart is
noted from the beginning). Some of these conversations could be said
to expose the family type, but others draw us intensely close to
characters and their feelings and provoke our intense feeling for them
in passages appropriate to pathos but impossible to successful
apologue: "Yet the morning was brought to a violent end by Morgan's
suddenly leaning his arms on the table, burying his head in them and
bursting into tears" (p. 429).

The scene of Morgan's sudden death is touching indeed, but James
chooses to "cool it" by reserving the final sentence in the story to the
Moreens and their reaction—Mr. Moreen "took his bereavement like
a man of the world" (p. 460). The novella thus ends with a judgment
on the Moreens.

In fact, many of the distancing devices usual to apologue come into
play—for example, the final line is one of several repetitions of the
statement that the Moreens are "perfect men of the world." There is
some diffuseness about character (critics, despite James's own
decision in the preface, have had trouble deciding who is the title
character, and whether the main character is Morgan or his tutor,
who is much more than a "ficelle" kind of consciousness). There is
also the handling of time, which occasionally draws us away from the
immediacy of the action into the present of "Pemberton's memory
today" of what happened back then (a decision I am not even able to
explain in terms of example apologue, except perhaps as a matter of
tone which balances the heat of the drama elsewhere in the story),
and the easy leaps across three years—"But it was during the ensuing

time that the real problem came up—the problem of how far it was excusable to discuss the turpitude of parents with a child of twelve, of thirteen, of fourteen" (p. 427). Terence Martin has pointed out that there is significance in the name Moreen: "A fabric of coarse, stout wool or wool and cotton; usually it is watered or embossed. In short, it presents one kind of surface to the eye when underneath it is intrinsically coarse." [10] Given James's extraordinary general interest in the problem of names for his characters, I would not wish to make too much of this as a signal of apologue, but it seems true to say that in other stories his names are at most suggestive and not so directly translatable as this one.

One surely feels a dominant pathos as Morgan is forced under by his family, but all the devices previously described then seem perversely calculated to draw us somewhat away from that drama as a formal principle, as do the long, general statements about what is to be *learned* from identifying the Moreens as a type, a group in which Pemberton is imprisoned as an "inmate" and of which even Morgan himself is a youthful example—"a pale, lean, acute, undeveloped little cosmopolite." They live less as individuals than as persons governed by laws of a type, about which one may moralize:

> . . . It pointed a moral, and Pemberton could enjoy a moral. The Moreens were adventurers not merely because they didn't pay their debts, because they lived on society, but because their whole view of life, dim and confused and instinctive, like that of clever colour-blind animals, was speculative and rapacious and mean. Oh! they were "respectable," and that only made them more *immondes*. The young man's analysis of them put it at last very simply—they were adventurers because they were abject snobs. That was the completest account of them—it was the law of their being.
>
> [P. 426]

This kind of lengthy entry into the speculative consciousness of someone who is not the main character (or is he?) could be sustained in an action the size of *The Ambassadors* and leave it formally an action. In a novella, working together with the other devices I have cited, it throws the weight in another direction.

Since I have been both moved and puzzled by *The Pupil* for a long time, I was charmed upon rereading it to find a line in the novella which seems to suggest that James himself, however confident about the story consciously, unconsciously saw the problem I see. Pemberton, the tutor, remarks to Morgan at one point: "If it were not for the hitch that you and I (feeble performers!) make in the *ensemble*, they would carry everything before them" (p. 441).

My purpose in discussing this story is by now, I hope, clear: to demonstrate that the forms of the novella, far from being a series of Procrustean beds, are capable of illuminating both the more and the less perfect formal achievements, the first goal of all being to illuminate the given story "as in itself it really is." Any appreciative reader of *The Pupil* will have perceived that formal imperfection is not necessarily the same thing as ugliness.

4
LOOSER AND TIGHTER PLOTS AND THE POCKET OF GOOD IN NOVELLA SATIRES

The ultimate wellspring of the satiric spirit is
perhaps benign.

Edward W. Rosenheim, Jr.

'Tis a sort of writing very like tickling.

Alexander Pope

How can one consent to make a picture of the
preponderant futilities and vulgarities and
miseries of life without the impulse to exhibit
as well from time to time, in its place, some
fine examples of the reaction, the opposition
or the escape?

Henry James

Satire, by its very nature, works at any length and in all genres—drama, poetry, essay, and prose fiction—but it has some interesting formal features which especially aid in its recognition and appreciation in the novella. For example, it exhibits not one, but two characteristic structures: the episodic plot; and a tighter plot, much closer to that of actions, which, so far as I am aware, occurs only at the novella length.

The first of these (and, curiously, the more contemporary) is the traditional structure one finds in Swift's *Gulliver's Travels* and Voltaire's *Candide*: a loosely plotted journey, taken by a central character, during which he experiences a series of episodes which structurally may have little to bind them together except the one character and which mostly gain their unity from the organizing principle of satire in general—that is, the imaginative presentation for ridicule of any number of objects in the world outside the story. (My reason for saying "mostly" is that I shall be pointing out later that all the parts of satire are not designed to ridicule, an observation which will become much larger than parenthetical.)

It is natural for writers like Kurt Vonnegut, Jr. and Evelyn Waugh, who vent a great deal of *saeve indignatio* against society, to choose the Swiftian structure and some of Swift's devices within that structure. The episodes are, however, fewer and more concentrated than in Swift. They are governed not by the number of items that have aroused the writer's spleen—it is not so scattered as that—but by a few (or oftener, one) general objects the author wishes to attack. In the all-encompassing ridicule of Swift's work, readers have identified such major objects of ridicule as government, human pride, academic posturing, travel literature, and at least a dozen others. The largeness of the subjects, as well as the wide variety of objects of ridicule available within each subject, makes Swift's book a lengthy one.

The Swiftian-Voltairian debts of Vonnegut

In two contemporary novellas of Kurt Vonnegut, the general object of ridicule is narrowed to war in *Slaughterhouse Five* and to the amorality of atomic science in *Cat's Cradle*; accordingly, the novellas are much shorter than *Gulliver's Travels*, though they approach the novella's outer size-limit of 50,000 words. Here there is a clearer attempt than in Swift to stick to the one subject, though satire of any age never gives up its natural advantage of being able to pick up along the way many minor objects of ridicule within the larger subjects. While Vonnegut does not risk extreme length in satire (perhaps for some of the same reasons that modern apologues tend to be short), neither does he miss the many opportunities for ridicule that lie naturally in the areas of war and atomic science.

The concentration and resulting length, however, place Vonnegut's works less in the mode of *Gulliver's Travels* and more in the mode of *Candide,* perhaps the first and most famous novella-length satire.[1] *Candide* takes as its general object of ridicule the philosophical optimism of which Pangloss is the fictional representative, then picks up along the way of Candide's travels a variety of human quirks and crimes which make ridiculous the view that this is "the best of all possible worlds." More confined to identifiable real-world locales than *Gulliver's Travels,* it is also a touch more realistic in its attention to a central consistent character (which Gulliver is not). In *Slaughterhouse Five* Vonnegut makes a comparable but more urgent effort to lure the reader, at least at the start, into a realistic immediacy involving a single character: the technique is a purposeful attempt to fuse (confuse?) into one the author, the first-person narrator of chapter 1 who is about to write the story, and the main character, significantly named Billy Pilgrim. The effect is paradoxically to keep the reader in touch with the real world by means of a realism employed to confuse and diffuse—a kind of "real toads in imaginary gardens" effect.

By these means Vonnegut makes a bow to the age of realism in fiction and to the modern taste for keeping moralizing ridicule focused within stricter length limits; but it represents also a curious structural return to the tastes and devices of the age of Swift and Voltaire. Somewhere around mid-twentieth century, realism as we have been discussing it has loosened its hold, and the term "modern" must be adjusted to the recognition that writers later than James, Forster, and Woolf are not necessarily so devoted to "hugging the shore" of reality but choose something like the old structures and devices when these are suited to the formal needs of the given work. It is the choice of the *kind* of "given work" that can make a term like "modern" meaningful, and thus there occur at least two structures of satires within the body of "modern" novellas.

The editors of a recent anthology of novellas have remarked: "Anthologies that claim to be modern are anachronistic. 'Modern' usually means a period beginning as early as the 1860's and ending sometime before World War II."[2] —So that now, presumably, we must watch out for the literary habits of a novella that is no longer "modern" but "contemporary." The question is: shall we watch out for its habits as though it were all one thing, or continue to look at the formal necessities of individual novellas, which indeed may fall into kinds governed by the taste of the given time.[3] Philip Rahv risks the larger generalization, when speaking about the "decline of naturalism": "The younger writers are stirred by the ambition to create a new type of imaginative prose into which the recognizably real enters as one component rather than as the total substance. They want to break the novel of its objective habits; some want to introduce into it philosophical ideas."[4] One would wish to argue with Rahv about the danger of trying to find anything really "new" under the sun (except, as I suggested earlier, in the realm of new techniques). James, Forster, and Woolf represented an era with a "new" taste for the real as a major component, but so did Shakespeare. Moreover, I think I have demonstrated that realism is in any case best understood as a relative term, for art is never really real. The "real" is as real as it needs to be to work in a given form; and the reason that the term "naturalism," the extreme of realism, does not arise in a discussion of the novella is that the forms the novella takes are, especially because of the graceful, "shapely" middle length, all conspicuously formal (rarely indeed does one find an ambiguous form such as I have described in *The Pupil*) and do not lend themselves to the real-life quality which characterizes naturalism.

Further, my discussion will have shown, it is not only not new to introduce ideas into prose fiction, but to do so has been one of the habits of prose fiction since its inception, sometimes a habit governing the whole (apologue) form of the work. As we now observe, the mode of ideational emphasis can be and is borrowed from authors as far back as Swift. Once Vonnegut has borrowed Swift's or Voltaire's structure, he also freely borrows the other famous devices, such as imaginary kingdoms (Tralfamadore is visited by Billy Pilgrim for the making of ridicule against earthlings, as Gulliver visits Lilliput and Candide visits El Dorado); and the "excrement festival" and "corpse mines" of Vonnegut are highly reminiscent of Swift's making of disgust by physical means. The reason Vonnegut borrows them is surely not to "break the novel of its objective habits" by a return to the literary habits of the eighteenth century but rather because of his consciousness of the appropriateness of eighteenth-century structures and devices to the comprehensive moral anger, "catatonic with disgust," that he feels and wishes to embody in a given novella. To the extent that Vonnegut, Swift, and Voltaire share a disgust and moral anger with the society around them, and find similar structures and devices effective for embodying that anger in fiction, they are contemporaneous in a manner that transcends time.

When Northrop Frye discusses the nature of modern satire he claims that "for better or worse, it is the tiny David with his sudden and vicious stones who goes to battle now, and the great Rabelaisian bellow has dropped out of literature. . . . The less sure society is of its assumptions, the more likely satire is to take the line of irony."[5] One can accept this, depending upon how one understands the term "now" (Frye was writing in 1944). Writers nearer to the contemporary scene, like Vonnegut and Waugh, are very sure of their assumptions and anger against war and society, and have (paradoxically) "gone back" to roaring. To find the tiny David and "the line of irony" one looks back in time to once "modern" novellas by Mann and James, whose satires are quieter and more ordered to a single subject, certain of their social assumptions only each-by-each, therefore not prone to large fantastic structures, but to the portrayal of characters and events which the reader can more readily imagine encountering in the world right around him; and because of the narrow thrust, built on a tighter, more plotted, structure.

Parodic plot in Mann's TRISTAN

In his title for *Tristan* Thomas Mann offers his opening suggestion of the parodic plot as his mode for telling a story that could be puzzlingly "real" even with its elements of distortion.[6] It has as its dominant aim the ridicule of two opposing stereotypes ever existent in the bourgeois world, types whose excesses (including excessive confidence in their own type) are fatally crushing to more ordinary and complex human beings. Thus the use of a plot proceeding toward an unhappy ending becomes here, as we shall see again in James's *The Death of the Lion*, an ideal device of the satire. To choose to parody the plot of love and death in the Tristan legend adds an obvious satiric dimension by means of irony.

The first of the two major types gets its satiric representation in

Detlev Spinnell, the type of the overrarefied artistic sensibility who throws "an aesthetic fit at the sight of beauty."[7] His nostrils distend at this sight, and he habitually responds to it by "flinging his arms blindly round the neck of anybody" while he shouts "My God! look, how beautiful!" (p. 139). A more mundane character refers to him by an "epithet," the "dissipated baby" (p. 138). His is the kind of sensibility which would cause him to reside at a sanatorium ("I'm having myself electrified a bit") out of feeling for its "perfect Empire" style (p. 141). It is quite in keeping with the opposition of the two types in the world outside the book, that we should get from Spinnell a denunciation of the second type, represented by Herr Klöterjahn, "a well-fed, trading, tax-paying citizen; a capable, philistine pillar of society; in any case, a tone-deaf, normally functioning individual, responsible, sturdy, and stupid" (p. 161). Klöterjahn twice labels himself as one who has "got my heart in the right place" (pp. 163–64), though we see that the pressures of business make it annoying for him to be called to the bedside of his fatally ill wife.

The opposition between the bourgeois mercantile mentality and the artistic sensibility was an ongoing problem in Mann's works which he solved in various literary forms—for example, "Little Herr Friedemann" and the serious action of the novella *Tonio Kröger*—but never better than when he chose satire, with the major narrative device of parodying the Tristan legend: a rather ordinary and gentle woman who plays the piano a little and has a weakness of the trachea (nothing so grand as the lung!), elevated in Spinnell's overblown imagination to an Isolde with a "little gold crown" which only he can see, is squeezed to death between Spinnell (Tristan) and her husband, Herr Klöterjahn, the "klutz" who parodies King Mark. The romantic notion of a *liebestod*, Wagner's music-to-die-slowly-by, is ideal for Mann's purpose:

> Oh, tumultuous storm of rhythms! Oh, glad chromatic upward surge of metaphysical perception! How find, how bind this bliss so far remote from parting's torturing pangs? Ah, gentle glow of longing, soothing and kind, ah yielding sweet-sublime, ah, raptured sinking into the twilight of eternity! Thou Isolde, Tristan I, yet no more Tristan, no more Isolde....
>
> [P. 155]

In the context of parody, and at the confined novella length, such effects are hilarious. But overblown diction like this combined with overblown characters who, as agents of satire, concentratedly point up overblown-ness of the one type or the other, could very well come to bore the reader were it not for the tight plot that is carrying all this to a prearranged finish. (By contrast, the loose journey-structure leaves room for countless diverting episodes and satiric subjects.) Moreover, there is the ironic interest of comparing this plot with the original legend, a comparison that deepens the satire as the reader is forced for the moment to disabuse himself of all attraction he ever felt either for the old legend or for Wagner's music.

Plotted as it is, as against the journey structure, *Tristan* is not without resources, credible and realistic, for picking up minor objects of ridicule along the way. The setting of a sanatorium is not only an ideal one for the rather maudlin love-death but for encountering a variety of flawed types, in this case not to the apologue end, discussed earlier, of enlarging our sense that the statement of the work applies to all humanity, but to reinforce our sense of ridicule by encounters with lesser stereotypes such as Fraulein von Osterloh, who represents the eternal housekeeper, and the doctors for whom the "dictates of science" are repeatedly reduced to treatments of "morphia, little pieces of ice, absolute quiet" (p. 156). Our sense of the absurdity and threat presented by the two major types is reinforced by making us feel that the world is full of human beings who reduce themselves narrowly to types. Set over against this, and not absurd at all, is the comparative innocence and goodness represented by the dying woman. She presents a formal problem of satire which I shall return to later in this chapter.

Henry James, THE DEATH OF THE LION,
and the plot question

When James chooses, as he does in *The Death of the Lion,* to satirize a single minor crime of middle-class society, the "lionizing" of noted authors, it is a subject even more amenable than that of Mann's story to realistic treatment and to the structure of the relatively plotted story. (Perhaps it is time for me to reiterate that I recognize the paradox in joining realism to plot, which is a structure of events totally opposed to the disorderly structure of real life. I know no other way to account for the paradox except to suggest that the "rage for order" and escape which drives us to fiction often allows for less plot when there is more fantasy (Swift, Voltaire, Vonnegut), and calls for more plot when the materials become more real (Mann, James). Fiction—from its beginnings in Homer, never mind "modern"—comes to us sternly, unalterably opposed to lifting life intact onto the printed page, and the complaints of Woolf and Forster against plot shall not prevail against this. In any case, as my quotation from *A Room of One's Own* (chap. 2, n. 10) makes clear, Woolf contradicted herself theoretically, as Forster did in practice.

I say "relatively plotted" because plot is ultimately one structure a satirist *may* choose, not a necessity he must choose, as it is for the author of effective actions (one thinks, of course, of Aristotle calling plot the "soul" of tragedy since "it is by his actions that a man is happy or unhappy"). If, however, What Happens has an end in the world outside the story—that is, the power to make us feel the ridiculousness, even the criminal absurdity, of one or another kind of recognizable, real-world human activity—plot can function relatively loosely or tightly according to the needs of the particular absurdity. Evelyn Waugh, setting up shop to show the absurdity of the welfare state in *Love Among the Ruins*, in his second chapter introduces a love-story plot for the "hero" Miles Plastic, full of expectations and humorous suspense (what will our hero do with a bearded lady?). The plot suddenly peters out because the particular objects in the English welfare state which it was designed to ridicule have successfully been ridiculed. The novella can then drop the plot on its head and move on to new events and characters, to display new objects of ridicule.

By contrast Henry James, having a much more particular object of ridicule in view, can well afford to hang onto the plot expectations of the death of the "lion," precisely because his death is best for showing the fatal absurdity of the whole lionizing process. As James himself said of this novella:

> Hadn't one again and again caught "society" in the very fact of not caring in the least what might become of the subject, however essentially fine and fragile, of a patronage reflecting such credit on all concerned, so long as the social game might be played a little more intensely, and if possible, more irrelevantly, by this unfortunate's aid? Given the Lion, his

"death" was but too conceivably the issue of the cruel
exposure thus involved for him.

[*Art*, p. 226]

James was even more bloodthirsty in his preliminary notebook plans
for the lion:

They must *kill him, hein?*—kill him with the very fury of
their selfish exploitation, and then not really have an idea of
what they killed him for.... The whole intention of the tale
should be admirably satiric, ironic.

[*Notebooks*, p. 148]

Not only is the lionization process fatal, but it is hungry for new
victims to devour, and thus it becomes appropriate to plot the killing
of a major victim within the story so as to leave room for the new
victims to appear even while he is breathing his last.

What distinguishes these plots of satires is that plot and character
need not hang together, as in actions. As the satire demands, one
may either sacrifice the plot to the single character (as in Waugh's
Love Among the Ruins) or sacrifice the single character to the plot,
the latter being James's mode in *The Death of the Lion*.

The character of the "lion," Neil Paraday, is as "fine and fragile"
as James intended, but James has several devices for keeping us at a
satiric remove from him.

1. Little or no "dramatization" of the character. The novella
contains a number of lively conversations, but Paraday is rarely
encountered in direct speech, and we are excluded from his consciousness.

2. First-person narration by a character who is almost as much
fixed on the plot and the subsidiary love story involving himself as he
is on Paraday. What we know of Paraday is filtered through the
narrator's consciousness and our ironic perception of it. And the
narrator ends the story on what comes next for *him* and the girl he
"loves." The dying old lion cannot hope to compete with that love
affair. It is not necessary that he do so, for the story is not primarily
"about" Paraday, but about the ridicule of lionization; and the
character of the narrator makes its own strong satiric contribution—
everything about him, including his falling in love, helps build our
sense of the comfortable selfishness and blindness that accompanies

even those who are indignant about lionization but help it along in their own ways.

3. The name "Paraday" could be one of those merely suggestive ones employed by so many authors in all literary forms, but in the satiric context of a whole series of names which turn their bearers into "species characters," Paraday's name also reduces both his stature and his complex humanity.[8] In context, the names have something like the following effects:

Pinhorn	=	pinheaded tinhorn
Lord Crouchley	=	weak changeling
Mrs. Bounder	=	a personal gossip
Mr. Morrow	=	the wave of the ugly future
Mrs. Wimbush	=	ambush for the lion
Mr. Rumble	=	"circus" director
Miss Hurter	=	ironically, the only character not prepared to hurt
Pretidge	=	the locus of false prestige
Neil Paraday	=	nothing ("nil") but a "parody" of what a true lion should be, he lacks courage and strength to keep lesser animals off his back

To make Paraday more sympathetic than this (the weakness of his self-defense becomes, in fact, increasingly reprehensible as the net closes on him) would be to increase our concern for him at the risk of our appreciation of the criminal absurdity of the whole lionizing process, which depends in part on a successful appeal to the lion's own vanity and blindness.

The incidents of the plot (marked by chapters), will, I think, be readily granted by any reader to be not only contributory to the approaching "death of the lion" but especially to the illumination of the lionization process itself, as it might happen to *any* lion":

1. The narrator's initial cheerful plan to get to Paraday for publicity purposes and to "touch" him "under the fifth rib!" (p. 78).[9]

2. The winning of Paraday's "kindness, hospitality, compassion," and the narrator's announced "change of heart" (p. 82) which the reader apprehends as little change except for the worse.

3. The appearance of major newspaper publicity which "waked up a national glory" for Paraday. "A national glory was needed and it was an immense convenience he was there" (p. 86). Diction carefully designed to reduce Paraday to a mere device to feed the glory-hungerers.

4. Mr. Morrow, the extreme of rapacious reporters, visits Paraday, an incident to expand our sense of the collaboration between lions and lion-hunters.

5. The making of our sense that publicity is always about the "larger latitude" of trivialities, with no serious central relation to an author's literary works.

6. The sinking of the "king of the beasts" (p. 93) into the Wimbush ambush, also called a "menagerie." A diction of animal life is an obvious reductive device in this novella.

7. The introduction of Miss Hurter, the sudden good, which will require extended separate comment.

8. The "circus" (p. 104) develops as an ironic reversal of the Roman circus—here the lion is thrown to the Christians.

9. The scene (cena!) in which the lion proves too "beastly intelligent" (p. 110) to save himself, or even to save his last and greatest manuscript.

10. The lion dies amidst "the unconscious, the well-meaning ravages of our appreciative circle" (p. 113), his death pushed to the background by the arrival of the new lions.

Among these chapters, number 7, the appearance of the angelic, self-sacrificing Miss Hurter, is a serious departure from the order of satire as it is usually defined. She represents the good—what the world would be like if lionizers could perceive the evil absurdity of their ways. Quite like Gabriele, the dying patient in Mann's story, she is there to *be* good, distinct from characters who are there to be agents of satire. It seems to me necessary to pause for a serious redefinition of satire to account not only for these two aberrations but for similar ones to be found in all novella satires and in fact in all the satires I know of—they are simply more conspicuous at the novella length.

The positive heart of satire

Readers usually recognize the signs that a work is a satire more easily, I think, than they recognize the often difficult and relatively ambiguous signs I previously suggested that differentiate apologue from action. The exaggerated put-down, traditionally accompanied by humor and by a structure built on open reminders of *Gulliver's Travels* and *Candide*'s travels, tells us what it is about with almost as few problems as the traditional allegory that employs obvious personified abstractions to tell us what it is about—Frye, in fact, calls such satire "allegory in reverse gear." Episode after episode comes into being to provoke a large laugh at the pride, venality, and cruelty of mankind. Diminished to the pettiness of Lilliput, blown up out of proportion in Brobdingnag so that every ugly pore is on view, splashed with blood and excrement, the old satires (like some of the new ones already cited that employ the same devices and structure) are so clearly what they are that we can be forgiven if we fail to take into account a fact that I think has been inadequately examined but which forces itself upon us much more vividly in novella-length satires, especially the plotted ones. *Viewed as literary wholes, satires are ever ninety-nine parts ridicule, but always at least one part ray of light. The ray of light arises from humor, and from at least one overt demonstration of the good.*

I have stressed the question of "wholes" because it is of coherent form that I continually wish to speak, and then to accept what follows from that. Theorists abound who have helped us refine our sensitivity to aspects of satires we read, but their discussion of aspects alone cannot help us when the problem is one of formal coherence—that is, when parts fall outside the satiric order to which a fiction seems to have committed itself *as a whole.* And in fact we do need help in resolving our puzzlement or disappointment with such characters as Gabriele (the gentle "Isolde" of *Tristan*) and Miss Hurter in the James story, characters who stand out the more because they appear in novellas, from which we have come to expect shapeliness. If satire is the principle of wholeness, do not these characters, as parts, weaken it?

Sheldon Sacks's definition of the principle of coherence in satire is, "A work organized so that it ridicules objects external to the fictional world created in it" (*Fiction,* p. 26). And he goes on to say that "Unless *all* the elements of a work make such contribution [that is, to ridicule], we will temporarily refuse to classify it as a coherent satire." Thus, Sacks's formal commitment is thoroughly responsible, at the same time as it seems insufficiently inductive in that his principle, as enunciated, does not include two important elements that readers encounter in all the works they commonly call satires: humor and the overt demonstration of the good. Sacks almost prescriptively rules out demonstrations of the good in satire—as a form it is "essentially limited to the negative pattern" (p. 49) and "the demonstration of what is admirable is irrelevant to the artistic end common to satires" (p. 48). As one who has learned much from Sacks's formal method, I should like to insist, on the evidence, that the overtly "admirable" is not only relevant to satire but integral to it, that it is connected with humor in the formal power of satire, and that the novella-length satires expose this principle with particular vividness.

Since I shall argue that humor makes room for the good in satires, I should like to begin with it. I recognize that humor could be conceived to be implicit in the term "ridicule"; yet ridicule is sometimes dangerously bitter, relatively humorless, as in an occasional satire like George Elliott's *The NRACP*. By humor I shall mean something more "good"-natured and insist that the most effective satires contain it in their formal power. Looking at just those few examples already mentioned, one can see that humor is of the laugh-out-loud variety in the episodic satires of lesser realism—novellas such as *Candide*, Vonnegut's *Cat's Cradle* and *Slaughterhouse Five*, and Waugh's *Love Among the Ruins*—which evoke laughter by means of gross exaggeration and excesses of various kinds. In the more realistic novellas of Mann and James, one finds the quieter humor of overelaborate diction and parody in *Tristan*, and the exaggerated stock characters which, in *The Death of the Lion*, are partly delivered to us by their laughable names.

Nobody, whether reader or critic, denies that humor occurs in satires, but I would insist with Northrop Frye that it not only occurs but that it belongs to the very essence of satire. The reasons seem to me to lie in the approach satire wishes to make to the reader's psyche *for purposes of amelioration* of all that is being ridiculed in the world outside the book. Jonathan Swift remarked that "satire is a sort of glass wherein beholders do generally discover everybody's face but their Own; which is the chief reason for that Kind Reception it meets with." And the technique for producing that kind reception surely must be the humorous mode of narrative. Swift, examining his own intentions, cannot have failed to understand that satire does ask us to perceive the evil in ourselves (certainly, it *is* our face in the glass) but by methods designed to leave intact a measure of our amour-propre ("He can't mean me," imagines the reader, "for I shall never carry things that far.") Humor makes space for the good. We are left with a superior smile and enough dignity to move toward the amelioration satire aims at, that is toward the positive good.

This positive good appears as an overt integral part of the geometry of all the satires I know. I use the term "geometry" with care, for I do not suggest an arithmetical alignment wherein ninety-nine parts of ridicule stand together with the addition of one portion of good cheer—as Elder Olson has pointed out, a "whole" is not the same thing as a "total."[10] A total alignment of parts applied to *The Death of the Lion* would leave us looking at nine chapters of ridicule, with Miss Hurter's chapter still standing outside the fold. What I do mean is that, integral to the geometry of the literary form we call satire, is a positive wedge of suggested good which works together with one degree or another of humor to turn away the despair ridicule might cause and to promote amelioration. Without this good the circle of satire does not complete itself. I shall summon evidence that in practice this positive wedge is as organically a part of satire as the heart is of the body. As Maynard Mack, without any necessary commitment to formal coherence, points out: "Rhetorically considered, satire belongs to the category of *laus et vituperatio*, praise and blame."[11]

Blame is where Sacks leaves us. As a result he accounts only awkwardly and unconvincingly for the presence of the kindly Portuguese sea captain near the end of *Gulliver's Travels*, as I believe he would be unable to account for Gabriele, Miss Hurter, and all the other conspicuous aberrations from his principle. I doubt that readers really apprehend the sea captain as "one last bitter thrust, to show even the best of men as hardly a justified cause for human pride" (*Fiction*, p. 44), as I doubt they would apprehend Miss Hurter's sweet wisdom as one last bitter thrust at all the lionizers who are not like her.[12]

My own proposal is that these two characters, and their counterparts in other satires, represent an overt ethical center which is lodged in the very nature of satire. The consequences, if I am right, are serious for formal theorists: if we are not to redefine satire as something other than a coherence totally centered on ridicule (certainly the steady put-down is always our major clue), at least we must add to that and suggest that the definition must somehow account for the positive element that appears in satiric works in all genres and media.

For the sake of conviction it may not be out of order here to point to a few satires in other genres before returning to the extraordinarily conspicuous evidence in novella satires.

In James Joyce's rather long and episodic story called "Grace," instance after instance of failed grace culminates bitterly with the priest whose sermon turns Christ himself into a kind of money changer in the temple. The mystery of the story, however, is that the relentless ridicule gets under way only after the early brief appearance of the Good Samaritan figure of the young cyclist who is a living example of grace and sets our standard for judging the ensuing failures of grace.

In the midst of Shakespeare's *Troilus and Cressida,* an almost overwhelmingly bitter ridicule of "war and lechery" (which gets its humor by employing, as Mann's novella does, the device of parodying great legends), Hector suddenly rises above himself to a moral prescription which, if followed, could change the entire moral situation: "Let Helen go." At another point in the play we listen with a sense of conviction to Ulysses' speech of warning not to "untune that string" of degree and order among men. It is very hard to account for those moments except by the question, Is it not a necessity for us overtly to hear the tuned string before we can be successfully summoned to an attack on the untuned? And a successful summons suggests change for the better.

In a recent film called *Playtime,* Jacques Tati once again plays a character who fumbles around like Gulliver or Billy Pilgrim in a world he never made, exposing in one incident after another the trashy and uncomfortable world we have built of neon lights, foam rubber, squeaky plastic, and easy cash. Our hearts quail while we laugh at the sight of American tourists moving through Paris from sterile airport to slick tour-bus to jerry-built night club, snapping camera shutters which, like small crocodile jaws, eat up sights while blocking perception. The old gracious city of Paris is not even sighted except when reflected in the glass of a swinging door which the tourists are too hurried to note (though the cathedral is there for *us*). Yet within the order of this ridicule there walks, out of step, a girl in green, much like a hopeful fertility figure borrowed from medieval literature. Her eye, like her camera, not only looks but sees and translates. She, like the figure of Tati himself who (both as actor within and satirist without) significantly hands her a bunch of flowers, is in the scene but not part of its ridicule. At the very last moment of the film, she looks up at a series of triple-pronged highway lights and wistfully sees them in her mind's eye translated into fragrant *fleurs de lys*.

Less skillfully and more sentimentally, Chaplin's film, *The Great Dictator,* tries to contain the heights of ridicule of fascism together with the idealism represented by the Jewish barber (interestingly, Chaplin himself plays both the barber and the Hitler-figure) and by Hannah, the barber's woman friend, with her list of "Wouldn't it be wonderful if ..."

This list could easily be a device borrowed straight from Swift's fictive essay, *A Modest Proposal.* Midway in this second most famous satire of Swift, the speaker breaks off from his hideous proposal to say "Let no man talk to me of other expedients ...," after which he lists—in italics, lest they be missed by the reader—the ten positive proposals which would make the cooking and eating of one's children an unnecessary solution to poverty and overpopulation.

Purposely skipping around in literary history, we can move to satires in modern drama. In Edward Albee's *The Sandbox,* a satire on the treatment of old age and death, the sturdy character of Grandma exists not only for what "Daddy" and "Mommy" can try to do to her but also as an overt standard of the good; she is the one who understands and who takes control of what she understands.

Another short play, Elaine May's *Adaptation*, is a satire exposing youth looking for answers by hopping from square to square of the checkerboard of life. A narrator on the sidelines tells us that there *is* a square that has the answers, the suggestion being that the audience can find it even though the character onstage serves to ridicule youths in the real world who grow old ignoring the truths in front of them.

The good in social protest novellas
of Elliott, Orwell, and Vonnegut

As soon as we begin to speak of "social protest" in fictional satires, the need for the demonstration of the positive good becomes more obvious—one does not protest with no end in view. It then especially becomes the author to employ the novella's balanced length, which allows this contradicting good particularly to shine through.

In George Elliott's epistolary story, *The NRACP,* there appears a character called O'Doone, whose refusal to accept genocide of American blacks, and cannibalism, hangs on to haunt the narrator's (and the reader's) acceptance after O'Doone is dead. There is no other accounting for the presence of O'Doone that I can see except to suggest overtly that not all men can be conditioned to genocide. Incidently, Elliott's satire is the only one I have ever encountered which tries to get along with little or no humor (except perhaps for the "black" humor of the title which sounds like NAACP). The result is clear in the horror with which the story's original publication was greeted. Readers retreated in shock, with little thought that so desperate a fictional possibility could leave room for amelioration in the world outside the story. Elliott's satiric intuition was right in the production of O'Doone, perhaps harsh in the death of O'Doone, and perhaps wrong in the humorlessness which leaves the reader no useful way to respond to a particularly loathsome fantasy.

George Orwell, in *Animal Farm,* shares Elliott's aim of satire produced as social protest, but he has a surer hand in moving his reader toward the good. Both works are protests against the threat of totalitarianism. Orwell, in "Why I Write," tells us that "Every line of serious work that I have written since 1936 has been written, directly or indirectly, against totalitarianism. . . . *Animal Farm* was the first book in which I tried, with full consciousness of what I was doing, to fuse political purpose and artistic purpose into one whole." The positive sound of the word "purpose" is carried out fictionally. It falls accidentally to the lot of Boxer, the best of the animals, to be the first to kill one of the human oppressors. He is stricken with remorse, which causes his comrade, Snowball, to accuse him of sentimentality: "War is war. The only good human being is a dead one."[13] But Boxer remains stricken: "'I have no wish to take life, not even human life,' repeated Boxer, and his eyes were full of tears" (p. 37). There is an irony in that the compassionate speaker is an animal. Nevertheless, it is an interval of genuine compassion which reminds us subconsciously of the existence of *human* compassion; it is directly opposed to all that Snowball satirically represents, and it would be out of place in an artistic economy aimed totally at ridicule. In such an economy, Boxer ought to be busy every minute serving to ridicule humans who, given a chance, invariably turn into oppressors. Instead, he injects the impression that compassion does, and ought to, exist.

There is a similar quality in the scene where Boxer is trapped in a van to be taken to his death. Clover, who has been a cloddish mare, suddenly perceives the danger and warns him. The warning is picked up by the other animals who beg the horses drawing the van to stop: "Comrades! . . . Don't take your own brother to his death!" (p. 102). What is the residue this scene leaves in the reader's mind?—is it the fact that Boxer's death is nevertheless carried out, or is it the possibility that his comrades might have cooperated to save him? I believe the final effect combines both.

Does tingeing these positive demonstrations with irony cause them to be, after all, merely devices of ridicule? (Irony, in fact, is the essence of Sacks's assessment of the Portuguese sea captain; the goodness of the captain, in Sacks's reading, is subsumed in our simultaneous awareness of how bad most men in the real world are—an awareness which adds to our hopelessness.) In Kurt Vonnegut's *Cat's Cradle*, another Swiftian "history of human stupidity," an American ambassador arrives in mythical San Lorenzo just before its destruction by "ice-nine," a fictional equivalent of atomic warfare. The ambassador arrives bearing a wreath inscribed "PRO PATRIA" and, as readers, we are all prepared for the ultimate stupidity of a superpatriotic outburst one minute before the end of the world. Instead, the ambassador suddenly reinterprets the message he bears: "This wreath I bring is a gift from the people of one country to the people of another. Never mind which countries. Think of people . . . " When we examine the passage after a first reading, the irony of the good man appearing at the last moment is dreadful, and indeed the good man dies. Yet, even then, it is not irony as a device of ridicule but rather an ironic vision which juxtaposes the end of the world equally with the possibility, offered by a good man, of cooperation among peoples (which, dear reader, will you choose?). Our reaction as the scene comes to us is a positive shock which offers us hope that the real world outside the book still contains a chance of betterment. To the extent that irony is defined as a rationale aroused in readers gradually and after the events, we may not be dealing here with irony at all. For while the ambassador is delivering his message, we are for the duration of it (and it goes on for many more lines) not aware of ridicule at all—he represents pure hope and is the character we are to emulate after we close the book.

Immediate and pure reader responses to the good are, by the way, made more available by the episodic structure in satires like Vonnegut's which imitate the disconnected travels of Gulliver and Candide, or are broken by leaps in time as in Orwell's history of the animal farm, or are disconnected by drastic scene shifts as in the shifts between Trojan and Greek camps in *Troilus and Cressida*. Audience responses are not conditioned to either hope or despair by rigidly controlled expectations as they are in actions, which involve us in middles that derive from beginnings, and endings which derive from both.[14] Even in the plotted satires, the distance on character achieved by diffusion, exaggeration, and humor prevents us from carrying the kind of emotional baggage that ties one episode to the next; so that shocks of the good do not violate the kind of unity established by this type of fiction. What *is* disturbed by such scenes as the ambassador's speech is the reader's expectation of continued ridicule, but that disturbance is at the service of the organization of the satiric whole as I would define it.

Miss Hurter and the positive good in plotted novella satires

The foregoing theoretical considerations are obviously of interest in all satires, but they are especially helpful to the reading of satire in the *plotted* novella. If readers were to depend on literary theory for their appreciation of literature, the love of literature had died out long ago. But this truth does not obviate the helpfulness of theory in cases of the Sore Thumb character like Miss Hurter (own cousin to Swift's Portuguese sea captain, who is less conspicuously a "sore thumb" only because he is a much more minor character than Miss Hurter in a much longer work than *The Death of the Lion*). The incurious reader accepts Miss Hurter and is pleased to have the hint of a love story between her and the narrator. The reader who wants all of the interest and pleasure the story affords, however, cannot get it until he understands Miss Hurter's crucial function in the novella's satire.

Miss Hurter appears on the scene of the lion hunt with her autograph book in hand (or, more appropriately, her friend's

autograph book, for she is quite willing to spend herself in
thoughtfulness to others even on a vacation that has brought her
from America to England). The narrator tells her the truth he
scarcely apprehends himself: that the best tribute to a great author
is to refuse to trouble him with visits, to go away and not even meet
him, to substitute for interest in his autograph interest in reading his
books. Miss Hurter listens, thinks, and does exactly as advised. That
is to say that, as an agent of ridicule of the lionization process, she
serves the satire not at all *if* satire is conceived wholly as ridicule.
Indeed, by letting go, she seriously weakens the fatal pile-up of
evidence proving that lionizers *never* let go short of killing their
victim.

The rest of the group surrounding the lionized author proceeds
relentlessly to one of the ancient satiric situations, the *cena*—or what
Gilbert Highet calls the "horrible party"—at the Wimbush estate. We
find there some of the typical *cena* guests listed by Gregory Fitz
Gerald: "not only gluttons and topers, but sycophants, hypocrites,
fops, intriguers, and debauchers . . ." (*Satiric Stories*, p. 38). Everyone has come to Prestidge except genuine readers of the author's
books, *and Miss Hurter.* She has come into the novella in order *not*
to attend the party—in order to demonstrate the reverse of the
problem being ridiculed, to display the positive good, the absence of
which is under attack. She remains in the outskirts of the story as a
reminder of the good, as well as to allow the narrator who "loves" her
and admires her behavior to reveal himself absurdly incapable of
similar action (he sends her letters describing the party, and she
replies by wondering why he remains at it). She is the fictional
"objective correlative" of the list of positives that Swift enumerates
in *A Modest Proposal.* She is literary cousin not only to the
Portuguese sea captain, but to Gabriele in *Tristan,* the girl in green
in Tati's film, and the young Samaritan of Joyce's "Grace" who
exhibits grace and leaves a little room for hope that all of us might
do the same.

As part to whole, Miss Hurter is a "sore thumb" only if we
conceive satire as an entity without purpose. I do not mean authorial
purpose but formal purpose, though they may often be the same.
Sacks suggests that

> To separate authorial intention from artistic end [which theo-
> rists of form wish to do] does not, of course, commit us to

> reject such a useful distinction as that made by some
> critics between mimetic and didactic works; it simply means
> that we would make the distinction according to how the
> work is organized, never according to what it is organized
> *for*.
>
> [*Fiction*, p. 247]

I can only answer, with the stories themselves in evidence, that part of *how* satires are organized is to be *for* something. Part of their "artistic end" is to try to take power over the reader's behavior, not only his feelings as is the case in actions. The artistic function of satires is to ridicule evils fictionally while suggesting the good that ought to drive the reader to correct the ridiculed evils after the story finishes with him. That the story's power remains within its formal borders is obvious—what the reader does with its effects is his own business (lionizers, alas, are alive and well long after the death of James), just as the original intention is the author's own business. What I have tried to do is account for *all* the power or potential that lies inside the formal borders of these satires.

In novella-length satires, identifying the representation of the good for what it is and what it formally means is a special pressure on the reader-critic. The briefer and more shapely the form, the more the stand-out part stands out. We might slip carelessly by the Portuguese sea captain in the diffuseness of length—Miss Hurter, never.

The satirist and the didact

These examples from the novella, and the foregoing ones from other genres, will have made clear that when I speak of overt demonstration of the good, I really do mean overt—one part or more which *openly* departs from the order of attack or ridicule. I am scarcely the first critic to observe that moral norms appear in satire, but I wish to call attention not just to the existence of the norms but to their significant conspicuousness in the form of satire. For of course in every form of fiction there must be implicit moral standards, signals that tell us what characters to trust or mistrust, where the good lies, where the bad, how to judge what happens.[15] Satires are like all other fictions in this use of implicit norms, in their almost line-by-line appeals to the reader's judgments. Where satires differ is in their apparent need to make an overt, often interruptive, sometimes lengthy exposition of the good in the very midst of the evil that is being ridiculed.

Gregory Fitz Gerald, like other theorists, says that satire "implies an unstated ideal" and goes on to say that "The objects of attack, the satirist believes, *could* choose differently if they only *would*" (p. 46). My evidence suggests that the satirist does not leave that matter open to chance—he specifies positively what the different choice ought to be. In that formal moment, the satirist meets the didact.

So strong a didactic quality in satire would seem to place it in the same formal camp as apologue, which also reaches out for reader acceptance of a truth, even sometimes for moral activity based on that truth. Frye borrows an image from Dante for stating the matter: "If we persevere with the satirist, we shall pass a dead centre, and finally see the gentlemanly Prince of Darkness bottom side up" (p. 89). That is, we shall be viewing the evil as increasingly ridiculous but from a position in sight of the potential good. In fact, previous to Sacks's delineation of three types of fiction—actions, satires, and apologues (and he is prepared to add others)—Elder Olson had viewed fictional works as divided between the "mimetic" (the realm of what Sacks calls actions) and the "didactic."[16] My analysis might seem to revert to that division, to have somewhat collapsed the distinction Sacks makes between apologue and satire, viewing them both as "didactic" in the sense of that which summons the reader's positive response or acts as his instructor in what to do and how to live. Indeed, I do think satires and apologues are much more alike in their ultimately didactic ends than either is like actions, and accordingly, their artistic procedures show many likenesses—my description of the devices of satire has found me often repeating some of the devices of apologue: "story line" structures, distance on character, exaggerated diction.

I do not intend, however, a collapse of distinctions which I have long found useful, nor would readers of fiction allow it even if I did. Since long before Sacks began his work, readers and critics have been employing (sometimes loosely) such terms as "satire" and "burlesque" to mean something quite distinct from "allegory," "parable," and "apologue." (Nor, in fact, does Olson really collapse the distinction—he knows what satire formally does but classes ridicule as one kind of didactic activity, perhaps because he senses, as I do, an ameliorative end underlying it.) The prime element of the great put-down, infused with dark humor, has always made satire the most recognizable of forms. The large task Sacks undertook was to make sure that terms were employed accurately and responsibly and that definitions were supported empirically. But I think that his distinction between satire and apologue can be clearer, and that his definition of satire can be yet more accurate and possibly more "true" to actual satires than it now is. Picture the difference between a workman tearing down bricks with a better building in mind (satire), and another workman at the quite different job of laying up bricks in the construction of a new building (apologue). These activities are not only different, they are indeed "mutually exclusive." But what satire is *not*, is a simple tearing down, a pure destruction. The "demonstration of what is admirable" that crops up in the midst of satires, even the most punitive satires, is the indispensable aid authors provide for keeping the better building in mind.

Should all of the works we call satires prove to contain this positive heart (and I have presented much evidence for expecting this), we shall want to expand the definition of satire as a fictional form and agree that *it is that kind of whole where the parts cohere in humorous ridicule of objects in the real world that depart from a good that is clearly suggested within the work itself.* With such a definition we shall heal the Sore Thumbs in our novella examples and draw them back inside the circle of understanding.

5
DEGENERATIVE "TRAGEDY" IN THE NOVELLA

That chill air where man's fate is determined,
and spirit withers at the mercy of punishing
circumstances.

Richard Hayes

They are those [tragedies] in which the
suffering finds no vent in action; in which a
continual state of mental distress is prolonged,
unrelieved by incident, hope, or resistance; in
which there is everything to be endured,
nothing to be done.

Matthew Arnold

A simple plot is one that moves in a single
direction, as when the fortunes of the protagonist steadily decline.

Elder Olson

Contemporary criticism frequently takes note of relationships between satire and tragedy.[1] If one looks at the limited tragedy that occurs in the novella, one finds in it an element of satire's dark irony. In a kind of double vision, there prevails over our tragic involvement a cold and dreary sense that the character of persons, events, and of modern life itself, can bring men relentlessly down, their fall seldom or never broken by that mitigating good that provided part of the *katharsis* of emotion in what we were wont to call "high tragedy."

Maurice Shroder, properly in my view, sees irony as a limitation on the scope of tragedy: "As the novel becomes more thoroughly tragic, it passes beyond irony" and is "open to more cosmic and more reflective visions of the world."[2] This is not to say (at least I do not say) that tragedy ever tries to do without irony entirely—ever since Oedipus, there is before us the irony of high aspirations brought down more visibly for the audience than for the protagonist—but rather that the highest tragedy encompasses the irony, does not allow it to prevail as a major effect. We shall later watch gradations of this encompassing process from the prevalent irony in James's *Daisy Miller* to the more acutely tragic in *Washington Square* and *The Beast in the Jungle*—and thus appreciate the limits of tragedy in the novella. Formally tragic in the minimal sense of a thoroughly prepared unhappy ending, the story is in varying degrees ironic in its distance on the sufferer, and it usually offers little overt good, mitigating its icy sadness only by its stylistic and formal perfections.

The class into which most "tragic" novellas fall is actually something more properly termed pathetic. They lack the nobility of an Oedipus or a Hamlet. They lack the high-minded moral certainty (though they also lack the hand-wringing helplessness) of a Clarissa Harlowe. They exhibit the relentless downswing of Thomas Hardy's novels but lack his large sense of the tragedy which rises from a social landscape as much as from an individual. George Steiner (in what sounds like another implicit relation to satire) notes that "in tragedy, there is a wildness and a refusal running against the grain of middle-class sensibility. Tragedy springs from outrage; it protests at the conditions of life."[3] Obviously, such a description is no equivalent for my term "icy sadness" in works which are private in scope, realistic in character delineation, yet severely plotted in the relatively hopeless struggle of their protagonists.

What we usually find in novellas in place of the "wildness" of high tragedy is an effect similar to that produced by what Norman Friedman has called the "degeneration plot."[4] In the degenerative action the protagonist encounters a change, sometimes drastic, sometimes not—it could be a new situation, a loss, a temptation or test of his own strength of character—and succumbs gradually to some kind of unhappy ending. The end could be disillusionment, but in the novella it is also frequently death. An end so dramatic is often necessary to lend importance to the process of succumbing—the "hero" can be less than heroic yet able to hold our sympathy as we see coming on the heavy price of his failed struggle. For in these works there is no "running against the grain of middle-class sensibility"; quite the reverse—the protagonist is often deeply trapped in, or by, that sensibility. As against the plot of high tragedy with its large rises and falls of hope, the degenerative action runs relentlessly downward for the central figure. It is obviously tempting to stylistic masters of the cumulative effect—Thomas Mann, Henry James, Franz Kafka, Gertrude Stein.

And this in itself is ironical. In his excellent essay on *Death in Venice*, Erich Heller speaks of the "ironical and weightier task of giving the highest degree of compositional order to this story of increasing disorder and decomposition."[5]

Degeneration in Mann's DEATH IN VENICE

We begin our experience of degeneration in *Death in Venice* with a protagonist whose powers are already waning—he is past fifty and the "wear and tear upon his system had come to make a daily nap more and more imperative" (p. 378).[6] Such initial small signs of trouble are augmented by the "mock summer," by sunset in the North Cemetery with its ironically inscribed mortuary chapel (inscriptions "all of them with a bearing upon the future life, such as: 'They are entering into the House of the Lord' and 'May the Light Everlasting shine upon them'"), and by the encounter with the Mephistophelean stranger who silently stirs in Aschenbach a desire to travel. The diction is fraught with dour expectations: "ruthless," "blinded," "hostility," "unpleasant twinge," and the description of the visionary landscape imagined by Aschenbach, where "eyes of a crouching tiger gleamed" (p. 380).

Yet, remarkably, these heavy expectations are aroused in us for

Aschenbach without arousing the kind of affectionate concern for
him as a potential sufferer that we feel in what we commonly call
tragedy. We understand Aschenbach to have virtues that are human
but also questionable: a proud self-discipline, enough self-knowledge to allow him to appreciate the truth that "his work, for which
he lived" has resulted in "rigid, cold, and passionate service"
(p. 381). This is to be pitied, and it is admirable that Aschenbach
wishes to live to old age because, as he sees it, "only the artist to
whom it has been granted to be fruitful on all stages of our human
scene can be truly great, or universal, or worthy of honors" (p. 383).
A man whose ambition is of this nature stands high enough in our
respect that his systematic degeneration must affect us; yet we have
much more distance from him than we can have on Oedipus, or
Hamlet, or Frederic Henry, or Meursault, all of whom are capable
of, *and have time and space for*, struggle against their fate and a
profounder understanding of it than Aschenbach, for all his intel-
lectuality. In the novella we have time only to watch a man whose
motto was "Hold fast" gradually, relentlessly, release his grip,
poisoned by "the unexpected contagion" in which, like Milton's
Satan, "myself am Hell."

Aschenbach's attempt to flee Venice is technically as gripping as
any tragic hero's struggle, but it is not a moral attempt, being caused
merely by the physical enervation of the sirocco. It holds our interest
like the struggle of the fly already partly enmeshed in the spider
web, though lifted much higher than that by the fact that this is a
human being, with whom we are acquainted very intimately by
reason of being directly in his consciousness every waking minute
and in his revealing dreams as well. It has been noted that in the
Visconti film of *Death In Venice* Aschenbach appears in "practically every frame of the picture,"[7] and this seems a proper filmic
translation of the hothouse (though, I insist, less than personal)
intimacy of the story. This intimacy is broken only very rarely by the
narrator speaking of "our solitary" and "our sufferer," the effect of
which is to keep us at just that storied distance which will make the
degeneration acceptable regardless of how physically and mentally
close to it we are brought.

I stress the nature of our concern for Aschenbach as accurately as
I can, for this kind of interest in the *outcome* for the character, more
than for the character himself, is one of the distinctions one might

make between what this kind of novella does as against what the long tragic novel does, where concern and interest in character must run deeper, become much more heart-stopping, if our attention is to be held. It is possible to weep for Clarissa Harlowe or for Frederic Henry partly because of the depth of moral character they present which makes us cling to the moments of high hopes for their happiness—the hopes followed by powerful "reversals" which Aristotle noted as ingredients of high tragedy. Onstage, visual immediacy allows us to accept such drastic changes as credible within the space of an evening's viewing, while in prose fiction they take lengthy preparation.

In this regard, it once again becomes interesting to compare an action like *Death in Venice* with the definition of actions offered by Sheldon Sacks:

> An action is a work organized so that it introduces
> characters, about whose fates we are made to care, in
> unstable relationships which are then further complicated
> until the complication is finally resolved by the removal of
> the represented instability.
>
> [*Fiction*, p. 26]

Though all definitions suffer a bit from stiffness of language when they are set up against the live objects they intend to define, what is noteworthy here is an extremely careful choice of words to describe what in fact we find in *Death in Venice* and some other degenerative tragedies. Sacks speaks of unstable relationships involving "characters about whose fates we are made to care." The degree of our emotional involvement in the "caring" is wisely left unspecified; it is the character's *fate* we care about. Whether we care for the character himself, and the degree of our caring, are, formally, matters of the individual work (though, as distinct from apologue, the center *is* on the *character*). And this is one of the areas in which one can observe habitual differences between the novella and the long novel, especially in the realm of tragedy. For Aschenbach we cannot weep. We are thoroughly concerned with the relentless progress of his moral and physical decline, not because our affections have been aroused but because the slow avalanche of his "fate" is absorbing.

The depths of degradation are carefully avoided by Mann, and we are intellectually in sympathy as Aschenbach attempts in his own mind to elevate, by the analogy of Socrates and Phaedrus, the quality of his passion for the boy Tadzio. If, in fact, we think about the many philosophical allusions in this novella as carefully as it invites us to do, part of our sympathy and fear for Aschenbach must lie in the fact of his thoroughly un-Platonic aloneness. In a lecture on "charlatanism" in this novella, Eva Brann, discussing Mann's use of classical allusion as ironic, says that the text of Plato serves Mann "as an occasion for mimicry and reminiscence, not for responsible appropriation," and she goes on to say that

> perhaps the most telling reversal in Mann's use of the Platonic *Phaedrus* is that a *dialogue,* which deals with the relation of eros and rhetoric, suggests to him a *solilioquy,* that the writing Socrates has no way to form and control his love by logos, and that not a word ever passes between him and the Venetian Phaedrus.[8]

What has actually happened is that Brann has done the appropriating—turned a tragic work of the imagination into a philosophical tract, collapsed the distinction between Mann and his imaginary character (in the above quotation the first "him" is Mann, while "the writing Socrates" is Aschenbach), and missed the work's *intentional* pathos in Aschenbach's soliloquizing. (To appreciate Mann's "responsible" recognition of dialogue, one has only to turn to the much more hopeful *Tonio Kröger,* as I shall do later.)

Nevertheless, it remains half-sympathy that we feel for Aschenbach (we respond with appropriate revulsion to the relentless imagery of letting-go, of overripeness and its attendant smell, of the grotesque masque, and eventually of disease). We are with the narrator in the irony of the conclusion: "And before nightfall a shocked and respectful world received the news of his decease." (In this adroit translation we are left with an echo of the word "disease.")

Struggle against degeneration in Kafka's THE METAMORPHOSIS

An interesting variation on the degenerative tragedy is available to our study in Kafka's pathetic account of the man who awaked to find himself an insect. The rhetoric of character, plot, and narrative procedure all forbid us, in my view, from taking this odd "instability" as allegorical or as akin to a beast fable. In the most daring fashion, the novella explores this situation as a concrete (though, of course, also suggestive) human disaster which Gregor suffers from, and attempts to cope with, as we feel any human being would have to do who was similarly stricken. In truth, with all its basic ridiculousness and impossibility, Gregor's confrontation with his life as a dung beetle comes near to genuine tragedy.

Much more than *Death in Venice,* Gregor's struggle approaches for awhile the "wildness" which Steiner finds in high tragedy. Irving Howe, in his introduction to *The Metamorphosis,* points out that

> within Gregor's humiliating transformation there is also
> rebellion—desperate and dispirited but rebellion nonethe-
> less.... At one and the same time, the metamorphosis
> comes to seem a humiliation, a rebellion, a "cop-out,"
> and, finally, a preparation for death. Still, because the will
> to survive flickers in Gregor Samsa, there continues to
> stir within him those human impulses and desires which
> mingle, so pathetically and incongruously, with his physical
> needs as an insect.[9]

Howe cites as evidence Gregor's "last stand" when he tries to prevent the removal from his room of his favorite picture, having recognized that he must not allow the stripping of his room "at the price of shedding simultaneously all recollection of his human background." Howe further calls our attention to the agonizing climax—the "most unnerving incident in the story—when Gregor hears his sister playing the violin [his unselfish plan had once been to send her to study at the Conservatorium] and, strangely moved by the music, comes out to listen—quite as a brother might" (p. 404).

What, then, keeps *The Metamorphosis* in the realm of the pathetic, the degenerative, and out of the realm of high tragedy and the more intense feelings it arouses? First of all, we must count the sheer physical degradation of man into dung beetle and the accompanying choice the author makes to stress physical degenera-tion. As Howe points out, the author chooses to open the story "at the beginning of Gregor's end." Looked at one way, this could be said of all organically unified tragedies, great and small—the seeds of destruction are sowed in the diction, setting, and action of the opening pages of the novel, or the first scene of the drama where we are made instantly aware of fatal corruption in Thebes or Denmark. But the difference between the great tragic protagonists and Gregor

Samsa is not primarily that he is physically degraded, but that all chance of reversal of his fate is relentlessly ruled out in the presentation of his steady decline in spirit. Thus, I am more with Howe when he speaks of Gregor's flickering "will to survive" than when he lays the tragedy totally to situation:

> Nothing but death is possible to Gregor once he becomes (or is revealed to be) an insect. No complications or denouement are possible. "Gregor Samsa is an insect"—once the extension of that metaphor has been established, everything else follows with the necessity of a mathematical proof.
> The story must move steadily downward, showing Gregor's disintegration and suggesting what it means.
>
> [Howe, p. 401]

Nevertheless, I do agree that irreversibility of situation is obviously a factor, appropriate to and characteristic of the degeneration plot, and is found in many variations in the kinds of tragedy the novella allows. The essential helplessness of the insect in *The Metamorphosis* is matched by the essential helplessness of the child in other novellas. To the extent that one considers James's *The Pupil* to be a tragedy of young Morgan, it is true of that story: Morgan dies because adult understanding was thrust upon a child's heart which by the very nature of childishness was unable to meet it. It is true again in the brilliant novella of the Argentine author, Laura del Castillo, entitled *A Plum for Coco*.[10] The plum is the adult world which impinges hideously on Coco's child-world. The purity of perception that is available to children, and the possibilities inherent in the long life ahead of them, theoretically could provide a situation that is basically hopeful; but when these possibilities are rejected, childhood becomes as useful to novellas of degeneration as the shell of a dung-beetle. What world could be more relentlessly without hope than that world in which helpless children are the only ones who even begin to understand (as indeed no human in *The Metamorphosis* matches Gregor's beetle-understanding even when he has become more beetle than man). Coco picks the plum of understanding of the adult horror around him, but this is a source of ultimate despair to the reader for we see (again, in the opening lines) that "his helplessness grew and grew inside him," and we find out near the end that "All of us are filthy. Only the boy and the cat are worth a damn." And the boy is only a boy.

And in *The Metamorphosis* the bug is only a bug, even when a man's sensibility is trapped within that shell. It is well worth noting, however, that richly humane and appealing possibilities are made available by this very initial hopelessness of situation which are not available in a work like *Death in Venice*. There is nothing intrinsically degenerative in the opening situation of *Death in Venice*. Aschenbach's degeneration unto death is accomplished for the reader less by events than in some realm of ideas, less by event than by stylistic suggestions of disorder, contagion, temptation both physical and intellectual ("Not far—not all the way to the tigers."). It is a movement toward spiritual decomposition marked along the way by quasi-mythological guides who call to mind not only Mephistopheles but the boatman of Hades, the fallen angel in his pride, a medieval vice figure (in the hotel entertainment). Brilliantly, it is developed by ironical misuse of refined literacy. Can there be sin under the aegis of Eros? Can a distinguished author fail to love "Hyacinthus, doomed to die" (p. 416)? So the suggestions go.

Yet Aschenbach, unlike Gregor Samsa, is always free to choose, and when he does choose he refuses to give up what he reflectively understands to be a "fond man's folly" (p. 422). One is made to feel that Aschenbach's downfall results from his overrefined intellect forgiving itself a kind of artistic license, and from his being subjected to, and gradually smothered by, Mann's own "ironical elegance" of style—I think of the somewhat glittering equation of Aschenbach's corruption with the plague on a great city. It is one kind of systematic, valid construction of a character's destruction. When it is done this well, and done with the reasonable swiftness of the novella length so that exquisiteness has no time to become cloying, we grant it those high honors which have classed *Death in Venice* as a masterpiece of one kind.

But it is not a masterpiece of human interaction—as previously noted by Eva Brann, Aschenbach never even speaks with Tadzio, the other main character. Instinctively, I believe, we award higher honors (provided the skill of presentation is equal) to a work like *The Metamorphosis*, where the protagonist, though his situation is totally unfree, battles in a human arena with the impossibility which has him in a vise. Gregor will never escape his metamorphosis, but our hearts lift in common humanity as he wages a fruitless struggle—admittedly in small flutters with inadequate weapons—to hold onto the consciousness, even the responsibilities, of a man, while lodged in the body of a beetle.

What is pathetic is that the struggle is necessarily minimal and almost entirely hopeless from start to finish. Compare it, for example, to Hamlet's struggle and we can find no serious reversals, no recognition, no relief. Degeneration remains degenerative, not tragic. Compared with the end of the prince of Denmark who "was likely, had he been put on, to have proved most royally," Gregor Samsa's human spirit leaves no echoes for our comfort. His end is all dung-beetle, "dead and done for," the "flat and dry" corpse pushed aside by the charwoman's broom. The degeneration gets its share of pity in part from Kafka's spare, everyday style—no quarter asked or given from the harsh facts. The pitiless directness of the diction has its own peculiar elevation; it matches the lack of self-pity with which Gregor confronts his fate. But pitiless it is; that is its mode of arousing our pity for a character suffering degeneration brought on by the world's indifference.

In both *The Metamorphosis* and *Death in Venice,* the pathetic effect is driven home by a final ironic twist on the *katharsis* of high tragedy. In the case of Aschenbach, we are left with the feeling that the flower of evil that can bloom within a man and destroy him is not only uncut but unnoticed by those in the world around him—they are as "shocked and respectful" as they would be if the action had never taken place. Neither he nor the world has been changed by his struggle, except for the worse. And in the case of Gregor, there is the final horror of the instant rejuvenation of the family after his demise. They let "bygones be bygones" so easily as to cheapen his whole torment into a final nothingness. Like some heartless minor phoenix, the sister who once understood rises from her brother's ashes. A "warm sunshine" illuminates the total indifference.

Situational degeneration in three James novellas

What I have been describing is the pathos of character degeneration. Gregor Samsa's situation would seem to have brought on his tragedy, but what really happens (and similarly, to Aschenbach) is the degeneration of the spirit needed to meet the situation. Gregor does not die because of the infection caused when his father flings an apple at him (though that scarcely helps his view of himself). Rather, he dies instantly at the moment when the gradual debilitation of his human spirit—the progress from a "he" toward an "it"—reaches its culmination.

In another variation of the rhetoric of character versus situation in the tragic novella, the pathetic end derives not from degeneration of character but from degeneration of a situation which no strength of character is able to prevent, though some weakness in an otherwise strong character may ironically serve to augment it. Both kinds of degeneration are prominent as plots in the novella, and in their total effect irony and pathos arise together, though usually in inverse ratio to each other.

The gradations appear most interestingly in the novellas of Henry James in which he centers his attention on a young woman in the thrall of an insensitive man—and the gradual change in emphasis from irony to extreme pathos can be appreciated in progressive readings of *Daisy Miller, Washington Square,* and *The Beast in the Jungle.*

In *Daisy Miller* and *Washington Square,* particularly, we have a genteel version of *The Metamorphosis* situation: the character awakes, so to speak, to find her complex human spirit trapped in the body of a woman. It is infinitely more ironic than the situation of Gregor Samsa because the young women necessarily imagine themselves to be human, wage their struggles (with full support of the author) as though they *were* human, whereas Gregor is automatically forced to be more in touch with his limitations.

Let me stress at once that to describe the situation which will degenerate into an unhappy ending is not yet to say who the protagonist is. In two out of the three James novellas, it is not the trapped woman who is the protagonist but, rather more ironically, the man who has helped to trap her. This is to say that, in the case of *Daisy Miller,* I agree entirely with James Gargano that the reception of the novella as an "outrage on American girlhood" caused an "obsessive preoccupation with its heroine," and that

> This simplification ignores the fact that Frederick Winter-
> bourne, as the central intelligence, represents the conscious-
> ness upon which the events and characters of the novel have
> the greatest impact. Since he is always on the scene, ob-
> serving, discriminating, and seeking to unravel the mystery of
> the enigmatic Daisy, the drama must, if James's art can be
> said to have any intention, structurally center in him. He, I
> believe is the subject of the novel and not merely the lens
> through which Daisy's career is seen.[11]

I also agree, then, with Leon Edel in the emphasis he finds on the men, in this story and in *The Beast in the Jungle:* "What both these tales have in common are men who have no understanding of women." Edel, however, goes on to remark a crucial difference between the narrative modes of the two novellas: the "earlier James" of *Daisy Miller* (twenty-five years earlier than *The Beast in the Jungle*)

> was addicted largely to the recording of external action, allowing the characters to develop before us through the things they say and do. The later James, no less addicted to the theory of self-revelation of his characters, shows us the thoughts that govern their actions.[12]

In *Daisy Miller* an occasionally intrusive narrator indeed specifically disavows any knowledge of what goes on in the mind of the "point of view" character (that is, Winterbourne): "I hardly know whether it was the analogies or the differences that were uppermost in the mind of the young American." And he reports reasons for Winterbourne's behavior gleaned at second hand: "What I should say is, simply, that when certain persons spoke of him they affirmed that the reason of his spending so much time at Geneva was that he was extremely devoted to a lady who lived there" (p. 142).[13] This forces the reader into the stance of irony, the position from which we are forced to appreciate the pathos of the novella—for it is left up to us to discover in the frequent mentions of Geneva that, far from there being romance for him there, it is the seat of Winterbourne's prim attitudes. From "his old attachment for the little metropolis of Calvinism" (p. 142) he had become "perfectly aware" that "a young man was not at liberty to speak to a young unmarried lady except under certain rarely-occurring conditions" (p. 145). We come to see that these prim attitudes, which deceptively underlie a liberal exterior, can properly be said to result in the false judgments which, in turn, result in Daisy's despair and death.

In the actual reading of *Daisy Miller* across nearly a century, the lightly ironic tone, and the busyness with double vision which irony necessitates, apparently have cost the novella its pathetic force. Wayne Booth, for example, says that "His [Winterbourne's] slow caution and ready suspicions are admirably suited to make us aware of the pathos of Daisy, without giving our awareness much emotional force" (*Rhetoric of Fiction,* p. 283). Which leaves still open the question of the pathos involved in Winterbourne's own conduct in the degenerating situation. A troubling formal question arises here: how much pathetic power does this novella contain if one has to accept an ironic stance, weigh characters against each other, and conduct critical discussions in order to grasp that the power is there? And indeed the question has also to do with novella length: if the novella has not enough time to build a tragic effect of the highest intensity, it certainly cannot afford to misdirect such pathos as it does undertake, by an excessive ratio of irony.

Yet pathos *is* there in *Daisy Miller,* if only in some technical realm of discourse where one totals up effects but lets wholeness of emotional power alone. Booth refers to a "masterful" mixture of "what James called 'the tragedy and the comedy and the irony'" and (Booth says) they are "clearly distinguished ingredients" (*Rhetoric of Fiction*, p. 284). Ingredients of what whole? Nobody has called this novella faulty in its form, but how is there a coherent power of parts if the parts are so contradictory in effect as "tragedy" and "comedy," and lie "clearly distinguished"?

The coherence lies, in my view, in the pathetic effect of a potentially highly tragic situation (Daisy's increasing and finally fatal isolation) confronted, ironically, by a central character whose understanding is so flawed that he could be subjected first to Daisy's tragic recognition, then to his own ("You were right ... I was booked to make a mistake"—p. 206), and finally go "back to live in Geneva" as though nothing important had happened. But the importance was (or should have been) there for *us* even while Winterbourne's perception suppressed it. There is what James himself knew was a "brooding tenderness" inherent in the situation Daisy presents, but our pity is suppressed by Winterbourne's own inattention, so that the effect is a muted misery on our part that such inattention can exist in a supposedly sensitive character who is, after all, as much in love with Daisy as it is possible for him to be.

The risk James took was that we might share that inattention, that feeling of unimportance—as indeed many critics have.[14] James himself seems to have felt it: in his preface he speaks briefly of "a certain flatness in my poor little heroine's literal denomination," and he refers to Winterbourne not at all. He seems to have missed the ironic horror of instances of his own diction and scene-making. Winterbourne stands at Daisy's grave, to us a shocking "raw protuberance among the April daisies" and begins to comprehend in his "winter-born" soul that Daisy "would have appreciated one's esteem" (p. 206).

Not only is there that dreadful, accusing grave which he and we have to deal with (differently), but also the crucial night scene of recognition in the Colosseum which sets on Daisy's death, less from the "Roman fever" than from her having nothing left to live for, since Winterbourne has here made his rejection clear. But critics do not pick up the seriousness of the scene much more readily than Winterbourne does. For Stanley Geist, Daisy remains always the "perfectly detached spectator from an amusing comedy."[15] And William Wasserstrom goes so far as to seriously misread the facts of the Colosseum scene. For Wasserstrom, Daisy is "ignorant" and "infantile," and "plays with the tiger of passion" much as she plays with the ferocity of "one of the statues" in the Colosseum.[16] As a matter of literal fact, no statues are referred to in James's text. What really happens is that Winterbourne, imagining himself alone in his visit to the Colosseum late at night, "walked to the middle of the arena, to take a more general glance, intending thereafter to make a hasty retreat" (p. 201). He draws near to a cross in whose shadow he sees two people whose identity it takes him some time to make out. "Presently" the unknown woman, who is of course Daisy, comments aloud, "Well, he looks at us as one of the old lions or tigers may have looked at the Christian martyrs!" And her escort, Giovanelli, responds: "Let us hope he is not very hungry. . . . He will have to take me first; you will serve for dessert!" (p. 201). These are the comments Wasserstrom imagines addressed lightly to a statue. The text makes clear, however, that Winterbourne is "more brightly visible" (p. 202) than he supposes. In disgust at Daisy's compromising situation (as he sees it) he turns away to leave, and then Daisy speaks again: "Why, it was Mr. Winterbourne! He saw me—and he cuts me!" (p. 202). What can "was" mean except that Winterbourne was the unrecognized subject of their previous conversation?

If we are sensitive enough to the degenerating situation caused by Winterbourne's indifference to the real quality of Daisy, who is the *only* character of genuine goodness and honesty in the novella, we are bound to take this moment very hard—to make the equation between Winterbourne and the "lions or tigers," and the equation between Daisy and "Christian martyrs." If we stumble into viewing her in the remainder of the scene through Winterbourne's eyes, as a "clever little reprobate" (p. 202) who "chattered" on "about the beauty of the place" (p. 203), we shall have missed the fact that Daisy has not only been "cut" but cut to the heart by what is to her an increasingly dismaying recognition. She is by nature cheerful and forgiving, and she does recover enough to discuss the pleasant evening she has had, but Winterbourne delivers another cut, this time a fatal one, when he announces his indifference to whether or not she is engaged to be married.

And this is what Wasserstrom, against all the signs, refers to as mere toying with passion. In yet another misconstruction, he tries to summon James to his support: "She may be flirting, James says, but 'Mr. Giovanelli is not; he means something else'" (Stafford collection, p. 139). What Wasserstrom has done here is to take w rds not simply out of Winterbourne's consciousness but directly out of Winterbourne's mouth and lay them to James's own account as though the author's view and the character's view were the same and interchangeable. The effect is that Winterbourne thus gains the moral support of both James (which he certainly never had) and of Wasserstrom, even though the degeneration of the novella's situation, ending with Daisy's death, is directly attributable to Winterbourne.

As dismayed as one might be with such a reading, it must be remarked that James's excessively ironic mode opened a door to it, partly closing the door on pathos. Very likely *Daisy Miller* ought to have been the tragedy of Daisy herself, as James seems to have thought it was, and our feeling for her ought not to have been risked by filtering her character and her degenerating situation through the consciousness of the man who caused her downfall. The mode of irony in the story we have is a mode requiring thought, is double vision, is a retroactive perception that Winterbourne is really the pathetic central character.

But the mode of any tragedy ought to be in much larger ratio a mode of feeling. (My "ought," like Aristotle's "ought," is not prescriptive but experiential.) In tone, in distance, the ratio of irony to pathos in *Daisy Miller* is so heavily on the ironic side that one would have to say the final effect is less than tragic. As James admitted, in Daisy's case "Flatness ... was the very sum of her story." She keeps the pathos of Winterbourne from being effectively achieved—we have to think about it even to begin to feel it.

James seems to have intuited, in his later novellas, that works of this length were bound to lose the shapeliness he so cherished if the effect of pathos, slenderer in the first place than tragedy, became misdirected by excessive irony. In the case of *Washington Square* he risks no doubt that we are to place our sympathies from first to last with Catherine, whose fineness of character is no match for cleverer characters who have hemmed her in relentlessly from the other three points of the "square"—her father, her aunt, and her false lover. This situation is conspicuously degenerative and pathetic—much more so than that of *Daisy Miller* where irony largely kept back the pathos until the breakthroughs I have described near the end.

Despite pathos (or because of it?), the pleasure of *Washington Square* may be greater, because Catherine's character is *there* for us despite her fatal trustingness and docility, which are worse than Daisy's. At the end, at the worst point for her in the sense that her life is more clearly than ever reduced to nothing, there is some lift or relief for us. What has brought the situation to its inevitable end is the three characters who compose it—the hard father, the foolish aunt, the grasping lover. But the square is closed by Catherine's own character set up in opposition to the situation. So fine is her ultimate dignity and courage, and so directly is it presented to us, that she seems to take control of the closing, "for life, as it were," of the squares-within-squares that have trapped her: Washington Square, the square of the parlor, the square of the pathetic "morsel of fancy work."

James, who never lacks irony, does not lack it in *Washington Square*. The irony which makes the degenerating situation the more pathetic in this case is that the three "villains" are, in varying degrees, behaving well according to their own lights and necessities, and part of Catherine's trap is that she perceives this and perceives it less harshly than the reader is caused to do. This is part of her elevation, part of what causes pathos to predominate over irony in the effect of the novella as a whole.

The pathos of degeneration accompanied by "education"

In *The Beast in the Jungle* the protagonist's perception is employed in a different, more drastic degeneration. Here, as Leon Edel points out, is the mature version of *Daisy Miller*. Marcher, very much more clearly than Winterbourne, has the role of protagonist in the degenerative action. "Winterbourne and Marcher!" exclaims Edel:

> —and in the whole of James's fictions they stand as arch-examples of men who see life only in the flickering light of their own troubled egoes. At the end of each story, the one has failed to understand Daisy and the other May, and both are face to face with their failures, in a cemetery, by the graves of the women they should have loved.
> [Stafford, James's *Daisy Miller*, p. 154]

The *quality* (as against the amount) of irony in *The Beast in the Jungle* is immense—more so than in any other novella that comes to mind. Marcher, in his dignity as protagonist, does not understand May Bartram partly because she is for too long where he is, drawn into a struggle to uncover significance where there is no significance at all. She dies of her gradual awareness that his great secret is nothingness, but she has elevated the pathos of that nothingness and of Marcher's struggle toward nothing, by her loving involvement. The pathos (accompanied still by the thread of irony) is intensified also by that potentially highest of human experiences, a learning process. Awareness eventuates this time not only in the unfortunate woman but finally in the protagonist himself; but the lesson for Marcher is pathetically fruitless because he is, like Winterbourne, a static character. Marcher's basic insensitivity early in the novella warns us that he will not be able to profit from what he learns at the last moment, and the course of the novella is a downward movement bearing out the truth of the warning.

There is, in learning, so much intrinsic hope that we most frequently find the "education plot" (again I am indebted to Norman Friedman)[17] a serious one or, among long novels, even a comic one, as in *Tom Jones, Emma,* and *Pride and Prejudice.* After much difficulty, education can result in a happy ending. But education is also dangerous and can be rendered destructive to characters unable to respond to it. Authors of novellas appear to recognize the pathos of the conjunction between a learning situation and the kind of static character which renders the learning process merely degenerative, and one finds a number of works which combine, with some irony and great pathos, as in *The Beast in the Jungle,* the "education plot" with the "degeneration plot."

Chekhov's *A Woman's Kingdom* is another example. There the

action significantly ends with a chapter entitled "Evening." As night finally falls on our hopes, the protagonist, Anna, perceives by the end that "We are fools! Oh, what fools we are!"[18] But that *is* the end—no hope is left in us that she will do other than remain worse trapped than ever in the follies of the thinly aristocratic way of life which both attracts her and repels her. "Disgust at her own lack of spirit" has already "overwhelmed her completely." It is "too late to dream of happiness" and it is of no avail that she perceives the boundaries of her trap: "It was impossible to go back to the life when she had slept under the same quilt with her mother, or to devise some new special sort of life." Self-knowledge in such cases is a pathetic waste. It has been said that "The element of guilt in tragic suffering distinguishes it from the pathetic suffering of the guilt-less."[19] Anna feels guilt, as Marcher does, but the guilt is either too small or too late for it to make any difference in their lives, or any change in the world around them. What has eventuated is a pathetic stab of guilt or "disgust"—admittedly stronger in the one case than in the other—which we know (if indeed we are even caused to think about it) cannot result in the "readiness" of a Hamlet or the "ripeness" of a Lear.

The art of degeneration in MELANCTHA

In Gertrude Stein's *Melanctha* we are made to feel the irony least and the pathos most. Melanctha's life and situation as a black woman (actually mulatto, thus less securely black), who "wanders" because she has so little base, is pathetically limited; but we are caused less to notice those limits than the positive possibilities of her own response in her long effort to find "that certain way that was to lead her to world wisdom" (p. 103).[20] Chief among her possibilities is a successful relationship with the doctor, Jeff Campbell, who opposes a steadier character and a firmer but less spirited view of what is right "in the life of the colored people" (p. 111).

Stein produced in this 50,000-word novella a structure that rocks back and forth for a good part of the way between the consciousness of Melanctha and that of Jeff Campbell, though it easily becomes clear that he is there mainly for our sense of Melanctha. In one of the most remarkable feats in American literature, a white author, writing in 1902, enters into black consciousness both unblinkingly and without a word of condescension, so that the characters are very real to us, and deeply moving.[21] The situation degenerates and

finally founders, causing Melanctha to become so "awful blue" that
"consumption" is the proper name for her death. But in that process
the rocking of the story structure lifts us at moments to such heights
of a struggle for wisdom and the good that the novella comes as close
as any to high tragedy, even as we perceive that the rocking is not
really back and forth but steadily, almost imperceptibly, downward.

For the structure, like the diction, is not only rocking but
convoluted, carrying a residue of trouble past each climax. Doors
close at several points for Melanctha, and each time we are almost
relieved, because they close after struggles that have become gradually hopeless: "'I certainly got to go now Melanctha, from you. I go
this time, Melanctha really,' and Jeff Campbell went away and this
time he never looked back to her" (p. 206). For him, despite his
sadness, the break is good because of the residue he takes with him
of Melanctha, who broke his conservatism regarding "just living
regular and not having new ways all the time just to get excitements"
(p. 167). He has learned from Melanctha to open up, "to have real
deep feeling in him" (p. 143). And "that was very good to have inside
him."

Yet what is good for Jeff builds the pathos of Melanctha, for
whom the break is more threatening, since she will begin again to
"wander." She is always able to bring good to others by means of
character traits in her which never change and are fatal to herself.
Essentially, these traits are two: the taste for excitement
("Melanctha Herbert could not help it, always she would find new
ways to get excited"), the trait which, ironically, awakened Jeff
Campbell; and lack of memory for the wisdom she achieves, whether
"world wisdom" or other ("Melanctha Herbert had no way she ever
really could remember").

At the end the door closes again:

> Rose Johnson went into her house and closed the door
> behind her. Melanctha stood like one dazed, she did not
> know how to bear this blow that almost killed her. Slowly
> then Melanctha went away without even turning to look
> behind her.

[P. 233]

This time the closure is on the most precious of Melanctha's
friendships. Unlike Melanctha, Rose Johnson has memory and solid

practicality but is also "sullen, childish, cowardly" (p. 222). Unfortunately, she has once again illuminated Melanctha's need and ability to be better for others than she is for herself, and Melanctha is lost:

> Melanctha Herbert never had any strength alone ever to feel safe inside her. And now Rose Johnson had cast her from her, and Melanctha could never any more be near her. Melanctha knew now, way inside her, that she was lost, and nothing any more could ever help her.
>
> [P. 233]

The novella is subtitled "Each One As She May." What is crushing is that Melanctha's character reaches the heights of what "she may" in her relations with others, but it also remains fatally static in the harm it brings to herself. In structure the story appropriately begins and ends with what is in time the last episode: the break with Rose Johnson. All that became most hopeful to us in the events of the life of "the complex and less sure Melanctha" returns in a relentless circle back to the beginning which is also the end. There is something even more disheartening in this circularity than in the chronology of *The Beast in the Jungle,* where reckless leaps across time, "year after year," give us the dread sense of time passing to no useful end, of people growing old wastefully in the service of nothing.

To talk of time shifts in the service of tragic novellas, when I have once singled them out as appropriate devices of apologue novellas, is to recognize a difficulty that inevitably rises in an attempt to talk about the art of narrative connected to form. All modern critics seem to find it very much easier to talk about the art of actions, such as these novellas of degeneration, than about the art of apologue, or even of satire in its less obvious novella structures. For actions can be discussed in terms primarily of what is both central and very obvious in them: characters closely and emotionally apprehended, and plot. Thus, I can describe with conviction a rhetoric of character which builds our sense of extreme pathos in Melanctha by pitting the prime elements in her character against the prime elements in Jeff Campbell's character to bring good to him and at the same time (therefore, the more pathetically) to bring the destruction of her situation and death to Melanctha. These characters in this plot (which is essentially "simple" rather than "complex," in Aristotle's distinction) become obvious once they are pointed out. The interest for my reader will lie in recognizing the variations between emphasis on degeneration of character or degeneration of situation. The plot in each case will be simple and not of great length, without major "reversals" and with "recognition" occurring only at the end, if at all. In the one plot, character itself moves toward destruction under the pressure of situation and events (*Death in Venice, The Metamorphosis*). In the other, the situation degenerates for the character, who remains unchanged (as in the James novellas described, in *A Woman's Kingdom,* and in *Melanctha*).

By contrast, everything is somehow less clear if one depends for conviction on a rhetoric of diction and of narrative manner, as was partly the case in my descriptions of novellas in the class of apologue and its subclass, the example. I have cited as devices of apologue the manipulation of our time sense and repetition of words and images, and now I return to cite these among the very devices which produce the effectiveness of *Melanctha* as a degenerative action. If I do so with confidence, it is because devices *are* obviously portable, are simply stylistic components in the author's bag of tricks until one judges them within a story's commitment to formal wholeness, fortunately both intuited and apprehended more readily at the novella length than in novels. Time manipulation is not itself apologue. Repetition is not, of itself, apologue. Even generalized statements are sometimes apologue, sometimes not.

It cannot be repeated too often that the crucial difference lies in the centrally appealing character and what happens to that character, as against a *use-value* placed upon both the character *and* what happens to him, for purposes either didactic or satiric in their appeal. The same devices can then be employed, singly or in combination, with a relatively visible difference according to their subordination to the form at hand. I have already begun to suggest how this works in my contrast of *The Woman Who Rode Away* with *The Fox.* Let us again watch the workings in practice, in the degenerative tragedy of the novella.

I have already shown that time manipulation in apologue tends to disturb our sense of chronological time to the end that we will apprehend a message or statement which is not caught in time as the "history" of Daisy Miller is, or even that of Melanctha, who moves steadily toward death in however circular a fashion. In apologue we have the frequent use of present tense, I have said, to drive home the sense of that which is true now and always—the apologue statement. In example apologue, leaps of time stress in another way the unimportance of historical past, for the life or type which is exemplified remains true, does not "die" even though its exemplars—Maggie, Ivan Ilyich, Félicité—die in the story. The truth about Soviet labor camps exists as a truth appropriated from the real world and does not end when Shukhov's day ends. The truth about slum life exists similarly, whether Maggie lives or not. Her death is only a device to make slum life appear as dreary as, in the real world, it really is. Her death arrives suddenly, has no plot "necessity," is not an occasion which we are caused to feel acutely as the individually moving "fate" of Maggie. The circumstances and scene of her death are withheld; we are merely told of it, in order for a point to be made.

By contrast, nothing is more destined and heartbreaking in the reader's "caring" about it than the fate of Melanctha. Time is disturbed in her story so that we shall feel the pathos of degeneration more and more, as we come to see that the beginning of the story was really its end, that all hopes of reversal we had for Melanctha were merely circling back to the despair already revealed to us in the third page of the story, then repeated in much the same words near the end (p. 226):

> Sometimes the thought of how all her world was made, filled the complex, desiring Melanctha with despair. She wondered, often, how she could go on living when she was so blue.
>
> Melanctha told Rose one day how a woman whom she knew had killed herself because she was so blue. Melanctha said, sometimes, she thought this was the best thing for her herself to do.
>
> Rose Johnson did not see it the least bit that way.
>
> "I don't see Melanctha why you should talk like you would kill yourself just because you're blue. I'd never kill myself Melanctha just 'cause I was blue. I'd maybe kill somebody else Melanctha 'cause I was blue, but I'd never kill myself. If I ever killed myself Melanctha it'd be by accident, and if I ever killed myself by accident Melanctha, I'd be awfully sorry."   [P. 87]

Many of the techniques of the story can be sampled in this passage, which employs not only its placement in story time but all its other devices in ways not at all likely to be found in formally didactic works. We are made to feel the encircling borders of Melanctha's "world" through her own consciousness, to which we are brought pathetically close by the use of Melanctha's own awkward syntax, "her herself." We also get our first sense (and we will return again to Rose for our last sense) of how Melanctha's friends fail her with their views of life which are less "complex" than hers, and accordingly more confident. Even the humor in Rose's self-confident rejection of suicide we feel as a blow against Melanctha—it is Rose at her insensitive, practical worst. And much of what we are made to feel is in the convoluted repetition of "kill" and "killed."

Repetition here is not didactic as in apologue but simply emphatic. Melanctha's fate cannot recover, ever in another hundred pages, from those repeated blows, though she will try, and be defeated, try again, and again be defeated. And it is worth pausing to note that, because of the manner and context of the repetitions, the story could probably never—after this passage has placed us this close to Melanctha's fate—resolve itself formally into an apologue. I can offer no better proof, in an area where hard-and-fast proof is difficult, than to ask the reader to set up the text of Solzhenitsyn next to that of Stein and carefully observe the degree and manner of our closeness to character in each, as I shall presently do with Solzhenitsyn and James.

Repetition is also employed in a directly degenerative effect in the diction of this story. I shall accomplish both economy and illumination of Stein's almost incomparable art by listing page numbers and quotations without intrusive comment:

p. 219:   "Melanctha's joy made her foolish."

          "Melanctha's love for Jem made her foolish."

          "Melanctha put all herself into Jem Richards. She was mad and foolish in the joy she had there."

p. 220:   "Melanctha Herbert never thought she could ever again be in trouble. Melanctha's joy had made her foolish."

p. 221:   "Melanctha Herbert's love had surely made her mad and foolish."

> "Melanctha's love had made her mad and foolish, she
> should be silent now and let him do it."

p. 224:   "Poor Melanctha, surely her love had made her mad and
>   foolish."

Interspersed between these narrative summaries (which are worth studying almost word by word for their incremental threat) are passages in which Rose heartlessly describes Melanctha's affair with Jem Richards, passages in which the narrator describes the affair more anxiously, and passages of Melanctha's own troubled awareness of it—in that order, and thus, in increasingly strong appeal to our sympathy and fear. Far from building a statement about foolish, joyful women, repetition here is clearly at the business of corralling us into a pen of increasing hopelessness for Melanctha; and the repetitions I have quoted lead quite naturally into a greatly expanded repetition of the early discussion between Melanctha and Rose about whether to kill oneself over being "very blue."

Repetition of "always" and "now" builds a time sense in a manner that may seem perversely close to my discussion of "always" in example apologue:

> Melanctha Herbert was always losing what she had in
> wanting all the things she saw. Melanctha was always being
> left when she was not leaving others.
> Melanctha Herbert always loved too hard and much too
> often. She was always full with mystery and subtle
> movements and denials and vague distrusts and complicated
> disillusions. Then Melanctha would be sudden and impulsive
> and unbounded in some faith, and then she would suffer and
> be strong in her repression.
> Melanctha Herbert was always seeking rest and quiet, and
> always she could only find new ways to be in trouble.
> Melanctha wondered often how it was she did not kill
> herself when she was so blue. Often she thought this would
> be really the best way for her to do.   [P. 89]

The passage is long enough in its litany of "Melanctha" (in fact, seven ensuing paragraphs begin with her name, except for one break) that my reader will already have appreciated that the repetition is "about" Melanctha, personally and individually, and not about a type or a way of life which she exemplifies. Indeed, Melanctha is spoken of by her own name a dozen times on every page of the story, by contrast with "the woman who rode away" or the speaker in Dostoevsky's story who, perforce, is always referred to by readers and critics as The Underground Man.[22] Sometimes everything is in a name—one has only to sound "Melanctha" to pick up the equivalent in pathetic tone of the passages I have quoted.

This, then, is not a *way* of life but Melanctha's *own* life, "now," "often," "always," "all her life long" until death. She cannot change from what she "always" is already on the fourth page of the story, and that is the intense pity of it. In context, and retroactively, the passage above has another effect: it is a summary of the whole novella. Here in the beginning pages the whole degenerative action—Melanctha's fixed character against all that can happen—has been predicted in summary; the rest of the story expands the pathos by supplying the live evidence. When the word "now" occurs over and over, it is not in the apologue sense of "It is always like this," but rather a relentless introduction of a change in the action which, whether for apparent better or worse, will move Melanctha one step closer to disaster:

—"Mis' Herbert was now always getting sicker" (p. 126).
—"What was it that now really happened to them? What was it that Melanctha did, that made everything get all ugly for them?"
—"Now Jeff began to have always a strong feeling that Melanctha could no longer stand it, with all her bad suffering"(p. 162).

The "now," far from universalizing, serves to put us passionately into the here-and-now of either a new hope ("Always now he too wanted really to understand") to be destroyed, or a new degree of pain. Passionately, because here more than in any other novella I have read, the reader is compelled to undergo a passion in which a web of discouragement is spun around him at the same time as he is caused to struggle against it, in company with Melanctha, all the way to the last few pages. What keeps the affective power of such a passion from being unbearably painful is the novella length and perhaps precisely that repetition which, inside the story, drags the action downward. Roy Morrell, discussing the "psychology of tragic pleasure," reminds us of Freud's analysis (in "Beyond the Pleasure Principle") of examples of children's play wherein "sometimes, by persistent repetition, the child's psyche obtains control over a painful experience."[23] Surely the authors of some of these degenerative tragedies are correct in their intuition that repetition, reasonably controlled in length, is a device which can substitute for the "cathartic" effects realizable in high tragedy. We *have* to release Melanctha to her death—it is a relief to do so, once her repeated "wanderings" have (partly by sheer use of the same words) finally convinced us that her character, in so many ways admirable and worth our long attention, cannot prevail over the increasing unhappiness of her situation.

What requires the length of this particular novella is that the web is not spun around a hopeless fly. The author fixes Melanctha's character for us very early, but it is never fixed for Melanctha herself, and it is no brief task to spin a web of action that will finally quiet her fight for love and wisdom. Melanctha's worst flaw, never to be able to "remember"—that is, to reflect back—is also what keeps her trying to move forward. Some of the shorter degenerative novellas are concerned with a character who is (in a description by Joyce Cary) "like a shark whose teeth are all turned inward, toward the dark." Melanctha cannot "remember" the dark, so she gets up and moves toward it many times before it finally encloses her.

Tragic action vs. "tragical" apologue

Though I am uncovering devices shared, on occasion, by novella actions and apologues, and am forced by them to put most of my final faith in context as against devices, I am unchanged in the "fixity and density" I feel regarding most of the signals I have suggested for identifying apologue as distinct from action. Actions can make little or no use, for example, of overrefined effects in diction, imagery, or ritual *unless* in the rare context of a character who appears before us as *himself* cool, overrefined, ritualistic—that is, unless those characteristics are the very breath of his individual life, what lets us know *him* and care, before all, about what will happen to *him*. And we will feel that breath if we let the story "have at us," and feel the difference between such a character and a character subsumed to apologue. We will see that Marcher, at the end of *The Beast in the Jungle* (somewhat like Aschenbach at his end), is able because of the kind of man he is to reflect, as symbolically as James himself, about Beast and Jungle. But in what passionate context, to what end, in the making of what kind of formal pleasure? As I. A. Richards once said: "What would be

highly ambiguous by itself becomes definite in a suitable context."
But I would argue also the reverse: that the form of the context
becomes definite as we see a preponderance of certain signs working
together in one kind of rhetoric as against another, and at a length
that permits relative certainty. Literary devices are a bit like cronies
choosing a regular Saturday night bar. They know which "bar" they
will be most consistently welcome in, though upon occasion they will
be welcome in another. But dangerous confusion will result if they
try to overwhelm the strange bar by appearing as a group.

Major definitive points hold firm. Apologue, including example
apologue as a subclass, will never by any literary means bring us into
the intimacy with character which we have with Marcher, with
Aschenbach, with Melanctha, or even with the dungbeetle, Gregor
Samsa (it is absolutely important to note that Gregor has not been
reduced to dungbeetle by animal epithet—it has happened to this
suffering soul to *be* a dungbeetle). Though we are made to sense
heat and cold, hunger, narrowness, and deprivation in *One Day in
the Life of Ivan Denisovitch*, the sensations are not presented as
personal to Shukhov but as general to the camp. They have no
chance (and because of their formal aim of generalization, wish no
chance) of making us feel deprivation only intimately and individually, as we feel the deprivation of Catherine in that last calm,
dreadful line of *Washington Square*.

Let us look at the "raw glare ... of grief" illuminating the
graveside stranger in *The Beast in the Jungle* (so like the effect of the
"raw protuberance" of Daisy Miller's grave) and see what that
famous ending has the power to produce in our feelings even for so
insensitive a man as Marcher:

> A moan now rose to his lips as he remembered she had
> prayed he mightn't know. This horror of waking—*this* was
> knowledge, knowledge under the breath of which the very
> tears in his eyes seemed to freeze. Through them, none the
> less, he tried to fix it and hold it; he kept it there before him
> so that he might feel the pain. That at least, belated and
> bitter, had something of the taste of life. But the bitterness
> suddenly sickened him, and it was as if, horribly, he saw, in
> the truth, in the cruelty of his image, what had been
> appointed and done. He saw the Jungle of his life and saw the
> lurking Beast; then, while he looked, perceived it, as by a stir
> of the air, rise, huge and hideous, for the leap that was to
> settle him. His eyes darkened—it was close; and instinctively

turning, in his hallucination, to avoid it, he flung himself, face down, on the tomb.

[P. 402]

And then let us compare that with a scene of suffering and reflection in *One Day in the Life of Ivan Denisovich:*

> Fetyukov came through the barracks, sobbing. Humped over. Blood-smeared lip. He had been beaten up again for plate-licking. Without looking at anyone, not hiding his tears, he went past the entire brigade, climbed up to his bunk, hid his face in his mattress.
>
> If you stopped to think, you felt sorry for him. He wouldn't live through his term. He couldn't adjust.

[P. 649]

In context, the sufferer is Fetyukov, "the jackal"; thus he has already been disabused of our sympathy before this scene, by a reductive device usual to apologue. His suffering (though we will shortly be told it has fatal implications) is presented as physical, his reactions like those of a whipped child. The scene has neither the preparation nor the immediate shock value of Marcher's, because it is happening "again" as it often has before. And our feelings for the scene are finally cut off by "If you stopped to think." We are forced to stop and think as we feel sorry for Fetyukov, and we cannot get the sense of fatality *unless* we stop and think, and listen to what Shukhov tells us. The scene is there to make us feel a harsh truth: prisoners who can't adjust will not survive in labor camps. *All* of whatever life and appeal Fetyukov's suffering has for us is fully spent on that statement. Our entry into the reflective consciousness of Shukhov is not there for Shukhov's sake, either; such intimacy as we have with him in this passage helps to keep us at a distance from Fetyukov's feelings and is obviously also spent on statement-making. Our feelings have, in a word, been manipulated for an end beyond the scene itself.

By contrast, our entry into Marcher's combined suffering and reflection, even though it takes place in his intellect and his tears are frozen, is there for no other end than finishing what was fatally begun for *Marcher*, and our feelings for *that*. If we are responding as the novella intends, responding to the bitter "taste of life" James has built so carefully in the baring of Marcher's internal agony, we are bound to be with him, totally with Marcher, as he flings himself, "face down, on the tomb."

6
THE SINGLE CHARACTER REVEALED TO US, WHO MAY BE REVEALED TO HIMSELF, AND WHO MAY OR MAY NOT PROFIT BY IT

From this genre we gain a sense of character in depth, character as it reveals itself through a central test or crisis ... a single character as he approaches a turning point in his experience, often a point where he must discover what he really is as a human being.

Irving Howe

It is very much easier to shatter prison bars than to open undiscovered doors to life.

D. H. Lawrence,
The Virgin and the Gipsy

... Des drames silencieux qui se jouent dans un seul cerveau.

Charles Baudelaire

Either "character tyranny" or "plot tyranny" rules the novel, according to E. M. Forster. If one were to speak of tyranny at all in works so pleasingly balanced as most novellas, one would have to recognize a dominance of character. One remembers Aschenbach more than one does his travels, and Gregor Samsa more than the order of his getting sick and dying. One remembers Catherine of *Washington Square* more than the long, vague process of her being jilted—she seems in fact to sit still in the "portentous intelligent stillness" which is said to brood over James's works.[1] One surely remembers Melanctha's character in painful detail, but less in terms of What Happens to her than in terms of who and what she is and the threat which that presents to her future.

Yet, as the previous chapter will have indicated, without her "wanderings" and her conflicts with men like Jeff Campbell and Jem Richards, or with friends like Rose Johnson and Jan Harden, Melanctha's character alone could hardly have brought her to her end. As Aristotle pointed out, "It is by virtue of their characters that agents are of a certain kind" (thus Melanctha is prone to excitement, and never able to "remember"), "but it is by virtue of their actions that they are happy or the contrary" (thus Melanctha could never have become so "awful blue" that death was her only relief, if not for her active conflicts, especially with Jeff Campbell). Aristotle admitted, however, to a possible "tyranny" of character later in the same passage of the *Poetics* (1450a): "If one were to place together successive expressions which involve characters and are well made in respect of diction and thought, one might produce the function of tragedy"; but, he went on to say, "one could produce it better through plot." Supposing, however, that it is less tragedy than pathos that a work seeks (something "closer to life itself"), then the relative emphasis on character—where even the action itself is degeneration of character, as in *Death in Venice* or *The Metamorphosis* —and a deemphasis of action in a simple plot, produce the peculiar beauty and pleasure of the novellas described in the last chapter.

For a more even balance between character and plot, we must turn, oddly enough, to the serious action centered on a single character, which is the most typical novella form of all. The action is of three main kinds in terms of the change that takes place: the gradual revelation to the reader, by means of the events, of the protagonist's character; a gradual change toward increased knowl-

edge for the character himself—a plot of learning which is complete
when the protagonist reaches (or clearly fails to reach) the point of new
understanding; a change toward new knowledge in the protagonist
which is predictive also of improvement in his future behavior. Of
the three the learning plot is by far the most frequently encountered
in novellas, doubtless again for reasons of length.

Critics interested in a study of plot types owe much to the
distinctions elucidated by R. S. Crane: "plots of action, plots of
character, and plots of thought."[2] What we are looking at in this
chapter is not so much the plots of action as plots involving a change
in the "moral qualities of the characters and the operations of their
thought." In the elaboration of Crane's theory undertaken by
Norman Friedman ("Forms of the Plot," p. 161), he does not
classify any works in the first category I have described—the plot of
revelation to the reader—but I shall shortly claim Colette's *Julie de
Carneilhan* as one of these, and Melville's *Bartleby the Scrivener* is
recognizable as another. The second category I have dubbed "the
learning plot" rather than choosing Friedman's term, the "education plot," since not all of these stories are so positive as the word
"education" sounds. The third is very close to what Friedman calls
the "maturing plot":

> Our long-range hopes that the protagonist will choose the
> right course after all are confirmed, and our final response is
> a sense of righteous satisfaction. And it is this crucial element
> of choice, of coming finally to a radical decision, which is the
> distinguishing quality of this type.
>
> [P. 161]

Friedman notes, correctly in my view, that *Great Expectations* is
an example of this plot type in the novel, and he mentions *The
Portrait of a Lady*, as I have done in my opening chapter. However,
just the mention of these long novels may help to define the
difference one is bound to find between them and the novella of
maturing, where the struggle is a briefer and lonelier one. It tends to
depend on the character himself, "his will power, patience, and
self-confidence" (Friedman, "Forms," p. 157), rather than on
circumstances, events, and relations with other characters. And it
ends, at the appropriate length, not by conclusively demonstrating
maturity but by merely suggesting it in a way that leaves us confident
of the character's future without going forward with him. Among

novellas, Conrad's *The Secret Sharer* is as clear an example of this type as any of those to which I shall give more extended discussion: the protagonist begins as "a stranger to the ship" and "I was somewhat a stranger to myself." By the end, we share his self-confident appraisal that "already the ship was drawing ahead" with himself in good command. Like his secret double, he has become "a proud swimmer striking out for a new destiny."

In discussing these serious novellas of character and thought, I employ the term "serious" with as much formality as I would "tragic" or "comic." What happens in these novellas, especially the learning and maturing plots, is an arousal of our feelings that things could go either way—the emphasis is not on a certain movement toward a happy or an unhappy ending to the learning process but rather on "emphasizing the ambiguous consequences" to the "shifting relations" the character goes through in his learning process.[3] The outcome naturally remains doubtful for a long time (learning is hard!), but in coherent works it is never improbable. In the plot of character revelation, the reader is gradually placed in command and the outcome is thus satisfactory: whether the fictional character is pleasing or not, we do get to know him and that (we can look back and see) was what was prepared for. In the maturing plot the problems are not easy but, there too, a kind of happy ending is by the end rendered perfectly probable. In the learning plot, however, the shifting relations sometimes turn downward (though not tragically) by the end where the learner simply fails to learn what we were made to hope he would learn (novellas of this kind are Elizabeth Bowen's *Ivy Gripped the Steps* and Lionel Trilling's *Of This Time, Of That Place*).

Though we are now naming these novellas of "character" and "thought," I must stress again what I hope will be even clearer when I come to individual descriptions, namely, that no novella (or any other fiction) tries to get along without "action" of some sort. It will be obvious that there is always a What Happens, a To Whom, and operations of thought in every story we read. The formal question is partly one of a rhetorical moving to the forefront of one or two of these latter elements (internal action often occurs at the expense of external action), and novella length becomes an obvious formal choice. I have previously suggested that this group of novellas shows a balance (that is, one is more aware of something happening than in most of the degenerative tragedies) but the action is less for

the sake of What Happens, in the sense of relieving suspense, than
for the sake of revealing a character and his thought.

Character Revelation in Colette's JULIE DE CARNEILHAN

We find, then, plenty of absorbing activity in *Julie de Carneilhan*:
confrontations with *amours* of both sexes, with Julie's divorced
husband, Espivant, and with his wife, a "plot" to get money from
the wife, a suicide attempt by a rejected boy lover, a visit to a
fortune-teller, and finally Julie's somewhat uncertain decision—
arrived at almost as circuitously and without necessity as a cat's
wanderings—to return, possibly forever, to her early family home at
Carneilhan. These episodes are loosely grouped in blocks by seven
"chapter" breaks, but they are not of equal size or importance and
do not relate to each other out of the necessity of plot fulfillment.
They lack what Friedman has acutely called "magnitude of the
whole plot," in the sense of an action where What Happens is built
of expectations carefully fulfilled and is the key to the power of the
whole story. What we have in *Julie* are the activities of smaller scope
than plot, which Friedman lists as the *speech*, "in which one person
acts verbally without being answered" (in *Julie*, this is often one
side of a telephone conversation), the *scene*, "in which two or more
persons speak and act in a single closed situation, the number of
persons remaining constant throughout" (in Julie's case, rarely more
than two persons), and the *episode*, a "system" of such scenes
(Friedman, "Forms," p. 150). While I do not agree with Friedman
that episode is "the action represented in most short stories and
novelettes" (there would be, by his definition, several "episodes" in
Melanctha and *Washington Square*, to name only two), it is true of
Julie. If plot means a major change completed in action, *Julie*
cannot answer to it. The only necessity that guides the production of
scenes, one after another, is the gradual elaboration for the reader of
the complex character of Julie. She too, as we watch her, understands herself and parts of the world around her, but only in fits and
starts. There occurs no change in her character, very little change in
what she understands, no establishment of maturity.

What the reader learns (and that is What Happens that guides the
production of scenes) is the nature of this woman, a particular
dispossessed animal, intelligent and resourceful but not wise, who
practices flaring her nostrils in front of the looking glass because it

helps accentuate the "wild animal" side of her character. Over against her animal (Carneilhan) character is opposed her demimonde Parisian character which she has developed in order to conduct a sophisticated, citified animal-survival process, protecting an "unprotected life" by setting up mechanical barriers of things, people, and her own flesh.

The art of the story is predominantly one of physical objects, natural and artificial, literally objective correlatives of Julie's character. She often confronts her "unframed" looking glass naked (thus vulnerable, in our view) in order to keep close track of the set of her neck, the "shape and firmness" of her bust, the curl of her ringlets. Any physical change for the worse (she is acutely conscious of her forty-four years) will interfere with her "frequent changes of mount" (p. 92), the farm-girl outlook from which she views her husbands and lovers.[4] The quality of her relations with people (chiefly men) is suggested by the frequent appearance of telephones in the story. Telephones are "symbols of activity" to her former husband, but in Julie's case, "like many creatures leading an unprotected life, she regarded the telephone as her only source of help" (p. 98). It puts her in touch with people but at one remove—a mechanical, unnatural remove which drives home how seriously she is caught between the values of her half-world of Paris and those of her Carneilhan country source.

The Carneilhan world supplies the "faded grey corduroy riding breeches" from which Julie cuts out a "triangular cushion" for her tiny Paris studio. Significantly,

> A fine-linked steel chain, which had once belonged, so Julie de Carneilhan said, to a monkey (though according to her brother the monkey had belonged to the chain) was to be sewn on one side of the cushion in the shape of a C, or possibly a J. "C would be easier to sew, but J is more decorative: it'll look terrific."
>
> [P. 77]

The studio is airlessly packed with trivial items like the cushion: "the Empire teacup, the Swedish spoon and the ryebread folded in a rough silk Turkish napkin." And again:

> The room was encumbered with a twelve-sided bronze tray-table from Indo-China, an armchair of South African

oxhide, bits of tooled leather from Fez, and basket work
which had originally been plaited round English tobacco tins
by the natives of the Gold Coast.

[P. 78]

We are never caused to imagine that Julie has ever traveled along
wide horizons to find these things, but quite the reverse—that every
trivial artifact has come together to crowd out nature and blur
horizons in the place where Julie is now.

Surely it was this kind of description that caused Willa Cather to
complain in 1936, within a few years of Colette's story, that "the
novel, for a long while, has been overfurnished." Speaking specifically of Balzac, she goes on: "To reproduce on paper the actual city
of Paris; the houses, the upholstery, the food, the wines, the game of
pleasure, the game of business, the game of finance; a stupendous
ambition—but, after all, unworthy of an artist." Cather later admits
that "Tolstoi was almost as great a lover of material things as
Balzac":

> But there is this determining difference: the clothes, the
> dishes, the haunting interiors of those old Moscow houses,
> are always so much a part of the emotions of the people that
> they are perfectly synthesized; they seem to exist . . . in the
> emotional penumbra of the characters themselves.[5]

Colette, by this measure, would seem to derive less from Balzac than
from Tolstoi, for it is by means of materiality more than action that
she builds for us the "emotional penumbra" in which we see Julie.
The complexity of this character is made for us not by a commonplace contrast between country and city but also by Julie's helpless
attraction to a highly material middle ground which represents the
values of one of her divorced husbands, Espivant. She visits him in a
"forbidden zone" of luxury where there are windows instead of
looking glasses, where there is such brightness that Julie is "as
happy as a wasp in the sun" (p. 105), and where the material things
inside have come from the outside garden, not from exotic foreign
craftsmen. There is a "yellow rose standing next to a pot of fresh
cream" and the tables are laden (Julie "could cope with anything
except hunger") with "late cherries, rose-colored peaches, thin-
skinned Marseilles figs, cloudy hot-house grapes that had been

carefully protected from the wasps" (p. 104). As the hothouse is next
to the garden, so the champagne which "trembled in thick cut-glass
jugs" stands next to the iced water which is Julie's favorite drink all
through the story ("A glass of cold water swept away the morning
fog"—p. 125). But it is the champagne that she drinks with
Espivant, and she is "fanned into flame" by it and by his life in a
way that her Carneilhan strengths cannot overcome. In the Espivant
house there are as many "closed doors" as there are windows, and
behind the doors seems to wait the rich wife. The Espivant source of
life is not the natural aristocracy of Carneilhan, "half manor and
half farmhouse" (p. 113), but tainted money which Espivant
describes as deriving ultimately from the artificial, from "reams and
reams of paper, portfolios, calculating machines, arctically cold
offices in impossible parts of the town, hideous malformed little
brats carting piles of documents about, and lawyers better dressed
than I am" (p. 118).

Julie's whole character, its animal strengths and hothouse weak-
nesses, is built for us thus economically in terms of objects that
range from the artificial to the relatively natural, and the problem of
where on the scale Julie will range herself is made for us but not
solved for her. She is dependent on her telephone, but Espivant also
has an "array" of them which Julie "can never quite believe" he
really needs. By a joint trick to get a piece of the wife's money (most
of which Espivant keeps when they get it) Julie is given her final
chance to leave with her horsy brother for Carneilhan. "But she still
felt uncertain of her departure" (p. 213), as do we, for we have had a
long encounter with her vacillation and her ups and downs with
Espivant, who is no good but who is the "man of my life," and who
has his own animal strength (even at the last he is still playing "the
mouse" Julie would like to trap, and "He's tougher than a seven-
year-old hen"—p. 217). Because of the ambivalence which characterizes Julie, Carneilhan enlarges to a symbol when she asks her brother
how long it will take them to return there, and he answers: "Three
weeks ... three months ... all our lives" (p. 219).

Just before what may be the last journey (Leon, the brother, says,
"The road to Carneilhan will be a one-way journey for me. Do you
think you can say the same?"—p. 218), the looking glass returns to
the story: "Julie's face materialized in the looking glass" and she
saw "her washed-out reflection" (p. 217). Like some of the mirrors

which we shall encounter in the novellas of learning and maturing, it gives her little information, though it is very useful to the reader, framing a picture which *he* is to look at. For Julie it is the "dead glass" of a Wallace Stevens poem

> ... which can reflect
> Only the surfaces—the bending arm,
> The leaning shoulder and the searching eye.[6]

We see all, but for Julie the looking glass is as unrevealing as the window of the lawyer's office in Melville's *Bartleby the Scrivener,* which looked out on blank walls. That lawyer's character, too, was presented to us by means of significant material objects which reveal the "emotional penumbra" of a life: "I make some mention of myself, my employes, my business, my chambers, and general surroundings; because some such description is indispensable to an adequate understanding of the chief character about to be presented." Far from knowing himself, he does not even know that the "chief character" about to be presented is actually himself.[7] However, in his case as in Julie de Carneilhan's, what keeps the power of the story "serious" and not pathetic is that they had at least the strength of the "searching eye" of Stevens's poem. "How many crazy decisions and allegiances to successive aspects of the truth!" (p. 145) Julie perceives in herself.

The nature of the pleasure for the reader is twofold: the superiority of knowledge which we achieve over these characters and the fine art with which the portraits are made for us. It is as like an art of painting—distinct from sketching—as successive words can be. In the Melville story it is a study by Daumier: a central character illumined by surrounding minor characters (Turkey, Nippers, Ginger Nut, and pale Bartleby himself) and dusty but precise material details (Turkey's spilled sandbox and inkblots, Nipper's shaky table, Ginger Nut's ginger nut—"small, flat, round, and very spicy"—and Bartleby's "high green folding screen" which blocks the central character's view).

Julie is a painting by Matisse, "unframed" to herself but framed and glassed for us: a single blonde female figure of immense interest and sensuality, her inner nature made for us by the gaudy background, the fruit and flowers on the table, the looking glass "festooned" with a "sheaf of dog whips and riding switches" (p. 79), her clothing "a white tailored shirt, a skirt with a pattern of black and white birds' feet and a black jacket that flouted every current fashion" (p. 98). To pursue a difficult analogy a bit farther: where the art of these novellas departs from the art of painting is not at all that they are less framed—the art of these character elaborations is as refined and shapely as novella form can be—but that they are spatially larger. Quite unlike the characters in example apologues, whose character delineation is narrowed to the limits of that which is to be exemplified,[8] we feel in *Bartleby* and *Julie* that we have it all, that we have an individual—live, complex, complete. In order to have an action, which is of the essence of "story," there must be a problem of "right now," but the character rises to the problem from the background of his own life fully made for us, exists to reveal his or her central and individual self in that problem, perhaps the more richly if he struggles unavailingly.

There is in the novella nearly ideal time and space for keeping the light on the one character while opening up scenes and episodes enough to throw varying, therefore fuller, sometimes even sociological as well as psychological, light on the character. In fact, one interesting variation on the plot of character, *The Pilgrim Hawk* by Glenway Wescott, focuses on two characters, a married couple who are not only fully presented to us as characters by the first-person narrator observing them, but he takes space also for at least minimal maturing reflections on the meaning for him of their characters. It is clearly, then, a very different art from the character sketch that is typical of the short story. One would not give away the brilliant bitterness of the bare-boned character delineation in, for example, Hemingway's "Hills Like White Elephants," but neither would one claim for it the high seriousness and complexity of these rich novellas.

Questions with answers:
The learning plot in OLD MORTALITY
and THE VIRGIN AND THE GIPSY

I have made mention of the significant question toward the end of *Julie de Carneilhan*: "How long do you think it'll take us to get to Carneilhan?" and its uncertain answer based on Julie's characteristic uncertainty. By contrast, the learning plot—the second of the

serious actions typical of novellas—is marked and naturally proceeds by raising questions very early, questions to which we hope the
protagonist will find an answer by the end.

The purpose of *Old Mortality*, by Katherine Anne Porter, will be
to make our serious sense of a young girl who fails initially to
understand her relationship to an intriguing and oppressive family
background. The action of the story advances her into young
womanhood, toward that degree of knowledge of which we find her
conscious in the last paragraph:

> I can't live in their world any longer, she told herself,
> listening to the voices back of her. Let them tell their stories
> to each other. Let them go on explaining how things
> happened. I don't care. At least I can know the truth about
> what happens to me, she assured herself silently, making a
> promise to herself, in her hopefulness, her ignorance.[9]
>
> [P. 221]

The beginning of the action which will conclude with this partial
education of Miranda (Latin, "she who wonders") is composed of
items of experience, appropriately dated progressively—e.g., "Part
I: 1885–1902." The early experiences consist mainly in looking at
old photographs and mementoes, and listening to stories about the
past. The plotting of these experiences is curiously devised to include
jointly the musing and discoveries of both Miranda and her sister
Maria in the first two parts of the novella, after which Maria drops
out of the story forever.

The loss of Maria is an interesting lesson not only in novella
economy but in the subordination of plot expectations and their
fulfillment to the needs of this particular kind of plot and its power.
Maria seems to exist in the story to complicate the learning process
of Miranda. Maria is four years older, but as children they share
poetic imaginings about the past that can only be expressed in terms
of the music they have heard and the poetry they have memorized. It
is not clear in which girl's consciousness we are getting the response
to the end of the romance of dead Aunt Amy, who is reported to
have called out

> 'Good-by, good-by,' and refused her cloak, and said, 'Give
> me a glass of wine.' And none of us saw her alive again."
> "Why wouldn't she wear her cloak, Cousin Cora?" "Because

she was not in love, my dear." Ruin hath taught me thus to
ruminate, that time will come and take my love away.

[P. 176]

Gradually we learn, however, that it belongs to Miranda to believe
that "by some miracle she would grow into a tall, cream-colored
brunette, like cousin Isabel; she decided always to wear a trailing
white satin gown." By contrast, "Maria, born sensible, had no such
illusions" (p. 177). In the second part, two years later, this division
has widened to the point where many of Miranda's thoughts become
secret. Together they share the wonderful word "immured" to
describe their convent school "where they spent the long winter
trying to avoid an education" (p. 193); but when Miranda decides
she will become a jockey when she grows up, she cannot confide her
plan to anyone, "least of all to Maria" (p. 196). Maria leaves the
story, then, when she has served to establish the painful point where
Miranda, the more vulnerable because the younger, can and must
make up her own mind about the family, independent even of
Maria.

Maria can be seen, then, as part of the oppressive family
"furnishing" of the story. As in Colette's story, things even more
than people serve to build that oppressive sense. Miranda's mind is
not only crowded with old family tales, and poems, and snatches of
music, but the world in which she moves is full of old photographs
and paintings, attic trunks containing "Such dowdy little wreaths
and necklaces, some of them made of pearly shells; such moth-eaten
bunches of pink ostrich feathers for the hair; such clumsy big breast
pins and bracelets of gold and colored enamel; such silly-looking
combs, standing up on tall teeth capped with seed pearls and French
paste" (p. 175). Julie de Carneilhan would have simply found these
things "terrific," and they would have served in that kind of
character plot simply to help mark off her character. In Miranda's
case, the judgmental "dowdy," "moth-eaten," "clumsy," and "silly-
looking" belong to her growing consciousness; and they are judgments that free her gradually from things, free her to raise the
questions by which the learning plot moves:

—"And where were they now, those girls, and the boys in the odd-
looking collars?" (p. 175)

—"Who could have taken them seriously, looking like that?"
(p. 176)

—"Why should anyone need to recall the past?" (p. 179)
At the end of Part I, a partly false answer is reached by Miranda,
that "the letters and all the strange keepsakes ... seemed to have
no place in the world" (p. 193).

Two years later the sisters are still making half-blind decisions
between the artificial and the real. At ages ten and fourteen,

> They had long since learned to draw the lines between
> life, which was real and earnest, and the grave was not its
> goal; poetry, which was true but not real; and stories, or
> forbidden reading matter, in which things happened as
> nowhere else, with the most sublime irrelevance and
> unlikelihood, and one need not turn a hair, because there was
> not a word of truth in them.
>
> [P. 194]

Clearly, life still has only as much reality as a Longfellow poem, and
decisions for Miranda are as vacillating as wanting to be a nun one
day and a jockey the next: "It seemed too silly to be worried about
arithmetic at all, when what she needed for her future was to ride
better—much better" (p. 196). The pressure now is between
thoughts like these of her own and her father's view of her: "'You
ought to be ashamed of yourself,' said father ... 'I can see the sun,
moon and stars between you and the saddle every jump'" (p. 196).
Question: "Oh, what did grown-up people *mean* when they talked,
anyway?" (p. 197).

Yet, half-answers begin to appear as horse-racing becomes
enlarged into an instructive analogy: "The jockeys sat bowed and
relaxed, their faces calm, moving a little at the waist with the
movement of their horses. Miranda noted this for future use; that
was the way you came in from a race, easy and quiet, whether you
had won or lost" (p. 199). At the same moment she sees the suffering
horse, "Miss Lucy," who was "bleeding at the nose, two thick red
rivulets were stiffening her tender mouth and chin." And "Miranda
stood staring. That was winning, too" (p. 199).

By Part III, Miranda is eighteen, is alone in her learning, and her
questions are now invariably accompanied by partial answers. On a
train-ride home to a family funeral, she comes under the hardest
family pressure of all: Cousin Eva Parrington, the other family
dissident, unmarried and an old feminist activist. She remembers
Miranda's childhood plans: "You were going to play the violin and

walk the tight-rope at the same time" (p. 207). Miranda, who now wants to be an air pilot, has the problem of raising the question to which she already has begun to know the answer: "Across the abyss separating Cousin Eva from her own youth, Miranda looked with painful premonition. Oh, must I ever be like that?" (p. 208). Miranda is "dimly fired for the cause" of feminism herself, but she makes the break between herself and her cousin, because "Cousin Eva so plainly had swept the field clear of opportunity" (p. 210). Miranda is caught now between two family traditions: romantic Amy-ness, and militant Eva-ness. Question: "What was the end of this story?" (p. 214). Question: "Wasn't being alive enough?" (p. 215). Question: "Why was a strong character so deforming? Miranda felt she truly wanted to be strong, but how could she face it, seeing what it did to one?" (p. 215). As her questions become complex (even rhetorical) with these half-answers, she is pinned down by Cousin Eva's strongest statement: "'Ah, the family,' she said, '... the whole hideous institution should be wiped from the face of the earth. It is the root of all human wrongs'" (p. 217).

The ultimate pressure is her father's reception of Miranda: "There was no welcome for her and there had not been since she had run away" and eloped. Under this pressure, the final questions, with initial answers, begin to fall into place:

> He had not forgiven her, she knew that. When would he? She could not guess, but she felt it would come of itself, without words and without acknowledgment on either side.... Surely old people cannot hold their grudges forever because the young want to live, too, she thought, in her arrogance, her pride. I will make my own mistakes, not yours; I cannot depend upon you beyond a certain point, why depend at all?
>
> [P. 219]

The education has slowly taken place, but in the "arrogance" and "pride" is the narrator's warning that maturity remains outside the story and not yet certain. What nevertheless keeps Miranda high in our estimation is that she fights for knowledge, both questioning and answering, up to the end:

> I hate love, she thought, as if this were the answer....
> And her disturbed and seething mind received a shock of comfort from this sudden collapse of an old painful structure

of distorted images and misconceptions. "You don't know anything about it," said Miranda to herself, with extraordinary clearness as if she were an elder admonishing some young misguided creature. "You have to find out about it." But nothing in her prompted her to decide, "I will now do this, I will be that, I will go yonder, I will take a certain road to a certain end." There are questions to be asked first, she thought, but who will answer them? No one, or there will be too many answers, none of them right.

[P. 221]

No answers thus become part of the right answer, and give Miranda at least a minimal final strength.

The art of this novella, as against the art required for *Julie de Carneilhan*, is clearly less a matter of building significant material atmospheres (these count, but not as character indicators so much as aids to learning) than of making a world of experience to which questions are steadily directed by an interior youthful consciousness full of wonder and intelligence. The story is full of paintings and photographs rather than of mirrors because it is, for Miranda, less a matter of looking at her unadorned self (or of our looking at it) than of discovering what is true of herself relative to all those others whose portraits fill the walls of her life. Julie de Carneilhan gazes but doesn't "quite see" (p. 200), her eyes are "as unabashed as those of the blind" (p. 192), and "mixed up with luminous globules and zigzags, little mirages," her posture one of "deep passivity and entire ignorance" (p. 196). By contrast, the diction of Miranda's story is full of "watching," "wondered," "examined," "noted," "listened," "astonishment," "believed," "was pained to learn," "gathered," "discovered," "understood." Her "ignorance" at the end is clearly compounded with new knowledge, as Julie's hardly is.

In Lawrence's *The Virgin and the Gipsy* we have again the plot of learning, amazingly like *Old Mortality* in some respects but much more exterior and dramatic in its action. Again there are two sisters, who "seemed so free, and were as a matter of fact so tangled and tied up, inside themselves.... And they were, as a matter of fact, two poor young rudderless lives, moving from one chain anchorage [school] to another [home]" (p. 9).[10] They, too, feel the "full weight of Granny's dead old hand on their lives" and have to come to terms, as Miranda did, with a romantically defiant Aunt-Amy figure, who in this case is their runaway mother. Once again, the younger sister,

Yvette, singles herself out as the character to whose learning process we are to attend.

The difference is that Yvette, the "virgin" learner, depends for what she learns not on her own thought but upon a "flood" of "dark power" infused in her by her encounters with the gipsy. By the end—the extended metaphor of the destruction of her family home and the drowning of her grandmother in the flood—Yvette is only half-aware of the significance to her of the flood and of the gipsy, though she has achieved some sort of intuitive knowledge: "The grief over him kept her prostrate. Yet practically, she too was acquiescent in the fact of his disappearance. Her young soul knew the wisdom of it" (p. 81). The reader's awareness, as in the Colette story, is much greater than the protagonist's. As is the case with *Julie*, the story seems to exist for what *we* learn more than for what Yvette learns—though, unlike Julie, she does learn. (When I speak of "what we learn," I do not mean that the story elucidates a formulable statement as in apologue—our learning is as intuitive as Yvette's, even though greater than hers.)

Accordingly, there are artistic devices shared by Lawrence with both the previous novellas. There is extended business of windows, doors, and mirrors through which, and into which, Yvette gazes with little more effect than Julie. The windows, doors, and mirrors belong to the rectory home, and their function, as in *Julie*, is not to be opened or seen through in the sense of perception but rather to serve as artificial barriers to the lesson that is outside in the gipsy's natural world. Because what is out there must be journeyed toward, there is the additional metaphor of the "road curved up-hill" toward the gipsy camp. Out of "the mud and dark and dampness of the valley" (p. 17) containing the stone rectory one must "climb," "still upwards," "always climbing," toward "the naked tops" until one is "on the top of the world now, on the back of the fist. It was naked, too, as the back of your fist, high under heaven" (p. 18). The summit, where the gipsy is, is suffused always with the light of the sun.

By contrast with the "naked tops," the rectory is even more furnished, stuffed, and smelly with things than Julie's studio: "Roast beef and wet cabbage, cold mutton and mashed potatoes, sour pickles, inexcusable puddings" (p. 9). Again, in making the reader aware of a much more subtle gap, that between the natural truth ("the real thing") of the gipsy and the "bourgeois" civilized sexual revolt ("the abstract morality of the north"—p. 54) of the Eastwoods, who attract Yvette, Lawrence stifles the Eastwoods with material objects:

> The cottage was hired furnished, but the little Jewess had brought along her dearest pieces of furniture. She had an odd little taste for the rococo, strange curving cupboards inlaid with mother-of-pearl, tortoise-shell, ebony, heaven knows what; strange tall flamboyant chairs from Italy, with sea-green brocade: astonishing saints with wind-blown, richly coloured carven garments and pink faces: shelves of weird old Saxe and Capo di Monte figurines: and finally, a strange assortment of astonishing pictures painted on the back of glass ...
>
> [P. 53–54]

With the stroke of a master Lawrence suddenly, in this scene, turns the Eastwoods themselves into artifacts:

> And there was the tiny rococo figurine of the Jewess herself, in a perfect little frock, and an apron, putting slices of ham on the dish, while the great snowbird of a major, in a white sweater and grey trousers, cut bread, mixed mustard, prepared coffee.
>
> [P. 54]

There is a delicate but distinct difference between the fine, natural, sensuous sleep of "pure will-lessness" upon which the novella places its moral value, and the gentle anger of Major Eastwood, "of the soft, snowy sort, which comfortably muffles the soul" (p. 58). Lest anyone imagine that the education that takes place between the "virgin" learner and the "gipsy" is at all simple, Mrs. Eastwood represents still another complication. There must be a great temptation on the part of many readers to treat the stress on the "Jewess" (she is tagged as "Jewess" no less than forty-nine times in the novella, usually "the little Jewess") as brazen, gratuitous, therefore extrinsic, Lawrentian anti-Semitism which flaws the story intrinsically by bearing no part-to-whole relationship to the power of Yvette's learning process. Indeed it is hard not to lay such a charge against an expression like "the canny shrewdness of a bourgeois Jewess: a rich one, probably" (p. 49), an expression which comes from the omniscient narrator, not from the limited viewpoint of

Yvette or any other character. In context, however, Mrs. Eastwood's Jewishness seems to me to be employed by Lawrence with intrinsic control, in one of those economies of the novella which often make its effects so much more pure and intense than those of the novel.

For the hurdles that stand between Yvette and the knowledge of "the real thing" which the gipsy offers are not one and simple, but several and complex. She must come to terms with (1) the moral contents of the stone-walled rectory: the narrowness of Aunt Cissy, the "weak, feeble nullity" of her rector father, and the "blind" power of tradition which Granny wields; (2) the puerile, day-trip escapes from bondage carried on by her youthful peers ("So the young people set off on their jaunt, trying to be very full of beans"—p. 16); (3) the simple confrontation with the significance of money and material things in the affair of her "borrowing" from the Window Fund, a revolt against the social values around her which has about the importance of "Mary-Mary-quite-contrary"; (4) the larger, apparently more daring and portentous, social revolt of the Eastwoods, who are "on our honeymoon" (p. 50), though unmarried.

The problem Lawrence faces with this last hurdle is to show in a relatively short space the complex attraction of a revolution that takes place essentially inside the "establishment," partly so that Yvette can remain high in our estimation both when she is "rather thrilled by the Eastwoods" (p. 53) and when she more or less fails either to defend them against her father or to understand why she should not. The complexity is refined, then, by Lawrence in his presentation of Major Eastwood as a "pale-eyed" snow bird with a "sense of outraged justice, the abstract morality of the north blowing him, like a strange wind, into isolation" (p. 54). His is one kind of false moral authority, the military class. Set up in contrast, the Jewishness of "Mrs." Eastwood calls up a specific moral law backed by the whole Judaic tradition which turns false in her because of being mixed with her "bourgeois free-masonry" (p. 53). A remarkable effect of moral messiness results: "The little Jewess had a burning indignation against her first husband. She was intensely moral, so moral, that she was a divorcee" (p. 54). One feels that it is precisely a traditional Judaic moral sense that Lawrence would like to praise in her, were it not turned upside down by the bourgeois values which are her real religion and which cause her to look down on the gipsy as "one of the common men" (p. 51). In the

value system of the story, which Yvette only half-learns, the
Eastwood sexual freedom is no revolution at all because it requires a
man of one's own social level, is dressed in a fur coat "which seemed
to walk on little legs of its own" (p. 53), and is surrounded by
bourgeois safeguards, "pictures painted on the back of glass" (p.
54).

With social constructs like these set in her path, Yvette can only
"chip against the pillars of the temple, from the inside" (p. 67),
while the gipsy stands easily in open doorways. The doors of Yvette's
life are too hard to open. ("The keys of their lives were in their own
hands. And there they dangled inert"—p. 16.)

The windows in the story exist to be fought over, by the learner
who wishes to "see" through them against the "life unbelievers" (p.
28). Yvette ("one of the people who are conscious in visual images"
—p. 43) wishes to see through, and to open windows, and the
window on the landing of the rectory becomes her station for
watching for the gipsy to come, her place from which "to gaze
through the window that looked to the road and the bridge" (p. 35).
For her the window curtains exist to be pushed aside—"Yvette
stood close to the window and put the casement-cloth curtains
behind her" (pp. 36–37). For her father, the rector, they are
ramparts of "the establishment"—"he backed away from her,
against the window-curtains of his study, like a rat at bay" (p. 62). At
one point there is a symbolic battle with Granny over whether Yvette
shall open the window (for "the room was never fresh, she imagined
it smelt: smelt of Granny"). The battle is resolved when "the rector,
in silence, marched to the window and firmly closed it" (p. 11). After
the flood and the final drama in which the gipsy saves and warms
the "virgin," the window is appropriately seen "smashed."

For the gipsy has no barriers between his "dark conceited proud
eyes" (p. 22) and what he sees when he looks at Yvette, "not from the
outside, but from the inside, from her secret female self" (p. 40). By
contrast Leo, her beau from inside the walls of the Lambley Close
party, has a superficial "bold, meaningful smile" which "instead of
penetrating into some deep, secret place, and shooting her there . . .
only hit her on the outside of the body, like a tennis ball" (p. 44).

The diction of seeing, looking, staring, and awareness suggests the
learning process, as it did in *Old Mortality*, but it lacks the quality of
wondering, thinking, believing, and being "pained to learn" intellectually that belongs to Miranda. The phallic suggestiveness of the

contrast between the looks directed at Yvette by the gipsy and by Leo have to do with the kind of lesson to be learned. As in *The Fox,* the lesson Yvette must learn is an awareness of the flesh and of the spirit submitting to itself, not to the intellect: "The gipsy, supremely aware of her, waited for her like the substance of shadow, as shadow waits and is there" (p. 48). And the quality of her awareness begins to match his: "The childlike, sleep-waking eyes of her moment of perfect virginity looked into his, unseeing. She was only aware of the dark strange effluence of him bathing her limbs, washing her at last purely will-less. She was aware of *him,* as a dark, complete power" (p. 48).

Further comparing artistic devices, one cannot leave *The Virgin and the Gipsy* without noting the other conspicuous "seeing" artifact: the mirrors. In a kind of hodgepodge of symbolism, Yvette participates in an amateur theatrical called *Mary in the Mirror,* the proceeds of which are to go to Aunt Cissie's stained-glass Window Fund, which never results in a window but only in an "ugly little monument" (p. 25). In the same chapter there appear the "long mirror," in which Yvette views her "naked elbows," and a "second mirror perched perilously on the piano." Yvette, "flourishing her long, naked arms," stands "between the mirrors, to look at herself once more," and drops the small one on the floor. Aunt Cissie and Granny are aghast with rage and superstition ("... there shall be no mirrors broken in *this* house, if we can help it"), and Yvette's response is, "I may say it's my own looking-glass, even if I did break it" (p. 33). The scene ends with Yvette gazing "through the window that looked to the road" (p. 35). Uncannily like those in *Julie de Carneilhan*, mirrors have here been devalued to an artificial mode of viewing (connected to Paris values versus Carneilhan values, or rectory values versus gipsy values) which produces unreliable judgments of surfaces only.

In *Julie,* the plot of character, there is almost no learning to be done by Julie. Therefore there are untelling mirrors (which *we,* however, see into), windows from which Julie constantly leans out but sees nothing, doors which are only "half-open" or threateningly closed, lovers to be got rid of if they see too much (" 'The clear-sighted little wretch!' she thought. 'It makes his company intolerable' "), and only one large question, whose answer remains unclear.

In *The Virgin and the Gipsy*, a plot of learning of one kind,

windows, doors, and mirrors appear once more significantly dis-
valued—they belong again to the inside—and Yvette's outside road
leading upward to the gipsy becomes an equivalent of the "impend-
ing journey" to Carneilhan. But the Lawrence story adds the device
of questions which ally it to *Old Mortality* as a plot of learning:

—"Why did she go? Why did she burst away with such an éclat of
   revulsion . . . ?" (p. 3)
—"Outside the family, what was there for them but danger and
   insult?" (p. 7).
—"Why was that? Why, why was that?"(p. 27)
—"But where did the horrible wincing of her flesh come from?
   Why did she feel she had caught some physical contagion?"
   (p. 27)
—"Why are we all only like mortal pieces of furniture? Why is
   nothing *important*?"(p. 41)
—"Where among them was the subtle, lonely, insinuating chal-
   lenge that could reach her?" (p. 43)

Unlike the questions of Miranda—those of the probing intellect—
these remain more or less unanswered in Yvette's own mind, except
by the flood as the grand natural answer. And after the flood, there
is one large unanswered question, which at least Yvette has learned
enough to ask: "Where was the gipsy? This was the first thing in her
mind. Where was her gipsy? This was the first thing in her mind.
Where was her gipsy of this world's-end night?" (p. 79). The
question itself is phrased almost like a chant, suitable to a question
whose answers lie in the flesh and the spirit, unavailable to unaided
reason. The learning is only as great as Yvette's still-complex
situation allows: that is, the question has advanced to a *first*
question, the gipsy has become "her" gipsy, her old world has
reached "world's-end." What her new world will be like is left
unclear to us.

The maturing of Tonio Kröger and some others

The affection and praise with which Mann himself talks of *Tonio
Kröger* in his preface to *Stories of Three Decades* puzzled me for a
long time. Its large movements across time and space seemed to me
to thin its quality somewhat, to make of it less a novella like the
beautifully confined works we have been discussing, and more like a
failed long novel. Since I have reread it and compared it with the
others of its kind—the serious plots of character and learning—it

has revealed itself as one of the finest of this kind, an artistic summit which gathers to it the best of the foothills of Colette, Porter, and Lawrence, though its publication date (1903) predates all the others by three to four decades.

The problem of Tonio is to think his way past the emotional problem presented by his standing "between two worlds." Quite like the two worlds of "the virgin" and "the gipsy," or the Amy-ness and Eva-ness of *Old Mortality*, it is a conflict represented by a stern father and a "dark, fiery mother" whom Tonio views as "just a little wanton."[11] His childish decision is at times clear: "After all, we are not gypsies [!] living in a green wagon; we're respectable people, the family of Consul Kröger" (p. 91). Yet his estrangement from the blond children of the bourgeoisie like Hans and Inge causes him painful questions:

—"Why is it I am different, why do I fight everything, why am I at odds with the masters and like a stranger among the other boys?" (p. 88)

—"What is the matter with me, and what will be the end of it all?" (p. 88)

By age sixteen, his self-questioning both becomes more intense and begins to provide complex answers:

> For he was looking within, into himself, the theatre of so much pain and longing. Why, why was he here? Why was he not sitting by the window in his own room, reading Storm's *Immensee* and lifting his eyes to the twilight garden outside, where the old walnut tree moaned? That was the place for him! Others might dance, others bend their fresh and lively minds upon the pleasure in hand! ... But no, no, after all his place was here.
>
> [P. 96]

The self-questioning, which Tonio properly sees as Hamlet-like (" 'Is it to consider things not curiously enough, to consider them so?' "—p. 106), is the questioning of the interior intellect comparable to Miranda's in *Old Mortality*, with the difference that Tonio is not only resolving his own place in the world but resolving for himself the great human problems of "mind, and art, forsooth!" and of the bourgeois versus the "adorers of the beautiful." And it is not the pathetic and fatal mode of Aschenbach deciding alone. Tonio shares with Miranda the healthy desire to try out his questions on others.

Mann saw his own art in this story as excelling "its next of kin,

Death in Venice, in youthful lyrical bloom" and, considered as a
work of art, "its musical affinities may have been what endeared
it" to the readers.[12] He speaks of it as "a weaving of themes, as a
musical complex of associations," as an employment of the "verbal
leitmotiv." While I think such a description of structure is accurate
for *Death in Venice,* which achieves its pathos by *leitmotifs* of death
and decay sounded repeatedly in the attrition of Aschenbach's life
and moral strength, something greater and more complex is going
on in the structure of *Tonio Kröger.* In my earlier discussion of
Death in Venice (in chap. 5) I took issue with Eva Brann in her
attack on the "charlatanism" of the artist who, both as character in
the story and author of the story, proposes to give form to life as
Aschenbach does, by means of soliloquy rather than dialogue (she is
echoing, of course, Socrates' old suspicion not only of poetry but of
the written word as against the dialectical argument). My evidence
for partial disagreement, especially in the case of Mann, arises in an
analysis of *Tonio Kröger,* which makes both internal and structural
use of dialogue.

Internally, one feels that Tonio would have had far less chance of
coming to his mature understanding on the last page without his
extended conversation with Lisabeta earlier. More than "a good
friend of his, to whom he told all his troubles" (p. 100), she is an
opponent in argument who is able to be vexed with his opinions,
shame him when necessary, and provide a foil for his Platonism.
Admittedly, she does this rather two-dimensionally (so that the
spotlight remains on his own thought), but she reminds him of "the
purifying and healing influence of letters, the subduing of the
passions by knowledge and eloquence; literature as the guide to
understanding, forgiveness, and love, the redeeming power of the
word, literary art as the noblest manifestation of the human mind,
the poet as the most highly developed of human beings, the poet as
saint" (p. 106). Simply because of her exposure of "elevated
literature," he is forced to summon his counterthoughts:

> "Now for the 'Word.' It isn't so much a matter of the
> 'redeeming power' as it is of putting your emotions on ice and
> serving them up chilled! Honestly, don't you think there's a
> good deal of cool cheek in the prompt and superficial way a
> writer can get rid of his feelings by turning them into
> literature.... And will you seriously enter the lists in behalf

of this vain and frigid charlatan? What is uttered, so runs
this *credo,* is finished and done with. If the whole world
could be expressed, it would be saved, finished and done."

[P. 107]

Only their long argument makes possible her summary of Tonio:
"You are a bourgeois on the wrong path, a bourgeois manqué"
(p. 110). Tonio rather sarcastically thanks her (" . . . now I can go
home in peace. I am expressed"), and it is clear that he perceives her
"Word" as only half the truth, for there remains for him his voyage
of discovery. His questions are by no means ended:

—"What was at the bottom of this? What was it burning darkly
   beneath the ashes of his fatigue, refusing to burst out into a
   clear blaze?" (p. 112)
—"Where was he going? He scarcely knew." (p. 113)

But the questions begin, partly as a result of their conversation, to
attach themselves to half-answers:

—"Where was he going? It seemed to him the direction he took
   had a connection with his sad and strangely rueful dreams."
   (p. 113)
—"Where did he go? Toward home. But he took a roundabout
   way outside the walls." (p. 114)

The visit to his old home, which is now a public library ("What
were either literature or the public doing here?") ends with a
confrontation with local police in which Tonio is asked, significantly, to identify himself, and is faced with his childhood temptation: "Should he make an end of the business, by revealing to Herr
Seehaase that he was no swindler without specified means, no gypsy
in a green wagon, but the son of the late Consul Kröger, a member
of the Kröger family?" (pp. 117–18). The answer of his growing
maturity is, "No, he felt no desire to do that" (p. 118). Instead he
identifies himself as an author, a creative artist, by means of
showing the official his manuscript. Thus is resolved half of his
sense of himself.

What remains is to go north, then farther north, to reconfront his
ancient trouble with the "blond, fair-haired breed of the steel-blue
eyes, which stood to him for the pure, the blithe, the untroubled in
life" (for all that is not the "Word"). It is a confrontation which
results in the last darkness before the light, and in immense pain:

> He undressed, lay down, put out the light. Two names he
> whispered into his pillow, the few chaste northern syllables
> that meant for him his true and native way of love, of longing
> and happiness; that meant to him life and home, meant
> simple and heartfelt feeling. He looked back on the years
> that had passed. He thought of the dreamy adventures of the
> senses, nerves, and mind in which he had been involved; saw
> himself eaten up with intellect and introspection, ravaged
> and paralysed by insight, half worn out by the fevers and
> frosts of creation, helpless and in anguish of conscience
> between two extremes, flung to and fro between austerity and
> lust; *raffiné*, impoverished, exhausted by frigid and
> artificially heightened ecstasies; erring, forsaken, martyred,
> and ill—and sobbed with nostalgia and remorse.
>
> [P. 131]

It is typical of the plot of learning that concludes in maturity to
pay the price for maturity by one of these dark-before-the-dawn
scenes of painful recognition. The scene above has its equivalent in
Saul Bellow's *Seize the Day* (which, of course, is also preceded by the
dialogues with the father and with Tamkin) when Tommy Wilhelm
sobs in ecstasy before the coffin of a stranger who helps him back
from the brink toward control of his own life. What has brought
about both the recognition and the open hope for the future is not
only experience but the raising of questions and seeking of answers
(dialogue) about the experience.

The dialogue of Tonio Kröger's learning process is incomplete
without the expression (to Lisabeta) of the knowledge and sense of
the future that has arisen from his painful search:

> "I stand between two worlds. I am at home in neither,
> and I suffer in consequence. You artists call me a *bourgeois,*
> and the bourgeois try to arrest me.... I don't know
> which makes me feel worse. The bourgeois are stupid;
> but you adorers of the beautiful, who call me phlegmatic
> and without aspirations, you ought to realize that there is
> a way of being an artist that goes so deep and is so much
> a matter of origins and destinies that no longing seems to it
> sweeter and more worth knowing than longings after the bliss
> of the commonplace.... For if anything is capable of
> making a poet of a literary man, it is my *bourgeois*
> love of the human, the living and usual. It is the source

of all warmth, goodness, and humour; I even almost think
it is itself that love of which it stands written that one
may speak with the tongues of men and of angels and yet
having it not is as sounding brass and tinkling cymbals."

[P. 132]

This painful knowledge allows him to see into his future and accept
his work:

"I am looking into a world unborn and formless,
that needs to be ordered and shaped; I see into a whirl
of shadows of human figures who beckon to me to weave
spells to redeem them: tragic and laughable figures and
some that are both together—and to these I am drawn.
But my deepest and secretest love belongs to the blond
and blue-eyed, the fair and living, the happy, lovely,
and commonplace."

[Ibid.]

It is still in the spirit of the dialogue that anticipates opposing ideas
that he ends: "Do not chide this love, Lisabeta; it is good and
fruitful."

That the structure of this novella of learning and maturing can be
seen as musical is beyond doubt—here one thinks of novella length
as sonata length. One can find themes repeated and counterpointed
(the blond and the blue-eyed, the "gypsy in a green wagon" against
the "Consul Kröger"); leitmotifs like the recurring walnut tree
which serves the story like Proust's madeleine; rhythms of the
recurring dance scenes—"life's lulling, trivial waltz-rhythm"; and
the ending of the last "movement" with a maturer, more firmly
stated return to the identical theme (almost the identical words) of
the first "movement": "There is longing in it, and gentle envy; a
touch of contempt and no little innocent bliss" (pp. 92 and 132). But
that is the emotive structure of the novella only. Superimposed on
the loosely strung musical structure is the intellectual structure of
the dialectic: Experience—Questioning of Experience—Partial
Answer—Analysed and Formed Experience—Better Answer.

Watching this dialogue in *Tonio Kröger* by means of the chapter-
like breaks, one has (and has it very similarly in *Old Mortality*,
though there the Better Answer is not certainly one of final
maturity):

1. Childhood experience: frustrated love of the "blond and blue-eyed" Hans.

2. Adolescent experience: the "blond and blue-eyed" Inge, complicated by a new opposition from Tonio's sense of Magdalena, she who "often fell down in the dance." From this opposition arises a host of questions.

3. Out of questioned experience arises the partial and insufficient answer of youth: life is to be seen in extremes "between icy intellect and scorching sense" (p. 99).

4. The actual dialogue between Tonio and Lisabeta which concludes his youth (age 30), ending with his being "expressed" ambiguously—a prod to the next experiences which he approaches for the sake of analysis.

5. Experience is chosen for what it will reveal. The making of a decision as to where knowledge lies.

6. The journey home where the old experiences are given form by his analytical understanding—acceptance of his role as artist.

7. The journey out on the sea, open but formed by direction: northward, upward.

8. Recapitulation of the old bourgeois experience in the new and higher location. Acceptance of his role as bourgeois *and* artist.

Here in the eighth section the imagery of doors, curtains, and windows which we have found used more or less negatively in all the novellas of learning, including this one, reappears with a positive joyfulness as maturity sets in:

> The very opening of the day had been rare and festal.
> Tonio Kröger woke early and suddenly from his sleep,
> with a vague and exquisite alarm; he seemed to be looking
> at a miracle, a magic illumination. His room had a glass
> door and balcony facing the sound; a thin white gauze
> curtain divided it into living- and sleeping-quarters. . . .
> But now to his sleep-drunken eyes it lay bathed in a serene
> and roseate light, an unearthly brightness that gilded walls
> and furniture and turned the gauze curtains to a radiant pink
> cloud. Tonio Kröger did not at once understand. Not until
> he stood at the glass door and looked out did he realize
> that this was the sunrise.
>
> [P. 124]

What these eight sections have offered is the purely Platonic

movement of the character toward the truth of his own life: out of
the cave into the sunlight which dazes the learner so lately released
from the dark; up the divided line from the world of shadows and
experience to the world of forms and understanding; through the
oppositions of the dialectic toward the truth.

But there remains the ninth section. Here, Tonio writes a letter to
Lisabeta instead of talking with her. Quite unlike the last act of
Platonic thought, Tonio is prepared now to "say" what he has
learned, to write down the "Word," to "weave spells to redeem,"
clearly no longer the charlatan of his earlier view of himself. That
which is most touching about many of this group of novellas, I
would argue against Platonists like Eva Brann, is that implicit in
them is a final judgment that art has value. As often as the novellas
of learning and maturing offer windows, doors, mirrors, pictures
and photographs, journeys, and pathways to the sun as their devices,
they offer hints of art as the accompaniment and expression of
learning (as indeed Plato offers the myth).

It is not for nothing that Tonio's final "word" to Lisabeta about
all he understands and hopes for is spoken in the highest poetry of
St. Paul about the "tongues of men and of angels" which are *not* "as
sounding brass and tinkling cymbals." It is not for nothing that,
even in his childhood, Tonio begged Hans to give up the flatness of
books of "instantaneous photography" in favor of Schiller's *Don
Carlos*, in which there are places "so lovely they make you jump" (p.
89). It is not for nothing that Miranda in *Old Mortality* makes sense
of her life by thinking of Shakespeare's sonnets and Longfellow's
Psalm; that she assesses the reality of Aunt Amy to be "as real as the
pictures in the old Holbein and Dürer books were real"; that Uncle
Gabriel's love has the kind of truth one finds in "unworldly books,
but true, such as the Vita Nuova, the Sonnets of Shakepeare and the
Wedding Song of Spenser; and poems by Edgar Allan Poe" (p. 178).

It is not for nothing that the learner, Neil Klugman, of Philip
Roth's *Goodbye, Columbus* defends himself against the Patimkin
world of flat "photo-paintings" by means of what represents *him:* It
is a "broken wall of books, imperfectly shelved" (and seen, of
course, through glass and windows), but they will serve to describe
the world: "Doris? She's the one who's always reading *War and
Peace.* That's how I know it's the summer, when Doris is reading *War
and Peace.*" As the black child who is analogous to Neil finds the

best of life through Gauguin's paintings (*"Look, look, look* here at this one. Ain't that the fuckin' *life?"*), so Neil makes gradual sense of both his attraction to, and rejection of, upper-crust suburbia: "I started up to Short Hills, which I would see now, in my mind's eye, at dusk, rose-colored, like a Gauguin stream."

And it is not for nothing that Tommy Wilhelm in Bellow's *Seize the Day,* at the moment of his greatest flux between agonized confusion and dawning truth, hangs onto lifelines thrown out to him back in college from the "thin pages" of "Leider and Lovett's *British Poetry and Prose":*

> Since there were depths in Wilhelm not unsuspected by himself, he received a suggestion from some remote element in his thoughts that the business of life, the real business— to carry his peculiar burden, to feel shame and impotence, to taste these quelled tears—the only important business, the highest business was being done. Maybe the making of mistakes expressed the very purpose of his life and the essence of his being here. Maybe he was supposed to make them and suffer from them on this earth. And though he had raised himself above Mr. Perls and his father because they adored money, still they were called to act energetically and this was better than to yell and cry, pray and beg, poke and blunder and go by fits and starts and fall upon the thorns of life. And finally sink beneath that watery floor— would that be tough luck or would it be good riddance?

Here is the key question of this novella. We are given every reason to believe that without the help of Milton and Shelley, without even the most self-pitying statements of romantic art to help him make sense of his own temptation to self-pity, Tommy could not have answered it.

I am not saying merely that it is moving to find artists eloquently defending their art (giving the reasons Socrates begged them to give as to why they should be invited back into the ideal republic). Intrinsically, within the province of our discussion, it is moving to see the tradition of literature, painting, and music turned exquisitely to the achievement of the power of individual novellas. And in the art of the novella at large, we must also look and see how these devices that have moved us, move us most at that certain length or magnitude. Just as the plethora of unrevealing mirrors, of curtained windows, and closed or half-open doors would seem excessive in a short story (yet cannot work except by repetition), so the quotations from poetry are just right (that is, just at their emotive best) when they occur briefly in the representation of the learning struggle of a Miranda, who says "One should always have Latin or at least a good classical poetry quotation to depend upon in great or desperate moments," a Tonio Kröger, a Tommy Wilhelm, a Neil Klugman. With an effect of economy, and a kind of literate pleasure ("You caught that line from Milton, didn't you, Dear Reader?"), they keep the reader closely in touch with the learner, making us feel "It is by reason of what you and I together already know—you, the protagonist, and I, the reader—that you are able to learn what you have to learn." And the effect is not primarily in an intellectual reference to what we know. Rather, it is a calling back of the original stab at the heart caused in us by the poem that is referred to; thus, there is a powerful emotional economy in which literary tradition serves the individual talent as a kind of device.

I trust it will seem no book-burning operation when I say that these novellas have in fact an emotional economy, derived from this device, which novels cannot match when they attempt the same kind of thing. The discussions of music and the touches of old songs in Joyce's *The Dead* belong acutely to the characters and to what Gabriel must learn; they contribute every moment to the serious power of that novella. By contrast, the discussions of aesthetics in *Portrait of the Artist* bring a period of stasis into the action, as though it were Joyce working out his own problems rather than those of Stephen Dedalus.[13] And the greater the length, the greater the stasis and risk of loss of emotional power; witness the difference between the discussions of art in *Tonio Kröger* and those in *Doctor Faustus*. Proportionately as the number of pages increases, the shape can change from sleek thoroughbred to "baggy monster."

AFTERWORD

This book will by now have provided its own terminus if my reader has apprehended not only a definition of the novella as a distinct genre among prose fictions, but especially if I have provoked a fuller response to the beauty of individual novellas and their significant formal relations to each other. Both the formal perfections and the baggy-monstrousness of long novels have had their share of deference and analysis in modern criticism. So have the exquisite small scenes and line-drawing portraitures of the short story. My province has been to open up the territory occupied by the novella, to show that it is not limbo but a "blest" and shining place of certain boundaries, a place of its own.

To discover the territory has been to discover the counties within it, the "forms of the modern novella" which can be classified and spoken about in terms which, while open to discussion, become more definite as more readers examine a story together. Readers are a curious lot, and I have taken the risk of gratifying the kinds of curiosity my discussion has already aroused, by attaching an appendix which locates some of the best of modern novellas within the formal categories to which I think they belong—that is, which best reveal them for what they really are.

Ghosts of other formal critics, living and dead, expected and unexpected, have hovered over this work. None perhaps has been more unexpected yet more full of grace than Walter Pater, to whom I should like to give the final word:

"The concrete, and that even as a visible thing, has gained immeasurably in richness and compass, in fineness, and interest toward us, by the process, of which those acts of generalization, of reduction to class and generic type, have certainly been a part. And holding still to the concrete, the particular, to the visible or sensuous, if you will, last as first, thinking of that as essentially the one vital and lively thing, really worth our while in a short life, we may recognize sincerely what generalization and abstraction have done or may do, are defensible as doing, just for that—for the particular gem or flower—what its proper service is to a mind in search, precisely, of a concrete and intuitive knowledge such as that."

Appendix
A FORMAL LISTING OF NOVELLAS

Let the buyer be wary. Yet not so wary as to miss a new light which might be cast on some hitherto obscure novella by reason of seeing it afresh in relationship to other members of its kind.

APOLOGUES
Chekhov, Anton, *Ward No. 6*
Conrad, Joseph, *Heart of Darkness*
Crane, Stephen, *The Blue Hotel*
———, *The Monster*
———, *The Open Boat*
Faulkner, William, *Old Man*
———, *Red Leaves*
———, *Spotted Horses*
Flaubert, Gustave, *The Legend of St. Julian Hospitator*
Kafka, Franz, *The Burrow*
Kipling, Rudyard, *The Man Who Would Be King*
Lawrence, D. H., *The Man Who Died*
———, *The Man Who Loved Islands*
———, *The Woman Who Rode Away*
Mann, Thomas, *Mario and the Magician*
Maupassant, Guy de, *The Legacy*
McCullers, Carson, *The Ballad of the Sad Café*
Melville, Herman, *Benito Cereno*
———, *Billy Budd*
Sansom, William, *A Contest of Ladies*
Stead, Christina, *The Puzzleheaded Girl*
Stevenson, Robert Louis, *The Strange Case of Dr. Jekyll and Mr. Hyde*

Twain, Mark, *The Man That Corrupted Hadleyburg*
——, *The Mysterious Stranger*
Warren, Robert Penn, *The Circus in the Attic*
Wharton, Edith, *False Dawn*
Wright, Richard, *The Man Who Lived Underground*

EXAMPLE APOLOGUES
Anderson, Sherwood, *The Man Who Became a Woman*
Andreyev, Leonid, *The Seven Who Were Hanged*
Böll, Heinrich, *In the Valley of the Thundering Hooves*
Conrad, Joseph, *Youth*
Crane, Stephen, *Maggie, A Girl of the Streets*
Dostoevsky, Fyodor, *Notes from Underground*
——, *The Gambler*
Fitzgerald, F. Scott, *The Great Gatsby*
Flaubert, Gustave, *A Simple Heart*
Lessing, Doris, *A Home For The Highland Cattle*
Mailer, Norman, *The Man Who Studied Yoga*
Solzhenitsyn, Alexander, *One Day in the Life of Ivan Denisovich*
Tolstoy, Leo, *The Death of Ivan Ilyich*
Welty, Eudora, *The Ponder Heart*

SATIRES
Elliott, George P., *The NRACP*
Firbank, Ronald, *Concerning the Eccentricities of Cardinal Pirelli*
James, Henry, *The Death of the Lion*
Mann, Thomas, *Tristan*
Orwell, George, *Animal Farm*
Pynchon, Thomas, *The Crying of Lot 49*
Voltaire, *Candide*
Vonnegut, Kurt, *Cat's Cradle*
——, *Slaughterhouse Five*
Waugh, Evelyn, *Love Among the Ruins*
West, Nathanael, *A Cool Million*

DEGENERATIVE TRAGEDIES
Andreyev, Leonid, *The Dilemma*
Cather, Willa, *My Mortal Enemy*
——, *Neighbor Rosicky*
——, *Old Mrs. Harris*
Chekhov, Anton, *A Woman's Kingdom*
del Castillo, Laura, *A Plum For Coco*

Dostoevsky, Fyodor, *White Nights*
Huxley, Aldous, *After the Fireworks*
James, Henry, *The Beast in the Jungle*
———, *Daisy Miller*
———, *Washington Square*
Kafka, Franz, *The Metamorphosis*
Mann, Thomas, *Death in Venice*
Maupassant, Guy de, *Monsieur Parent*
Olsen, Tillie, *Tell Me a Riddle*
Porter, Katherine Anne, *Noon Wine*
———, *Pale Horse, Pale Rider*
Spark, Muriel, *The Go-Away Bird*
Stein, Gertrude, *Melanctha*
———, *The Gentle Lena*
———, *The Good Anna*
Steinbeck, John, *Of Mice and Men*
Turgenev, Ivan, *The Duelist*
Unamuno, Miguel de, *Abel Sanchez*
West, Nathanael, *Miss Lonelyhearts*
Wharton, Edith, *Bunner Sisters*

SERIOUS PLOTS OF CHARACTER REVELATION
Balzac, Honoré de, *Gobseck*
Cather, Willa, *Two Friends*
Colette, *Julie de Carneilhan*
Conrad, Joseph, *Typhoon*
Gide, André, *Pastoral Symphony*
James, Henry, *Diary of a Man of Fifty*
———, *The Turn of the Screw*
Melville, Herman, *Bartleby the Scrivener*

SERIOUS PLOTS OF LEARNING (OR FAILED LEARNING)
Bellow, Saul, *Seize the Day*
Boyle, Kay, *The Crazy Hunter*
Bowen, Elizabeth, *Ivy Gripped the Steps*
Chekhov, Anton, *A Boring Story*
Conrad, Joseph, *The Secret Sharer*
Crane, Stephen, *The Red Badge of Courage*
Eliot, George, *The Lifted Veil*
James, Henry, *The Bench of Desolation*
———, *The Lesson of the Master*
———, *The Aspern Papers*

Joyce, James, *The Dead*
Lawrence, D. H., *The Fox*
——, *Daughters of the Vicar*
——, *The Virgin and the Gipsy*
Lowry, Malcolm, *Elephant and Colosseum*
——, *The Forest Path to the Spring*
Mann, Thomas, *Tonio Kröger*
Moravia, Alberto, *Agostino*
Porter, Katherine Anne, *Old Mortality*
Roth, Philip, *Goodbye, Columbus*
Styron, William, *The Long March*
Trilling, Lionel, *Of This Time, Of That Place*

NOTES

Notes to Chapter One

1. A list of works on the novel which I have found most helpful appears in my selected bibliography. In the area of formal relations in the novel I find particularly useful the work of Sheldon Sacks on the general types of prose fictions: *Fiction and the Shape of Belief* (Berkeley: University of California Press, 1964); Wayne Booth on the rhetoric of narrative modes: *The Rhetoric of Fiction* (Chicago: University of Chicago Press, 1961); the articles on various novel elements collected by Philip Stevick, ed. in *The Theory of the Novel* (New York: The Free Press, 1967).

2. Austin McGiffert Wright, *The American Short Story in the Twenties* (Chicago: University of Chicago Press, 1961), and Eugene Current-Garcia and Walton R. Patrick, eds., *What Is the Short Story?* (Chicago: Scott, Foresman, 1961).

3. Howard Nemerov, "Composition and Fate in the Short Novel," *Graduate Journal* 5, no. 2 (Winter 1963): 375–91. This article contains insights into a number of individual novellas but treats the genre primarily as a "middle term," dependent for its visibility on "slighting" qualities of the other terms, short story and novel. Further, by treating novellas thematically ("appearance and reality," "freedom and necessity," "madness and sanity," all bound up in a main theme of "identity") Nemerov fails of his purpose to define the novella as "something in itself," especially something distinct from the long novel and its "problems of philosophy."

4. Edwin K. Bennett and H. M. Waidson, *A History of the German Novelle* (Cambridge: Cambridge University Press, 1965); John M. Ellis, *Narration in the German Novelle* (Cambridge: Cambridge University Press, 1974). These works attempt novella theory but are basically skeptical of achieving it: "One must be content with approximations; difficulties only arise if one seeks the abstract 'die Novelle'" (Ellis, p. 10). Their skepticism (conscious or unconscious) derives from their methods, in that these critics ignore the possibility of holistic forms governed by the length of the stories and turn instead to consideration of narrative techniques, "thematic complexity," and historical influences on the writer—all interesting considerations which cannot, however, advance the distinction between the novella and the novel because they manifest themselves in both.

Despite my examination of works by Mann and Kafka, I am moved to think my study has little to do with the German *novelle,* of which it is affirmed that its length may vary between "a few pages" and "over four hundred pages" (Bennett and Waidson, p. 1). At this latitude, Waidson is certainly right to say that "short story may merge into Novelle, Novelle into novel" (p. 245), and any attempt at generic definition is automatically blocked. Neither skepticism nor latitude, however, seems to kill the intuition of these critics that the "middle length" *is* something which could be defined if one could only find the most fruitful theoretical framework for the discussion. My book came into being because I believe formalism is that framework.

5. Gerald Gillespie, "Novella, Nouvelle, Novelle, Short Novel?—A Review of Terms," a two-part article in *Neophilologus* 51, no. 2 (April 1967), 119-27 and no. 3 (July 1967), 225-29. Gillespie properly sees this detailed historical study of terms as a "first step toward any discussion of form." I am indebted to him for saving me that step, and for concluding with an encouraging invitation: "The establishment of a qualitative definition [of the novella] is a worthwhile task for English criticism."

6. Norman Friedman, "What Makes A Short Story Short?" *Modern Fiction Studies* 4 (1958): 103-17.

7. Wright, *The American Short Story,* chapter on "Pathos."

8. Elizabeth Bowen, "The Short Story," in *The Faber Book of Modern Stories* (London: Faber & Faber, 1937), p. 15.

9. Martha Foley, ed., *The Best American Short Stories 1968* (Boston: Houghton Mifflin, 1968), pp. xi–xii.

10. The best of such anthology introductions are those by Ronald Paulson, ed., for *The Novelette Before 1900* and for *The Modern Novelette* (both from Englewood Cliffs, N.J.: Prentice-Hall, 1965).

11. Mark Schorer, ed., *The Story* (New York: Prentice-Hall, 1950), p. 432.

12. Quoted by Edward Weeks, ed., in *Great Short Novels* (Garden City, N.Y.: Doubleday Doran, 1941), Foreword, p. viii.

13. Henry James, *The Art of the Novel* (New York: Charles Scribner's Sons, 1948), p. 219.

14. "Katherine Anne Porter," *Writers at Work,* The Paris Review Interviews, 2d ser. (New York: The Viking Press, 1963), p. 162.

15. F. O. Matthiessen and Kenneth Murdock, eds., *The Notebooks of Henry James* (New York: Oxford University Press, 1947), p. 66.

16. F. O. Matthiessen, *Henry James, The Major Phase* (New York: Oxford University Press, 1963), p. 133.

17. Gillespie, "Novella," p. 225.

18. *Poetics,* trans. and ed. Kenneth A. Telford (Chicago: Henry Regnery Co., 1961), p. 16.

19. R. S. Crane, *The Languages of Criticism and the Structure of Poetry* (Toronto: University of Toronto Press, 1953), p. 189.

20. Quoted by David Lodge, *Language of Fiction* (New York: Columbia University Press, 1966), p. 34 n.

21. M. M. Liberman, "'Noon Wine,' Henry James, and the Novella," *Katherine Anne Porter's Fiction* (Detroit: Wayne State University Press, 1971), p. 56.

22. The term is R. S. Crane's ("The Concept of Plot and the Plot of *Tom Jones*," in Crane, ed., *Critics and Criticism* [Chicago: University of Chicago Press, 1952], p.

620). Crane usefully points out that the traditional view of plot as a change in action is too limited to cover what plot often does in modern fiction, namely, produce change not only in "action" but in "thought," or "character," as well—and that these can be distinct types of plot unity.

23. William Wasserstrom, ed., *The Modern Short Novel* (New York: Holt, Rinehart and Winston, 1965), pp. x–xi.

24. James, *Art of the Novel,* p. 111.

Notes to Chapter Two

1. Sacks, *Fiction,* p. 26.

2. *Other Inquisitions 1937–1952* (New York: Simon and Schuster, 1965), p. 154.

3. D. W. Robertson, Jr., *A Preface to Chaucer* (Princeton: Princeton University Press, 1962), p. 33.

4. *The Future of the Novel,* ed. Leon Edel (New York: Vintage Books, 1956), p. 263.

5. Sacks, *Fiction,* p. 5.

6. Robert Scholes and Robert Kellogg, *The Nature of Narrative* (New York: Oxford University Press, 1966), p. 88.

7. Ibid., p. 142.

8. Crane, *Languages,* p. 163.

9. "The Psychological Implication of Generic Distinctions," *Genre* 1, 2 (April 1968): 106–15.

10. I speak here of demands propounded by Forster (*Aspects of the Novel*) and Woolf as theorists, not as novelists. If they had carried out the demand in their own fictional works, it would probably become me as critic simply to report it, not complain of it. In their fictional works, both Forster and Woolf in fact give more form to the stuff of life than their theory would lead us to expect. And Woolf's theory of plot as "tyrant" (*The Common Reader* [New York: Harcourt Brace, 1925], p. 153) would seem to contradict that fine moment in chapter 4 of *A Room of One's Own* when she says: "On the one hand, we feel You—John the hero—must live, or I shall be in the depths of despair. On the other, we feel, Alas, John, you must die, because the shape of the book requires it. Life conflicts with something that is not life."

11. References are to the text in *The Complete Short Stories of D. H. Lawrence* (London: William Heinemann, 1955), vol. 2.

12. Kate Millett, *Sexual Politics* (Garden City, N.Y.: Doubleday, 1970), p. 286.

13. "Notes on the Decline of Naturalism," *Image and Idea* (New York: New Directions, 1949); reprinted in *The American Novel Since World War II,* ed. Marcus Klein (Greenwich, Conn.: Fawcett Publications, 1969), p. 27.

14. Eliseo Vivas shares this conviction about both author and reader when he says: "Let me assume for the moment, as *per impossibile,* that a poet can work without a more or less clear idea of the kind of thing he wants to make. Neither critics, nor teachers, nor readers, nor of course librarians, can dispense with some sort of classification. Classes, kinds, and genres there must be. We assume them unconsciously if we do not stipulate them explicitly" ("Literary Classes: Some Problems," *Genre* 1, 2 [April 1968]: 102).

15. References to Faulkner's *Spotted Horses* and *Old Man* are to the texts in *Three Famous Short Novels* (New York: Random House, Modern Library, 1931).

16. Rosemond Tuve, in discussing medieval figures, says, "The horse connected with the heedless will reappear infrequently" (*Allegorical Imagery* [Princeton: Princeton University Press, 1966], p. 220).

Faulkner himself is quoted as saying of the horses that "they symbolized the hope, the aspiration of the masculine part of society that is capable of doing, of committing puerile folly for some gewgaw that has drawn him, as juxtaposed to the cold practicality of the women whose spokesman Mrs. Littlejohn was" (*Faulkner in the University,* ed. Frederick L. Gwynn and Joseph L. Blotner [New York: Vintage Books, 1965], p. 66). When one reads the story, however, the horses also seem to have a nature of their own which cannot be dragged down to the level of men's "puerile folly." I suppose Faulkner to have been speaking somewhat loosely (in interview), wishing to say that the whole situation involving the horses was meant to be taken more than literally—as apologue.

17. "When major characters 'generate' subcharacters, fractions of themselves, these fractions have peculiar causal interrelations" (Angus Fletcher, *Allegory* [Ithaca, N.Y.: Cornell University Press, 1964], p. 182).

18. Paul Berchner, C.S.C., "The Allegorical Interpretation of Medieval Literature," *PMLA,* March 1967, p. 38.

19. "William Faulkner's Style," *American Prefaces,* Spring 1941; reprinted in *William Faulkner, Two Decades of Criticism,* ed. Frederick J. Hoffman and Olga W. Vickery (East Lansing, Mich.: Michigan State College Press, 1951), 150–51.

20. References, both here and later, to *The Open Boat* are to the text in *Men, Women, and Boats,* ed. Vincent Starrett (New York: Boni and Liveright, 1921).

21. Readers and critics do not mix forms in their apprehension of works as often as is commonly supposed—at least not without feeling either the puzzlement or disappointment I have suggested. In a review of the film *The Conformist* (*Newsweek,* 5 April 1971), Paul D. Zimmerman remarks: "It is a disappointing denouement, for we have seen him as a man and can no longer buy him as the agent of a thesis."

22. Toby A. Olshin, "Form and Theme in Novels About Non-Human Characters, a Neglected Sub-Genre," *Genre* 2, 1 (March 1969): 43–56.

23. Fletcher, *Allegory,* p. 35 n.

24. Sheldon Sacks, "Golden Birds and Dying Generations," *Comparative Literature Studies* 6, no. 3 (September 1969): 277.

25. Carson McCullers, *The Ballad of the Sad Café* (Boston: Houghton-Mifflin, 1951).

26. Mark Schorer, remarking on just this passage, assesses both the use of such passages and the difficulty the action-oriented reader has with them: "It is to do violence to the texture and feeling of Mrs. McCullers' work so to abstract the thematic core, and yet in at least one remarkable passage (the one on love), itself abstract, she gives us a certain sanction for this procedure" (*The World We Imagine* [New York: Farrar, Straus, & Giroux, 1968], p. 276).

27. "Art and Fortune," *The Liberal Imagination* (New York: Viking Press, 1950), reprinted in Klein, *The American Novel,* p. 93.

28. To try to specify the apologue statement of *The Ballad of the Sad Café* by now seems obligatory, though it is not necessary to my argument: Human affairs move as inevitably as the turn of a wheel. When the wheel is up, the instructive, healing, nurturing centers of humanity (home, store, café, medical office) provide some

temporary comfort against the inevitable downswing: the return (like a ballad refrain) to evil, lovelessness, and loneliness.

29. Herman J. Weigand, "Franz Kafka's 'The Burrow,'" *PMLA* 87 (March 1972): 156. Though Weigand's analysis of this novella is heavier with sexual psychology than I read the story to be, I take encouragement in my listing of apologue signals from some of the devices he observes in *The Burrow:* Main character as "hybrid of man and animal," the "realm of unreality," the heavy-handed "progressive recital" which describes rather than presents the action, the diffuse sense of time ("The ninety-minute recital and the life span of many years run on two parallel but qualitatively different rails"), and the diction not only of aphorism but of rhetorical questions.

30. Quoted from *The Circus in the Attic and Other Stories* (New York: Harcourt Brace, 1947), reprinted in *Stories From Six Authors,* ed. William E. Buckler and Arnold B. Sklare (New York: McGraw-Hill, 1960).

31. I am reminded of a reader whom I heard discussing *The Death of Ivan Ilyich:* "I despise this narrator—he doesn't let me alone for one moment." So intense a demand in contemporary readers for the dramatic mode of narration, even at the novella length, would seem to preclude its effectiveness at the novel length.

32. Quoted in Liberman, *Porter's Fiction,* p. 14.

33. The extraordinary proliferation of critical articles on "A Rose For Emily" (including a recent one which centers on the narrator as a sex-mad voyeur) suggests that the story lends itself, by lack of elaboration of its art of apologue, to gross impressionism. I take support for my own view from the careful analysis by Ray B. West, Jr. ("Atmosphere and Theme in Faulkner's 'A Rose For Emily,'" *Perspective,* Summer 1949, pp. 239–45).

It is worth studying this story in conjunction with Poe's Gothic horror story, "The Fall of the House of Usher," to appreciate the difference in techniques which an apologue calls up.

Notes to Chapter Three

1. Philip Rahv carries my dichotomy, between realism as an extrinsic taste and realism as a formal device, an interesting step further by saying that realism is an indispensable feature of prose fiction as a genre: "It seems to me a profound error to conceive of reality as merely a species of material that the fiction writer can either use or dispense with as he sees fit. It is a species of material, of course, and something else besides: it also functions as the *discipline of fiction*" ("Notes on the Decline of Naturalism," in Klein, *The American Novel,* p. 30). It is hard to see how this statement could hold true in the face of some of contemporary fiction such as Kurt Vonnegut's satiric fantasies, if indeed it ever held true for older works, for example, Joyce's *Ulysses.*

2. When I speak of "inductive apologues" I am referring to a classification of Elder Olson's which helps me make clear that the term "apologue" is not an "Ur-form" but is itself a class within the family of didactic literature, and has its own several species. Olson's classification mentions three kinds of proof: the inductive, the deductive, and the analogical. He characterizes allegory as deductive, parable and fable as analogical. It is not my province here to conclude this matter, but I suspect that both the novellas I have called "apologue" (the more general) and "example apologue" (a

narrower species which always makes the same kind of statement) belong to what Olson calls the "inductive" fictional argumentation. But I have saved his word "example" (also used by Sacks, somewhat unclearly in my view) for just that narrower species, because it is accurately descriptive of that particular apologue that is always a sampling or an example. Certainly example apologue must belong to the inductive species which, Olson says, "exhibits examples from which we as audience are to generalize" (*Tragedy and the Theory of Drama* [Detroit: Wayne State University Press, 1961], p. 71). See also Olson's "A Dialogue on Symbolism," in *Critics and Criticism*, ed. R. S. Crane (Chicago: University of Chicago Press, 1952), p. 592.

3. References are to the text of *Maggie* in *Three Great Novels by Stephen Crane*, ed. Arthur Edelstein (Greenwich, Conn.: Fawcett Publications, 1970).

4. Daniel Knapp, "Son of Thunder: Stephen Crane and the Fourth Evangelist," *Nineteenth Century Fiction* 24 (1969): 253-91.

5. Tuve, *Allegorical Imagery*, p. 220.

6. Edelstein, Introduction to *Three Great Novels by Stephen Crane*, p. 18.

7. References are to the Fawcett Publications translation by Thomas P. Whitney, reprinted in Wasserstrom, *The Modern Short Novel*, the only edition available to me of this translation, which I much prefer to the two others I have read.

8. "Preface to 'What Maisie Knew'," *The Art of the Novel*, p. 150.

9. References are to the text in *The Complete Tales of Henry James*, ed. Leon Edel, vol. 7 (Philadelphia: J. B. Lippincott, 1963).

10. "James's 'The Pupil': The Art of Seeing Through," *Modern Fiction Studies* 4 (Winter 1958-59), reprinted in Edward Stone, ed., *Henry James: Seven Stories and Studies* (New York: Appleton-Century-Crofts, 1961), p. 188.

Notes to Chapter Four

1. I am aware that *Candide* has been called a *conte philosophe* and that Sheldon Sacks, without saying why, calls it an apologue (*Fiction*, p. 60 n.). My own reading agrees with the view of Wayne Booth, Northrop Frye, and Edward Rosenheim, Jr., that it coheres as a satire. The statements about work and cultivating one's garden, which appear at the end, do not sway the balance against the build-up of ridicule all through Candide's journey. In fact I agree with Flaubert that "the claws of the lion are marked on that quiet conclusion, as stupid as life itself."

2. Charles Clerc and Louis Leitner, eds., *Seven Contemporary Short Novels* (Glenview, Ill.: Scott, Foresman, 1969), preface, n.p.

3. David Lodge (*Language of Fiction*, chap. 7) talks about Stephen Spender, in *The Struggle of the Modern*, emancipating "contemporary" as well as "modern" from chronological significance, dividing twentieth-century writers between those who deal optimistically in a "direct, prosaic way" with issues, and those who "distrust or detest their circumstances" and wish to "express poetically an inner crisis of sensibility." For formal reasons I am glad to get away from chronology, but not in Spender's way, which is enough to drive one away permanently from historical generalizations. Joyce and Woolf are cited by him among the "sensibility" group who fear "contemporary" issues. One has only to reread a hundred passages in *Ulysses* such as the satire on capital punishment, or Virginia Woolf in *Three Guineas* writing on war, women's rights, and education.

4. "Notes on the Decline of Naturalism," in Klein, *The American Novel*, p. 27.

5. Northrop Frye, "The Nature of Satire," *University of Toronto Quarterly* 14, no. 1 (1944): 82.

6. I owe my initial appreciation of this novella as a coherent satire to an excellently careful analysis in an unpublished essay on Mann's works written by Constance Nickel in fulfillment of requirements for the bachelor's degree at the New School College, New York, 1970.

7. References are to the text in *Thomas Mann: Stories of Three Decades,* trans. H. T. Lowe-Porter (New York: Alfred A. Knopf, 1936).

8. This naming principle is discussed in an analysis of the diction of satire by Gregory Fitz Gerald in a long introductory essay to *Modern Satiric Stories, The Impropriety Principle* (Glenview, Ill.: Scott, Foresman, 1971), 2–47. As an anthologist, Fitz Gerald produces what I find to be formally shaky categories such as "Satiric Allegories" and "Satiric Parodies" which seem to defy his own definition of satire: "By the term 'satiric short story' ... we mean a brief narrative *satire*, not merely a story in which satire occurs in an unsustained or incidental fashion." Nevertheless, this essay is one of the best I have encountered on the parts of satire, including not only its types of diction, but also character, point of view, and plot. In the plot discussion, he makes the distinction I have made between the Aristotelian plots of action and those of satire, though I find it hard to share his view that the journey is merely a "stock situation" of satire rather than one of the two most common structures of satire, as I have suggested.

9. References are to the text in *The Complete Tales,* vol. 9.

10. Elder Olson, ed., *Aristotle's Poetics and English Literature* (Chicago: University of Chicago Press, 1965), p. xvi. In "A Dialogue on Symbolism" Olson says again "The poet, it seems to me, builds wholes; in this he is unlike the binder of faggots or the money-tellers, who care only about totals" (in Crane, *Critics and Criticism,* p. 587).

11. Maynard Mack, "The Muse of Satire," *Yale Review* 41 (Autumn 1951): 85.

12. I am aware that, on the tortured question of Don Pedro de Mendez, I am disagreeing not only with Sacks, but with R. S. Crane (*The Idea of the Humanities,* vol. 2 [Chicago: University of Chicago Press, 1967], p. 265), and Edward W. Rosenheim, Jr. (*Swift and the Satirist's Art* [Chicago: University of Chicago Press, 1963], p. 222). I not only continue to disagree on the effect of these good and hopeful characters such as the sea captain and the Brobdingnagian king, but I disagree with the whole concept of Swift as a purely punitive satirist. Swift himself saw his writings as ameliorative, and Rosenheim seriously contradicts himself on the matter by providing even more evidence than I shall do in this chapter to demonstrate the "positive heart" not only of *Gulliver's Travels* and *A Modest Proposal* but also of *A Tale of a Tub.* He is able to do this because he does not, in the first place, view satire as a principle of coherence but simply as a technique of ridicule which operates in most parts of these works but not necessarily in all.

13. References are to the text of *Animal Farm* published by Harcourt Brace (New York), 1946.

14. Helpful discussions of the use of plot in satire occur in Alvin B. Kernan's *The Plot of Satire* (New Haven: Yale University Press, 1965), as well as in the previously cited essay by Gregory Fitz Gerald (see, however, n. 8 for this chapter, which differs with him on the journey structure which is often *the* favored "plot" of events in satire

—cf. Nathanael West's *A Cool Million,* a novella parody of *Candide,* itself a journey-structure satire).

15. One of the best of discussions about ethical judgments in literature appears in Elder Olson's "An Outline of Poetic Theory," in Crane, *Critics and Criticism,* 554–56.

16. "A Dialogue on Symbolism," in Crane, *Critics and Criticism,* 588–92.

Notes to Chapter Five

1. I refer to the previously cited essays on satire by Frye, Mack, and Fitz Gerald.

2. Maurice Z. Shroder, "The Novel As a Genre," *The Massachusetts Review* 1963, reprinted in Robert M. Davis, comp., *The Novel: Modern Essays in Criticism* (Englewood Cliffs, N.J.: Prentice-Hall, 1969), p. 55.

3. *The Death of Tragedy* (New York: Hill and Wang, 1961), p. 167.

4. "Forms of the Plot," *Journal of General Education* 8 (1955), reprinted in Philip Stevick, ed., *The Theory of the Novel* (New York: The Free Press, 1967), p. 163. Friedman provides an excellent "preliminary list of general possibilities" in kinds of plots, but the descriptions sometimes melt into each other in the actual working out of stories. In tragic novellas, for example, I have usually found a meld of the "degeneration plot" with the "pathetic plot."

5. "Autobiography and Literature," a critical essay printed with *Death in Venice,* trans. Kenneth Burke (New York: The Modern Library, 1970), p. 120.

6. References are to the translation by H. T. Lowe-Porter in *Thomas Mann: Stories of Three Decades.*

It is time for me to make a bow to the problem presented by close formal analysis of works in translation. My solution to the problem has been to ignore it. I have been encouraged in this by my discovery that the form of a novella that presents itself in an English translation presents itself still more conspicuously in the original. (I once found myself studying Mann's story, "The Infant Prodigy," which I felt certain was an apologue despite a narrative mode that seemed as "historical" as an action. It developed that, in the original German, the narrative device was present tense, which I have earlier suggested is a powerful device for universalization in apologue. It greatly strengthened the apprehension of the statement I had already intuited in the English.)

If one is not entirely at home with the original language, reassurance about form is still available in comparing translations. In the present case I have read both the "authorized" translation of *Death In Venice* by Kenneth Burke, cited above, and that of H. T. Lowe-Porter. There seems to me fair reason to "authorize" Burke for this novella (though someone who knew Mann at Princeton tells me he was both friendly with Lowe-Porter and much pleased with her translations of his works). Burke is somewhat more subtle in presenting the initial self-containment of Aschenbach, so that his later Dionysian surrender can seem more devastating. One brief example at the end of chapter 1 will reveal Lowe-Porter's somewhat more florid "interpretation":

Burke: "To travel, then—that much was settled. Not far, not all the way to the tigers. But one night on the sleeper, and a rest of three or four weeks at some pleasant popular resort in the South" (p. 10).

Lowe-Porter: "Good, then, he would go on a journey. Not far—not all the way to the tigers. A night in a *wagon-lit,* three or four weeks of lotus-eating at some one of the gay world's playgrounds in the lovely South" (p. 382).

It will be readily observed that Burke has rendered a more coolly Germanic consciousness for Aschenbach, while Lowe-Porter has tipped the hand of the story, become herself "sardonic," and sacrificed a little of our pity for Aschenbach's eventual fall by showing him already into "lotus-eating" (the word Mann chose was the Spanish *siesta*). Nevertheless, except for the rakish dash instead of the comma, the key sentence remains the same: "Not far, not all the way to the tigers." (Mann's choice was the comma.)

I might add that Lowe-Porter is now punished for her slight excesses by the recently changed meaning of the word "gay"—I doubt that she would have wanted to carry Aschenbach that far ahead of the story. My central point remains: the formal effect of the novella is not changed but simply reiterated, with variations of taste, in the two translations.

7. Hollis Alpert, "Visconti In Venice," *Saturday Review,* 8 August 1970, p. 17.

8. Eva Brann, "The Venetian Phaedrus," *The College,* 24, no. 2 (July 1972): p. 9 (a publication of St. John's College, Annapolis, Md).

9. Irving Howe, ed., *Classics of Modern Fiction* (New York: Harcourt, Brace & World, 1968), p. 401.

10. This novella was printed in *Prize Stories From Latin America* (Garden City, N. Y.: Doubleday, 1963). The book contains the winning stories from the *Life En Español* literary contest for the best Spanish-language short novel written by a Latin American. Both in terms of the rise of Latin American literature and of contemporary interest in the novella, it is interesting to learn that no less than 3,149 novellas were submitted in this contest.

In regard to the quality of tragedy in the novella, I was also interested to read the remarks of Arturo Uslar Pietri (Preface, p. ix), one of the contest judges. He speaks of "the preference for themes of fatality, loneliness, injustice and desperation, and for the feeling of man's insignificance before fate or nature."

11. "Daisy Miller: An Abortive Quest for Innocence," *South Atlantic Quarterly,* 49 (Winter 1961), reprinted in William T. Stafford, ed., *James's Daisy Miller* (New York: Charles Scribner's Sons, 1963), p. 150.

12. Leon Edel, Introduction to *Henry James: Selected Fiction* (New York: E. P. Dutton & Co., 1953), reprinted in Stafford, *James's Daisy Miller,* p. 154.

13. References are to *The Complete Tales of Henry James,* vol. 4.

14. Here I feel bound to record a conflicting opinion from Robert Bloom of the University of California at Berkeley, who knows the James novellas almost by heart, and who wrote me regarding my analysis of *Daisy Miller:* "We do not really share Winterbourne's 'inattention.' We regret it terribly, all the more because we see that it comes of what Europe has done to him. *Daisy* is a tragedy of misunderstanding; we are immensely moved that her capacity to love should have taken incomprehensible form for Winterbourne.... We absolutely must have Daisy filtered through Winterbourne. The story is not the 'tragedy of Daisy herself' but the tragedy of Daisy as misconstrued by Winterbourne, with all the appropriate American-European cultural implications at play. It takes two to misunderstand."

15. "Portraits From a Family Album: Daisy Miller," *Hudson Review* 5, no. 2 (Summer 1952): 203-6, reprinted in Stafford, *James's Daisy Miller,* p. 132.

16. *Heiress of All the Ages: Sex and Sentiment in the Genteel Tradition* (Minneapolis: University of Minnesota Press, 1959), reprinted in Stafford, *James's Daisy Miller,* p. 139.

17. Norman Friedman, "Forms of the Plot," in Stevick, *Theory of the Novel,* p. 163.

18. References are to the translation by Constance Garnett in *The Party and Other Stories* (New York: Macmillan, 1917).

19. Richard B. Sewall, "The Tragic Form," *Essays In Criticism* 4 (1954), reprinted in Laurence Michel and Richard B. Sewall, eds., *Tragedy: Modern Essays in Criticism* (Englewood Cliffs, N.J.: Prentice-Hall), p. 125.

20. References are to the text in *Three Lives* (New York: Vintage Books, Alfred A. Knopf and Random House, 1961).

21. Edmund Wilson contrasts this story with Flaubert's *Un Coeur Simple* (which I have called example apologue). He notes that Stein in her "closeness" to the characters in *Three Lives,* of which Melanctha is of course one, "seems to have caught the very rhythms and accents of her heroines" whereas, in the Flaubert story "we feel that the old family servant has been seen from a great distance and documented with effort" (*Axel's Castle* [New York: Charles Scribner's Sons, 1948], p. 237).

22. The subtitle of the chapter on Dostoevsky in Maurice Friedman's *Problematic Rebel* is "The Underground Man and Raskolnikov." What other name is possible?

23. Roy Morrell, "The Psychology of Tragic Pleasure," *Essays in Criticism,* 6 (1956), reprinted in Michel and Sewall, *Tragedy,* p. 278.

Notes to Chapter Six

1. Albert Cook, *The Meaning of Fiction* (Detroit: Wayne State University Press, 1960), p. 134.

2. R. S. Crane, "The Concept of Plot and the Plot of *Tom Jones,*" in Crane, ed., *Critics and Criticism,* pp. 616-48.

3. Sacks, *Fiction and the Shape of Belief,* p. 22.

4. References are to the translation by Patrick Leigh Fermor in *Gigi, Julie de Carneilhan, Chance Acquaintances: Three Short Novels by Colette* (New York: Farrar, Straus, and Young, 1952).

5. Willa Cather, "The Novel Démeublé," in *Not Under Forty* (New York: Alfred A. Knopf, 1936), reprinted in George Perkins, ed., *The Theory of the American Novel* (New York: Holt, Rinehart and Winston, 1970), pp. 283 and 285.

Cather half convinces one about "How wonderful it would be if we could throw all the furniture out of the window" and "leave the room as bare as the stage of a Greek theatre." But the formal question keeps re-raising itself: How much furniture do you need for the particular power of the story you are writing? How many blouses and teacups and yellow roses does it take to represent Julie for us?

Balzac has his defenders for similar reasons, for example, Felicien Marceau (*Balzac et Son Monde* [Paris: Gallimard, 1955]), who "shows how essential to the building up of character are those lengthy, overloaded descriptions of rooms and houses, and suggests that Balzac changes his style when he writes of Paris or of the provinces" (anonymous review, *The Times Literary Supplement,* 29 July 1955). And

Jules Romain says of Balzac's stories (some of which are character novellas, for example, *Gobseck*): "The object is present to the point of hallucination" and "For the first time perhaps in the history of literature, I believe in what I am told" (Introduction, *The Short Novels of Balzac* [New York: The Dial Press, 1948], pp. 11, 12).

6. The poem is "Blanche McCarthy."

7. For a fuller analysis of *Bartleby the Scrivener* as a plot of character, see Norman Springer, "Bartleby and the Terror of Limitation," *PMLA* 80 (1965): 410-18.

8. It is worth reflecting what might be the differences between an example apologue of miserliness and the delineation of a miserly character in Balzac's *Gobseck*.

9. References are to the text in *The Collected Stories of Katherine Anne Porter* (New York: Harcourt, Brace & World, 1930).

10. References are to the text in *The Short Novels of D. H. Lawrence*, vol. 2 (London: William Heinemann, 1956).

11. References are to the text in *Thomas Mann: Stories of Three Decades*.

12. Preface to *Stories of Three Decades*, p. vi.

13. The autobiographical quality of *Portrait of the Artist* is discussed by Ralph W. Rader in "Defoe, Richardson, Joyce and the Concept of Form in the Novel," in *Autobiography, Biography and the Novel* (Los Angeles: W. A. Clark Memorial Library, 1973). The stasis I have described in *Portrait* is seen by Rader to be appropriate to its form, which he calls "simular" or "an artificial simulation of the author's own life."

SELECTED
BIBLIOGRAPHY

Aristotle. *Poetics.* Trans. and ed., Kenneth A. Telford. Chicago: Henry Regnery, 1961.

Balzac, Honoré de. *The Short Novels of Balzac.* New York: Dial Press, 1958. Introduction by Jules Romains.

Beck, Warren. "William Faulkner's Style," *American Prefaces,* Spring 1941. Reprinted in Frederick J. Hoffman and Olga W. Vickery, eds., *William Faulkner, Two Decades of Criticism.* East Lansing, Mich.: Michigan State College Press, 1951.

Beja, Morris. *Psychological Fiction.* Glenview, Ill.: Scott, Foresman, 1971.

Bellow, Saul. *Seize the Day.* New York: The Viking Press, 1956.

Bennett, Edwin K. (revised and continued by H. M. Waidson). *A History of the German Novelle.* Cambridge: Cambridge University Press, 1965.

Berchner, Paul, C.S.C. "The Allegorical Interpretation of Medieval Literature." *PMLA,* March 1967.

Blackmur, R. P., ed. *American Short Novels.* New York: Thomas Y. Crowell, 1960.

Booth, Wayne C. *The Rhetoric of Fiction.* Chicago: University of Chicago Press, 1961.

———. *A Rhetoric of Irony.* Chicago: University of Chicago Press, 1974.

———. "Yes, But Are They Really Novels?" *Yale Review* 51, no. 4 (Summer 1962): 632-34.

Bowen, Elizabeth. "The Short Story." In *The Faber Book of Modern Stories.* London: Faber & Faber, 1937.

Brann, Eva. "The Venetian Phaedrus." *The College* 24, no. 2 (July 1972): 1-9. Publication of St. John's College, Annapolis, Md.

Burke, Kenneth. *The Philosophy of Literary Form.* New York: Vintage Books, 1957.

———, trans. *Death In Venice* by Thomas Mann. New York: The Modern Library, 1970.

———. "Formalist Criticism: Its Principles and Limits." Texas Quarterly 9 (1966): 242-68.

Burnett, Whit, and Burnett, Hallie, eds. *The Modern Short Story in the Making.* New York: Hawthorn Books, 1964.

Cather, Willa. "The Novel Démeublé." *Not Under Forty*. New York: Alfred A. Knopf, 1936. Reprinted in George Perkins, ed., *The Theory of the American Novel* (New York: Holt, Rinehart and Winston, 1970), pp. 283–87.

Chekhov, Anton. *The Party and Other Stories*. New York: Macmillan, 1917.

Clerc, Charles, and Leitner, Louis, eds. *Seven Contemporary Short Novels*. Glenview, Illinois: Scott, Foresman, 1969.

Colette. *Gigi, Julie de Carneilhan, Chance Acquaintances: Three Short Novels by Colette*. New York: Farrar, Straus, and Young, 1952.

Connolly, Cyril, ed. *Great English Short Novels*. New York: Dial Press, 1953.

Conrad, Joseph. *Three Short Novels*. New York: Bantam Books, 1960.

Cook, Albert. *The Meaning of Fiction*. Detroit: Wayne State University Press, 1960.

Cowley, Malcolm. "Storytelling's Tarnished Image." *Saturday Review,* 25 September 1971, pp. 25–54.

Crane, R. S. *The Languages of Criticism and the Structure of Poetry*. Toronto: University of Toronto Press, 1953.

————. "The Concept of Plot and the Plot of *Tom Jones*." In R. S. Crane, ed., *Critics and Criticism*. Chicago: University of Chicago Press, 1952.

————, ed. *Critics and Criticism*. Chicago: University of Chicago Press, 1952.

Crane, Stephen. *Three Great Novels by Stephen Crane*. Ed. Arthur Edelstein. Greenwich, Conn.: Fawcett Publications, 1970.

————. *Men, Women, and Boats*. Ed. Vincent Starrett. New York: Boni & Liveright, 1921.

Current-Garcia, Eugene, and Patrick, Walton R., eds. *What Is the Short Story?* Chicago: Scott, Foresman, 1961.

Davis, Robert Murray, ed. *The Novel: Modern Essays in Criticism*. Englewood Cliffs, N.J.: Prentice-Hall, 1969.

Dolley, Christopher, ed. *The Penguin Book of English Short Stories*. Harmondsworth, England: Penguin Books, 1967.

Dostoevsky, Fyodor. *The Short Novels of Dostoevsky*. New York: Dial Press, 1951.

Edel, Leon. Introduction to *Henry James: Selected Fiction*. New York: E. P. Dutton, 1953.

————, ed. *The Future of the Novel*. New York: Vintage Books, 1956.

Edelstein, Arthur. Introduction to *Three Great Novels by Stephen Crane*. Greenwich, Conn.: Fawcett Publications, 1970.

Elliott, George P., ed. *Types of Prose Fiction*. New York: Random House, 1964.

————. "The NRACP." *The Hudson Review* (Autumn 1949).

Ellis, John M. *Narration in the German Novelle*. Cambridge: Cambridge University Press, 1974.

Faulkner, William. *Three Famous Short Novels*. New York: Random House, 1931.

Felheim, Marvin. "Recent Anthologies of the Novella," *Genre* 2:1 (March 1969): 21–27.

Fitz Gerald, Gregory, ed. *Modern Satiric Stories: The Impropriety Principle*. Glenview, Ill.: Scott, Foresman, 1971.

Flaubert, Gustave. *Three Tales*. Harmondsworth, England: Penguin Books, 1961.

Fletcher, Angus. *Allegory*. Ithaca, N.Y.: Cornell University Press, 1964.

Flower, Dean S., ed. *8 Short Novels*. Greenwich, Conn.: Fawcett Publications, 1967.

Foley, Martha, ed. *The Best American Short Stories, 1968*. Boston: Houghton Mifflin, 1968.

Forster, E. M. *Aspects of the Novel*. New York: Harcourt Brace, 1927.

Friedman, Maurice. *Problematic Rebel.* Chicago: University of Chicago Press, 1970.

Friedman, Norman. "What Makes a Short Story Short?" *Modern Fiction Studies* 4 (1958): 103-17.

———. "Forms of the Plot." *Journal of General Education,* 8 (1955). Reprinted in Philip Stevick, ed., *The Theory of the Novel* (New York: The Free Press, 1967), pp. 145-66.

Frye, Northrop. *Anatomy of Criticism: Four Essays.* Princeton: Princeton University Press, 1957.

———. "The Nature of Satire." *University of Toronto Quarterly* 14 (October 1944): 75-78.

Gardner, Helen. *The Business of Criticism.* New York: Oxford University Press, 1959.

Gargano, James W. "*Daisy Miller:* An Abortive Quest for Innocence." *South Atlantic Quarterly* 59 (Winter 1961): 114-20.

Geist, Stanley. "Portraits From a Family Album: Daisy Miller." *Hudson Review* 5, no. 2 (Summer 1952): 203-6.

Gillespie, Gerald. "Novella, Nouvelle, Novelle, Short Novel?—A Review of Terms," *Neophilologus* (Groningen) 51:117-27 and 225-30.

Gwynn, Frederick L., and Blotner, Joseph L., eds. *Faulkner In the University.* New York: Vintage Books, 1965.

Hall, Lawrence Sargent. *A Grammar of Literary Criticism.* New York: Macmillan, 1965.

Hamalian, Leo, and Wiren-Garczynski, Vera Von, eds. *Seven Russian Short Novel Masterpieces.* New York: Popular Library, 1967.

Hamalian, Leo, and Volpe, Edmond L., eds. *Seven Short Novel Masterpieces.* New York: Popular Library, 1961.

Hamalian, Leo, and Karl, Frederick R., eds. *Short Fiction of the Masters.* New York: G. P. Putnam's Sons, 1963.

Heller, Erich. Autobiography and Literature." Essay printed with *Death in Venice* by Thomas Mann. Trans. Kenneth Burke. New York: The Modern Library, 1970, pp. 101-27.

Henn, T. R. *The Harvest of Tragedy.* London, Methuen, 1956.

Highet, Gilbert. *The Anatomy of Satire.* Princeton: Princeton University Press, 1962.

Hobsbaum, Philip. *Theory of Criticism.* Bloomington: Indiana University Press, 1970.

Holland, Norman. *The Dynamics of Literary Response.* New York: Oxford University Press, 1968.

Holmes, William, and Mitchell, Edward, eds. *Nineteenth-Century American Short Fiction.* Glenview, Ill.: Scott Foresman, 1970.

Howe, Irving, ed. *Classics of Modern Fiction.* New York: Harcourt, Brace & World, 1968.

James, Henry. *The Art of the Novel.* New York: Charles Scribner's Sons, 1948.

———. *The Notebooks of Henry James.* Ed. F. O. Matthiessen and Kenneth B. Murdock. New York: Oxford University Press, 1947.

———. *The Complete Tales of Henry James.* Ed. Leon Edel. Philadelphia: J. B. Lippincott, 1962.

Jessup, Bertram E. "Aesthetic Size." *Journal of Aesthetics and Art Criticism* 9 (1950): 31-38.

"Katherine Anne Porter." *Writers at Work.* The Paris Review Interviews, Second Series. New York: The Viking Press, 1963.

Kermode, Frank. "Novel, History, and Type." *Novel* 1 (1968): 231-38.

Kernan, Alvin. *The Cankered Muse*. New Haven: Yale University Press, 1959.

————. *The Plot of Satire*. New Haven: Yale University Press, 1965.

Kettle, Arnold. *An Introduction to the English Novel*. 2 vols. New York: Harper & Row, 1960.

Klein, Marcus, ed. *The American Novel Since World War II*. Greenwich, Conn.: Fawcett Publications, 1969.

Klein, Marcus, and Pack, Robert, eds. *Short Stories*. Boston: Little, Brown, 1967.

Knapp, Daniel. "Son of Thunder: Stephen Crane and the Fourth Evangelist." *Nineteenth Century Fiction* 24 (1969): 253-91.

Kumar, Shiv K., and McKean, Keith. *Critical Approaches to Fiction*. New York: McGraw-Hill, 1968.

Lawrence, D. H. *The Complete Short Stories*. 3 vols. London: William Heinemann, 1955.

————. *The Short Novels*. 2 vols. London: William Heinemann, 1956.

Lectures in Criticism. Bollingen Series 16. New York: Pantheon Books, 1949.

Liberman, M. M. *Katherine Anne Porter's Fiction*. Detroit: Wayne State University Press, 1971.

Lid, R. W., ed. *The Short Story*. Philadelphia: J. B. Lippincott, 1966.

Lodge, David. *Language of Fiction*. New York: Columbia University Press, 1966.

Lubbock, Percy. *The Craft of Fiction*. New York: Peter Smith, 1947.

Mack, Maynard. "The Muse of Satire." *Yale Review* 41 (Autumn 1951): 80-92.

Mann, Thomas. *Thomas Mann: Stories of Three Decades*. Trans. H. T. Lowe-Porter. New York: Alfred A. Knopf, 1936.

Martin, Terence. "James's 'The Pupil': The Art of Seeing Through." *Modern Fiction Studies* 4 (Winter 1958-59).

Matthiessen, F. O. *Henry James, The Major Phase*. New York: Oxford University Press, 1963.

————. *American Renaissance*. New York: Oxford University Press, 1941.

Matthiessen, F. O., and Murdock, Kenneth, eds. *The Notebooks of Henry James*. New York: Oxford University Press, 1947.

Maupassant, Guy de. *Miss Harriet and Other Stories*. Harmondsworth, England: Penguin Books, 1951.

McCullers, Carson. *The Ballad of the Sad Café: The Novels and Stories of Carson McCullers*. Boston: Houghton Mifflin, 1951.

Michel, Laurence, and Sewall, Richard B., eds. *Tragedy: Modern Essays in Criticism*. Englewood Cliffs, N.J.: Prentice-Hall, 1963.

Miller, James E., Jr. *A Reader's Guide to Herman Melville*. New York: Farrar, Straus & Cudahy, 1962.

Miller, James E., Jr., and Slote, Bernice, eds. *The Dimensions of the Short Story*. New York: Dodd Mead, 1966.

Millett, Kate. *Sexual Politics*. Garden City, N.Y.: Doubleday, 1970.

Morrell, Roy. "The Psychology of Tragic Pleasure." *Essays in Criticism* 6 (1956).

Neider, Charles, ed. *Short Novels of the Masters*. New York: Rinehart, 1948.

Nemerov, Howard. "Composition and Fate in the Short Novel." *Graduate Journal* 5, no. 2 (Winter 1963): 375-91.

O'Connor, William Van, ed. *Forms of Modern Fiction*. Minneapolis: University of Minnesota Press, 1948.

Olshin, Toby A. "Form and Theme in Novels About Non-Human Characters, A Neglected Sub-Genre." *Genre* 2, 1 (March 1969): 43-56.

Olson, Elder. *Tragedy and the Theory of Drama*. Detroit: Wayne State University Press, 1961.

——. "A Dialogue on Symbolism." In *Critics and Criticism*. Ed. R. S. Crane. Chicago: University of Chicago Press, 1952, pp. 567-94.

——. "An Outline of Poetic Theory." In *Critics and Criticism*. Ed. R. S. Crane. Chicago: University of Chicago Press, 1952, pp. 546-66.

——, ed. *Aristotle's Poetics and English Literature*. Chicago: University of Chicago Press, 1965.

Orwell, George. *Animal Farm*. New York: Harcourt Brace, 1946.

Paulson, Ronald. *The Fictions of Satire*. Baltimore: Johns Hopkins Press, 1967.

——. *Satire and the Novel*. New Haven: Yale University Press, 1967.

——, ed. *The Novelette Before 1900*. Englewood Cliffs, N.J.: Prentice-Hall, 1965.

——, ed. *The Modern Novelette*. Englewood Cliffs, N.J.: Prentice-Hall, 1965.

Pepper, Stephen. "The Justification of Aesthetic Judgments." *Problems of Literary Evaluation*, 2. Ed. Joseph Strelka (University Park: Pennsylvania State University Press, 1969).

Perkins, George, ed. *The Theory of the American Novel*. New York: Holt, Rinehart and Winston, 1970.

Phillips, William, ed. *Great American Short Novels*. New York: Dial Press, 1950.

Porter, Katherine Anne. *The Collected Stories of Katherine Anne Porter*. New York: Harcourt, Brace & World, 1965.

Prize Stories From Latin America. Garden City, N.Y.: Doubleday, 1963.

Rader, Ralph W. "Defoe, Richardson, Joyce and the Concept of Form in the Novel." *Autobiography, Biography, and the Novel*. Los Angeles: W. A. Clark Memorial Library, 1973, pp. 31-72.

Rahv, Philip. "Notes on the Decline of Naturalism." *Image and Idea*. New York: New Directions, 1949.

——, ed. *Seven Great British Short Novels*. New York: Berkeley Publishing Corp., 1963.

——, ed. *Eight Great American Short Novels*. New York: Berkeley Publishing Corp., 1963.

Reichert, John F. "'Organizing Principles' and Genre Theory." *Genre* 1, 1 (January 1968): 1-12.

Richards, I. A. *Principles of Literary Criticism*. New York: Harcourt, Brace, 1925.

Robertson, D. W., Jr. *A Preface to Chaucer*. Princeton: Princeton University Press, 1962.

Rosenheim, Edward W., Jr. *Swift and the Satirist's Art*. Chicago: University of Chicago Press, 1963.

Roth, Philip. *Goodbye, Columbus*. Boston: Houghton Mifflin, 1959.

Runden, John P., ed. *Melville's Benito Cereno*. Boston: D. C. Heath, 1965.

Sacks, Sheldon. *Fiction and the Shape of Belief*. Berkeley: University of California Press, 1964.

——. "Golden Birds and Dying Generations." *Comparative Literature Studies* 6, no. 3 (September 1969): 274-91.

————. "The Psychological Implication of Generic Distinctions." *Genre* 1, 2 (April 1968): 106-15.

Sartre, Jean-Paul. *What Is Literature?* New York: Harper and Row, 1965.

Scholes, Robert, and Kellogg, Robert. *The Nature of Narrative.* New York: Oxford University Press, 1966.

Schorer, Mark. *The World We Imagine.* New York: Farrar, Straus, and Giroux, 1968.

————, ed. *The Story.* New York: Prentice-Hall, 1950.

Scribner's Treasury. New York: Charles Scribner's Sons, 1953.

Sewall, Richard B. "The Tragic Form." *Essays In Criticism* 4 (1954).

Shroder, Maurice Z. "The Novel as a Genre." *The Massachusetts Review* 4 (1963): 291-308.

Sklare, Arnold B., ed. *The Art of the Novella.* New York: Macmillan, 1965.

Solzhenitsyn, Alexander. *One Day in the Life of Ivan Denisovich.* Trans. Thomas P. Whitney. Greenwich, Conn.: Fawcett Publications. Reprinted in William Wasserstrom, ed., *The Modern Short Novel* (New York: Holt, Rinehart and Winston, 1965).

Springer, Norman. "Bartleby and the Terror of Limitation." *PMLA* 80 (1965): 410-18.

Stafford, William T., ed. *James's Daisy Miller: The Story, The Play, The Critics.* Scribner Research Anthologies. New York: Charles Scribner's Sons, 1963.

Stein, Gertrude. *Three Lives.* New York: Vintage Books, Alfred A. Knopf and Random House, 1961.

Stein, William Bysshe. " 'The Pupil': The Education of a Prude." *Arizona Quarterly,* 15 (Spring 1959). Reprinted in Edward Stone, ed., *Henry James: Seven Stories and Studies* (New York: Appleton-Century-Crofts, 1961), pp. 193-98.

Steiner, George. *The Death of Tragedy.* New York: Hill and Wang, 1961.

Stevick, Philip, ed. *The Theory of the Novel.* New York: The Free Press, 1967.

Stone, Edward, ed. *Henry James: Seven Stories and Studies.* New York: Appleton-Century-Crofts, 1961.

Strelka, Joseph, ed. *Problems of Literary Evaluation*, 2. University Park: Pennsylvania State University Press, 1969.

Thurston, Jarvis. *Short Fiction Criticism.* Denver: Alan Swallow, 1960.

Tolstoy, Leo. *The Short Novels of Tolstoy.* Ed. Philip Rahv. Trans. Aylmer Maude. New York: Dial Press, 1949.

Trilling, Lionel. *The Liberal Imagination.* New York: Viking Press, 1950.

Tuve, Rosemond. *Allegorical Imagery.* Princeton: Princeton University Press, 1966.

Vivas, Eliseo. "Literary Classes: Some Problems." *Genre* 1, 2 (April 1968).

Voltaire. *Candide.* Bilingual edition. Trans. and ed. Peter Gay. New York: St. Martin's Press, 1963.

Warren, Austin, and Wellek, Rene. *Theory of Literature.* New York: Harcourt Brace, 1942.

Warren, Robert Penn. *The Circus in the Attic and Other Stories.* New York: Harcourt Brace, 1947.

Wasserstrom, William. *Heiress of All the Ages: Sex and Sentiment in the Genteel Tradition.* Minneapolis: University of Minnesota Press, 1959.

————, ed. *The Modern Short Novel.* New York: Holt, Rinehart and Winston, 1965.

Watt, Ian. *The Rise of the Novel.* Berkeley: University of California Press, 1965.

Weeks, Edward, ed. *Great Short Novels.* Garden City, N.Y.: Doubleday Doran, 1941.

Weigand, Hermann J. "Franz Kafka's 'The Burrow,'" *PMLA* 87 (March 1972): 153-65.

West, Anthony. "Books," *The New Yorker,* 8 May 1965, p. 177.

West, Nathanael. *A Cool Million: The Dismantling of Lemuel Pitkin.* London: Neville Spearman, 1954.

————. *Miss Lonelyhearts.* London: The Grey Walls Press, 1949.

West, Ray B., Jr. "Atmosphere and Theme in Faulkner's 'A Rose for Emily.'" *Perspective,* Summer 1949, 239-45.

West, Ray B., Jr., and Stallman, Robert Wooster, eds. *The Art of Modern Fiction.* New York: Rinehart, 1949.

Wickes, George, ed. *Masters of Modern British Fiction.* New York: Macmillan, 1963.

Wilson, Edmund. *Axel's Castle.* New York: Charles Scribner's Sons, 1948.

Winner, Anthony. *Great European Short Novels.* Vol. 1. New York: Harper & Row, 1968.

Woolf, Virginia. *A Room of One's Own.* New York: Harcourt Brace & World, 1963.

————. *Three Guineas.* New York: Harcourt Brace & World, 1938.

————. *The Common Reader.* New York: Harcourt Brace, 1925.

Wright, Austin McGiffert. *The American Short Story in the Twenties.* Chicago: University of Chicago Press, 1961.

Writers At Work. The Paris Review Interviews, Second Series. New York: The Viking Press, 1963.

Index

Actions: apologue devices in, 40; definition of, 10, 104; didactic emphasis
in, 31; direct speech in, 36; distinguished from apologues, 12, 20,
25–26, 30, 40, 49, 50–52, 64, 70, 74,
104, 119–27; distinguished from
example apologues, 56, 65–66, 68,
72; distinguished from satires, 84,
85, 95; plot and character expectations in, 30–31, 44; plot of, distinguished from apologue instability,
27; serious plot of character in,
129–60; statement-making as subordinate in, 40; tragic, 26; universality
in, 24

Albee, Edward, *The Sandbox,* 92

Allegory, 10, 98, 105; as deductive, 55,
169 n 2; devices of, 20; distinguished
from apologue, 55, 57; modern
distaste for, 20, 21, 56–57; personified abstractions in, 13, 42, 88;
pleasure of, 24; recognition of, 13,
23, 88; symbolic interpretation in, 35

Allusions to poetry and other arts: as
device of learning and maturing
plots, 138–40, 155–57

Ambassadors, The (James), 75

Amelioration, as formal purpose in
satire, 89, 98

Analogies of fiction with other arts:
with music, 150, 153; with
painting, 58, 136–37

Andreyev, Leonid, *The Seven Who
Were Hanged,* 41

Animal characters, 52; as device of
apologue, 41–42

Animal epithet, 126–27; in example
apologue, 67–68; in satire, 87

Animal Farm (Orwell), 93–95

Apologue: as alien to modern era, 21;
amount of dialogue in, 38; articulation of statement in, 28–30;
artificial elements in, 34; biblical
elements in, 37; character in,
25–30, 34, 120, 125–27; compendium of signals of, 39–51; cyclic
elements in, 33; definition of, 10,
40; devices of distance in, 40–42,
74; devices of, in satire, 98; diction
in, 28, 35, 37–39, 47–49, 50–51;
diffusion of characters as device of,
32–33, 41, 74; distance of character
as indispensable signal of, 40–42;
distinguished from actions, 12, 23,
30, 31, 40, 49, 50–51, 52, 64, 70, 74,
104, 119–27; distinguished from
allegory, 55, 57; distinguished from
parable, 46; distinguished from
"prophetic" actions, 24; distinguished from satire, 97–99; epic elements in, 34; epithet in, 34; generalization and overt statement as signal
of, 49–50; generic titles as signal of,
50; heavy-handed narrative as

Apologue (*continued*)
   signal of, 46; inductive, 49,
   169 n 2; intrusive narrator in, 38;
   irony in, 60; killing of character
   before story begins in, 41, 52; lack
   of dialogue as signal of, 48; length
   governed similarly to satire, 79;
   magnitude (length) of, 12, 19,
   51–53; not-naming and significant
   names in, 40–41; plot and character subsumed to requirements of,
   19, 31, 46–47, 60; plot of, distinguished from action plot, 25–26,
   29; present tense as device of, 43,
   121; relative plotlessness as signal
   of, 42–43; repetition of words and
   images as signal of, 33, 45–46;
   120–23; ritual and unnatural
   effects as signal of, 26, 34–35,
   44–45; as akin to satire in didactic
   ends, 98; short story length in,
   52–53; signals of, 39–51, 125;
   statement of, distinguished from
   "theme," 23, 37; statement *made*
   rather than *stated*, 46, 60;
   stereotypes in, 15; stylized prose as
   signal of, 50–51; symbolic interpretation in, 35; time manipulation in,
   43–44, 120–21; traditionally symbolic settings in, 46; universality in,
   23
Aristotle, 9, 10, 42, 51, 84, 104, 114,
   120, 129
Arnold, Matthew, 76, 100
Artificial elements, in apologue, 26,
   34–35, 44–45
Austen, Jane, 116; *Emma*, 116; *Pride
   and Prejudice*, 116
Authorial intention, 72–73, 96–97

Ballad of the Sad Café, The
   (McCullers), 43–44, 45, 46, 47, 48,
   49; apologue statement of,
   168–69 n 28
Balzac, Honoré de, 134
Bartleby the Scrivener (Melville), 4,
   130, 136–37
Baudelaire, Charles, 128

Beast in the Jungle, The (James),
   101, 110, 111, 116, 119, 125,
   126–27
Beck, Warren, 36
Bellow, Saul, 152, 156; *Seize the
   Day*, 152, 157
Benito Cereno (Melville), 4, 15,
   40–41, 42, 44, 47
Berchner, Paul, Rev., 35
Biblical elements, as device of
   apologue, 37; in *Old Man*, 37
Billy Budd (Melville), 4
Bleak House (Dickens), 20
Blue Hotel, The (Crane, S.), 41, 43,
   46, 57
Boccaccio, Giovanni, 17
Booth, Wayne C., 10, 18, 21, 22, 23,
   47, 52, 63, 111–12
Borges, Jorge Luis, 21
Bosch, Hieronymus, 58
Bowen, Elizabeth, 3; *Ivy Gripped the
   Steps*, 131
Brann, Eva, 105, 108, 150, 155
Bunyan, John, *Pilgrim's Progress*, 13,
   19, 42
Burke, Kenneth, 10
Burrow, The (Kafka), 40, 42, 43;
   animal character in, 41

Camus, Albert, *The Stranger*, 66, 103
Candide (Voltaire), 78–81, 88, 89, 95
"Caring," in apologue, 25–30
Cary, Joyce, 125
Castillo, Laura del, *A Plum for Coco*,
   107
Cather, Willa, 134
Cat's Cradle (Vonnegut), 12, 78, 89,
   94
Character: in actions, 56, 119,
   125–27; animal and subhuman, 41,
   126; in apologue, 15, 20, 33, 35,
   40, 41, 51, 52, 55, 125–27; in apologue and action, compared, 120;
   degeneration of, as a major plot
   type in tragic novellas, 102–9; in
   degenerative tragedy, 101–5,
   107–9, 115–20, 124; degree of
   realism of, in apologue, 40, 55;

Character (*continued*)
delineation of, in short story, 137;
diffusion of, as device of apologue,
32-33, 41, 74; diffusion of, in
satire, 95; distance-making devices
in delineation of, 40-42; "drop-
out," 138-39; in example apologue,
56, 59, 65, 67, 68, 70; killing of,
before story begins, 41, 52; in
maturing plot, 130-31; moral
norms for judgment of, 97; as
personified abstraction, 13, 20, 42;
relations in maturing plot, 150-53;
in satire, 79, 85-86, 95-99; "sore
thumb," in satires, 95-99;
"species," 42, 86; type, in example
apologue, 68; type, in satire,
81-83. *See also* Rhetoric of
character
Character plots: as one novella form,
12; novella length appropriate to,
131; reader's learning in, distinguished from apologue, 143;
serious power of, 13; three kinds
of, defined, 129-30
Character revelation plot, 131-37;
defined, 129; distinguished from
learning and maturing plots, 132,
142; doors in, 135; events governed
by achievement of reader's knowledge, 132; looking and seeing in,
142; material objects and furnish-
ings in, 133-35; novella length
ideal for, 137; windows in, 135-36;
as variation of character plot,
defined, 12
Chekhov, Anton, 117; *A Woman's
Kingdom*, 117, 120
Circus in the Attic, The (Warren),
41, 43, 51
Clarissa Harlowe (Richardson), 101,
104
Classification: defense of, 14-17, 31,
159-60, 167 n 14; overelaborate, 3
Coherence: in example apologue, 68;
of parts of satire, 88; versus
realism, 25
Colette, 149; *Julie de Carneilhan*, 12,
130, 132-37, 139, 142, 143, 147

Comedy, 112, 116, 131; as one formal
principle in actions, 10; lack of
comic form in novellas, 13; slippery
definition of, 13-14
Conjecture and hypothesis: in diction
of apologue, 38, 50; in diction of
example apologue, 67
Conrad, Joseph: *Heart of Darkness*,
2, 44, 46; *The Secret Sharer*, 131
Conspicuous narrator. *See* Intrusive
narrator
Contemporary: authorial certainty of
social assumptions in satire, 81;
debts to older authors and fictional
modes, 80; versus "modern,"
79-80
Crane, R. S., 1, 10, 11, 24, 39, 48,
50, 130
Crane, Stephen, 45, 49; *The Blue
Hotel*, 41, 43, 46, 57; *Maggie, a
Girl of the Streets*, 13, 42, 46, 56,
57-64, 65, 68, 72, 121; *The
Monster*, 57; *The Open Boat*,
38-39, 41, 42, 45-46, 48, 49-50, 57
Critical disagreements, 16-17
Cyclic elements, in apologue, 33

Daisy Miller (James), 4, 101,
110-15, 126
Dante, 42, 57, 98
Daumier, Honoré, 136
Dead, The (Joyce), 4, 157
Death in Venice (Mann), 4, 7, 12,
13, 102-5, 106, 108-9, 120, 125,
129, 149-50
Death of Ivan Ilyich, The (Tolstoy),
2, 41, 43-44, 65, 72, 121; apologue statement of, 56
Death of the Lion, The (James), 12,
81, 83-87, 88, 89, 90, 95-97
Deductive allegory, 55, 169 n 2
Degenerative tragedy: character in,
101-9, 115-20, 129; character
degeneration as a major plot type
in, 102-9; contrasted with "high"
tragedy, 106-7, 109, 117-18;
defined, 12, 101-2; diction of, 102,
109, 122-25; distance in, 103-5;

Degenerative tragedy (*continued*)
distinguished from apologue and
satire, 119–27; "education" in,
116–17; helpless children in, 107;
death as end of, 102; irony in,
108–9; lack of "reversal" in,
103–4, 107; length of, 12, 115,
125; as a major novella form,
100–127; "middle-class sensibility"
in, 101–2; pity aroused by, 102–5,
109; two plots of, 120; repetition in,
120–25; simple plot of, 101–2, 120,
129; situational degeneration as a
major plot type in, 102, 109–25;
time manipulation in, compared
with apologue, 119–21; universalization in, 123–24. *See also*
Tragedy

Dialogue: relative lack of, as signal of
apologue, 48, 52; underplayed in
satire, 85

Dickens, Charles: *Bleak House*, 20;
Great Expectations, 130

Diction: in apologue, 35, 38, 50–51;
artificial, 34, 52, 58; in character
plots, 129; in character revelation
plot, 142; of conjecture and hypothesis in apologue and example
apologue, 38, 67; in *Daisy Miller,*
113; in degenerative tragedy, 102,
109, 122–25; exaggerated, in satire
and apologue, 98; governed by
form, 15, 36; in learning plots,
142–43, 146–47; in satire, 82–83,
87, 89; overbrilliant, obscures
character, 51; of universality, in
apologue, 37–39; of universality, in
example apologue, 66. *See also*
Rhetoric of diction

Didact and satirist compared, 97–99

Didactic: classes of didactic literature, 169–70 n 2; distinguished from
mimetic, 96–97; functioning with
realism, 62–63; historical movement of, toward realism, 57;
making use of feelings for didactic
ends, 13; and mimetic not
"mutually exclusive" narrative

procedures, 52; modern inclination
toward, 31; related to realism, 21;
tone in apologue, 49. *See also*
Allegory; Apologue; Example
apologue

Didactic power, 9

Diffusion of character: as device of
satire, 95; as distance-making
device of apologue, 41

Direct speech, in actions, 36

Disappointment of reader: assuaged
by recognition of form, 40; based
on imperfect form, 168 n 21; based
on misapprehension of form, 25

Distance: in apologue, 31, 40–42,
74, 98; by means of reductive epithet, 59; on character as indispensable sign of apologue, 40; in
degenerative tragedy, 103–5; devices
of, listed, 40–42; in example
apologue, 57–58, 68, 127; and
length, 52; and intrusive narrator,
38–39, 47, 48; and realism, 55;
in satire, 85–86, 95, 98

Doctor Faustus (Mann), 157

Doors: in character plot, 135, 157;
in learning plot, 143, 146–48; in
maturing plot, 154–55

Dostoevsky, Fyodor, 58, 60; *Notes
from the Underground*, 4, 54, 66,
70, 124; ——— apologue statement
of, 56

"Drop-out" characters, 138, 139

Dynamis, 11, *passim*

Edel, Leon, 111

Edelstein, Arthur, 64

Editors' constriction of novella
length, 6–10

Education, as destructive force in
tragedy, 116–17

Eliot, George, *Middlemarch*, 46

Elliott, George P., "The NRACP,"
89, 92–93

Ellipsis, in example apologue, 70

Emma (Austen), 116

Emotional power, 11, *passim*

Epic elements, 58; in apologue, 34; in *Old Man*, 37

Episodic structure: plot of satire, 89, 91; affords pure reader response to the good in satire, 95

Epithet: animal, 126-27; in apologue, 34; in example apologue, 58, 63; generic, 40; Homeric, 42; reductive, 59, 67, 82

Ethical judgment: overt in satire, 90; provided by animal narrator, 41-42; related to rhetoric of character, 97

Everyman, 20

Example apologue, 43, 54-76, 120; use of animal epithet in, 67-68; character in, 56, 59, 60, 65, 67, 137; definition of, 13; distinguished from action, 56, 65-66, 66-67, 68, 72; use of ellipsis, 70; future tense in, 67; generalization in, 69; implicit statement in, 13, 56; as inductive, 169 n 2; length limits, 72; use of names, 69; pleasure in, 71; realism in, 63; repetition in, 67; rhetoric of plot in, 60, 71, 72-73; rhetorical questions in, 67; "scene of suffering" in, 126-27; selectivity of events in, 63, 68; suspense in, 65, 70-72; time gaps in, 72, 121; universalization in, 123-24

Fable, 10, 42; as analogical proof, 169 n 2; length of, 52; recognition of, 23; revealed by tacked-on statement, 13

Farewell to Arms, A (Hemingway), 103-4

Faulkner, William, 36, 57; "A Rose for Emily," 41, 52, 53, 72; *Old Man*, 37-39, 40, 42, 43, 45, 46; ——— apologue statement of, 70-71; *Red Leaves*, 41; *Spotted Horses*, 32-37, 41, 45-46, 51, 70; ——— apologue statement of, 32

Finnegan's Wake (Joyce), 54

Fitz Gerald, Gregory, 96, 98

Fitzgerald, F. Scott, *The Great Gatsby*, 46

Flaubert, Gustave, 58; *A Simple Heart*, 43, 121; ——— apologue statement of, 56; *The Legend of St. Julian Hospitator*, 44-45, 48

Fletcher, Angus, 42, 43, 45

Foley, Martha, 3-4

Form: critical recognition of, 23; critical suspicion of formal analysis, 14; definition of, 10-11; disappointment in failure to recognize, 25; disappointment resulting from misapprehension of, 25, 64; distinguished from structure, 11; distinguished from total of parts, 11; forms as "mutually exclusive," 10; governs use of devices, 120, 125-26; hypothesizing of, 24; as illumination of both more and less perfect works, 72-76; intuitive recognition of, 64; length governed by, 6, 9; list of novella forms, 11-13; narrative manner related to, 119; new variations of old forms, 23; not prescriptive, 76, 114; and emotional power, 11; not a "total" but a "whole," 90; plural forms in each genre, 5; polemic on value of formal analysis and classification, 14-17; psychology of, 19; related to historical period, 78-80; revealed by grouped devices, 126; of satire, 88; of satire, not limited to the negative, 89-90; study of, as freeing activity, 14; textual comparison as indicator of, 122

Formal principle: of actions, 10, 104; of apologue, 10, 40; of satire, 10, 99

Formal purposes, related to length, 9-10

Forster, E. M., 8, 24, 25, 79-80, 84, 129

Fox, The (Lawrence), 30-32, 40, 41, 120, 147

Frame, 59. *See also* Distance

Freud, Sigmund, 124
Friedman, Norman, 102, 116, 130, 132
Frye, Northrop, 81, 88, 89, 98
Future tense, in example apologue, 67

Galsworthy, John, 5
Gargano, James, 110
Geist, Stanley, 113
Generalization: and overt statement as signal of apologue, 49-50, 52; in example apologue, 66-67, 68, 69, 126; not always apologue signal, 120
Generic titles as signal of apologue, 50
Genre: definition of, 4-5; encompasses several "kinds" or forms, 5
George's Mother (Crane), 64
German novelle, 2, 165-66 n 4
Gillespie, Gerald, 2, 9, 17, 166 n 5
Goodbye, Columbus (Roth), 155-57
"Grace" (Joyce), 91, 96
Great Dictator, The (Chaplin), 92
Great Expectations (Dickens), 130
Great Gatsby, The (Fitzgerald), 46
Gulliver's Travels (Swift), 12, 78-81, 88, 91, 95

Hamlet, 65-66, 101, 103, 109, 117, 149
Hardy, Thomas, 101
Hawthorne, Nathaniel, 52
Hayes, Richard, 100
Heart of Darkness (Conrad), 2, 44, 46
Heavy-handed narrative or authorial commentary, as signal of apologue, 46. See also Intrusive narrator
Heller, Erich, 102
Hemingway, Ernest, 20; A Farewell to Arms, 103-4; "Hills Like White Elephants," 137
Highet, Gilbert, 96
Hobbes, Thomas, 41

Homer, 42, 84
Howe, Irving, 106, 128
Howells, William Dean, 8
Humor: as device of distance in satire, 95; distinct from ridicule, 89; effect of humorlessness in satire, 93; as integral to definition of satire, 89; related to ameliorative purpose of satire, 89-90

Interpretation, changes of, 17
Intrusive narrator: in Daisy Miller, 111; in example apologue, 70, 127; function of, 47; not pleasurable at great length, 52; positive effect of, 48; realism versus, 38; in modern fiction, 38, 46-47; as signal and unifying device of apologue, 46-48
Intuition: in apprehension of form, 24-25, 64; in interpretation, 35; related to novella length, 120
Irony: in animal narrators, 93; in apologue, 60; in Daisy Miller, 110-11; definition of, 94; in degenerative tragedy, 105, 109; excess of, can lead to misreading, 114; in example apologue, 64; in inverse ratio with pathos in degenerative tragedy, 110; as limitation on tragic power, 101-2, 111-15; in parodic plot of satire, 81, 83; related to the good in satire, 94; in significant names, 86
Ivy Gripped the Steps (Bowen), 131

Jackson, Shirley, "The Lottery," 52
James, Henry, 1, 6-10, 15-16, 21-22, 46, 47, 55, 73-74, 75, 77, 79-80, 102; The Ambassadors, 75; The Beast in the Jungle, 101, 110, 111, 116, 119, 125, 126-27; Daisy Miller, 4, 101, 110-15, 126; The Death of the Lion, 12, 81, 83-87, 88, 89, 90, 95-97; The Lesson of the Master, 6; The Portrait of a Lady, 12, 130; The Pupil, 72-76, 107;

James, Henry (*continued*)
  Washington Square, 101, 110, 115, 129, 132
Johnson, Samuel, 19, 20, 21, 29
Journey structure of satire, 83, 88
Joyce, James, 54; "Counterparts," 52; *Finnegans Wake,* 54; "Grace," 91; *The Dead,* 4, 157; *A Portrait of the Artist as a Young Man,* 157; *Ulysses,* 72
Julie de Carneilhan (Colette), 12, 130, 132-37, 139, 142, 143, 147

Kafka, Franz, 120; *The Burrow,* 40, 42, 43; ―――― animal character in, 41; *The Metamorphosis,* 105-10, 120, 129; "animal" character in, 41
Kellogg, Robert, 24, 52
Killing of characters before story begins, 41, 52
King Lear, 117
Kipling, Rudyard, *The Man Who Would Be King,* 50

Langland, William, 57
Lawrence, D. H., 34, 41, 44, 50, 55, 128, 149; *The Fox,* 30-32, 40, 41, 120, 147; *The Man Who Died,* 50; *The Man Who Loved Islands,* 40, 47, 50; *The Virgin and the Gypsy,* 137, 142-48, 149; *The Woman Who Rode Away,* 25-32, 38, 40, 42, 44, 48, 50, 55, 120
Learning plots, 137-48; allusion to poetry and art in, 138-40; as common novella form, 130; defined, 129-30; diction of looking and seeing in, 142; material objects in, 139; may end in failure to learn, 130-31; plot in, 138; as variation of character plot, defined, 12
Leavis, F. R., 27, 64
Legend of St. Julian Hospitator, The (Flaubert), 44-45, 48
Length: of apologue, 51-53; of char-

acter plots, 131; of character revelation plot, 137; of degenerative tragedy, 103, 108, 115, 124, 125; editor's constriction of, 6-10; of example apologue, 72; of learning plot, 130; of maturing plot, 130-31; and formal purposes, 9-10; and the good in satires, 89, 93; and narrative progressions, 63; and realism, 55; and repetition, 124-25; related to simple plot, 120; related to story line structure, 42; in satire, 83, 97; of satires and apologues, 79. *See also* Magnitude
Lesson of the Master, The (James), 6
Literary devices: as "cronies," 126; as subservient to form, 20
"Little Herr Friedemann" (Mann), 82
Looking and seeing, in character revelation and learning plots, 142
Lorenz, Konrad, 16
"Lottery, The" (Jackson), 52
Love among the Cannibals (Morris), 54
Love among the Ruins (Waugh), 84, 89
Lubbock, Percy, 4, 32

Mack, Maynard, 90
McCullers, Carson, *The Ballad of the Sad Café,* 43-44, 45, 46, 47, 48, 49; apologue statement of, 168-69 n 28
Maggie, a Girl of the Streets (Crane), 13, 42, 57-64, 65, 68, 72, 121; apologue statement of, 56
Magnitude: of apologue, 51-53; related to "likely and necessary," 9; related to narrative progressions, 63-64. *See also* Length
Mailer, Norman, *The Man Who Studied Yoga,* 43, 50
"Man" and "Woman," in generic titles of apologue, 50
Man Who Corrupted Hadleyburg, The (Twain), 50
Man Who Died, The (Lawrence), 50

Man Who Lived Underground, The
(Wright), 50
Man Who Loved Islands, The
(Lawrence), 40, 47, 50
Man Who Studied Yoga, The
(Mailer), 43, 50
Man Who Would Be King, The
(Kipling), 50
Mann, Thomas, 172 n 6; *Death in
Venice*, 7, 12, 13, 102–5, 106,
108–9, 120, 125, 129, 149–50;
Doctor Faustus, 157; "The Infant
Prodigy," 172 n 6; "Little Herr
Friedemann," 82; *Mario and the
Magician*, 46; *Tonio Kröger*, 12,
82, 105, 148–57; *Tristan*, 81–83,
87, 88, 89, 91, 96
Mario and the Magician (Mann), 46
Material objects, 135–36; in learning
plots, 139, 142–44; in *Old Mortal-
ity*, 139, 142
Matisse, Henri, 136
Maturing plot, 148–57; defined, 130;
in novella contrasted with novel,
130–31; as variation of character
plot, defined, 12
May, Elaine, *Adaptation*, 92
Melanctha (Stein), 117–25, 129, 132
Melville, Herman, 21, 55; *Bartleby
the Scrivener*, 4, 130, 136–37;
Benito Cereno, 4, 15, 40–41, 42,
44, 47; *Billy Budd*, 4
Metamorphosis, The (Kafka), 4,
105–10, 120, 129; "animal"
character in, 41
Middlemarch (Eliot), 46
Millett, Kate, 26, 29
Mimetic, distinguished from didactic,
96–97
Mirrors (or looking glasses): in character revelation plots, 132–36; in
learning plots, 142–43; in both,
147–48, 156–57
"Modern" versus "contemporary,"
79–80; less-certain social assumptions distinguish satirists of, 81
Modest Proposal, A (Swift), 92, 96
Monster, The (Crane), 57

Morrell, Roy, 124
Morris, Wright, *Love among the
Cannibals*, 54

Nabokov, Vladimir, 5
Names: in degenerative tragedy,
123–24; effect of proper, as against
generic, 41; humorous, in satire,
89; not-naming in apologue, 27,
37, 40–41, 52, 124; significant, in
apologue and example apologue,
41, 58, 68, 69, 86; suggestive and
ironic, in satire, 86
Narrative: animal, 41–42; commentary in actions, 36; progression,
distinguished from plot, 60–64; in
satire, 85–86. *See also* Rhetoric of
narrative manner
Naturalism: declining in contemporary fiction, 80; uncongenial with
strict form, 80
Necessity: in character revelation
plots, 132; of plot elements in
degenerative tragedy, 121; of plot
elements in example apologue, 121;
related to Aristotelian magnitude, 9
Nemerov, Howard, 1
Noon Wine (Porter), 11
Not-naming, in apologue, 27, 37,
40–41, 52, 124. *See also* Names
Notes from the Underground (Dostoevsky), 4, 54, 66, 70, 124; apologue
statement of, 56
Nouvelle, 6–7. *See also* Terminology
Novel: compared to novella, 4, 8, 11,
13, 15, 41–42, 64, 75, 120, 145,
148, 157; definitions of, 3, 8; differences from short story, 5; formal
consideration of, 2; maturing plot
of, contrasted with novella, 12,
130–31
Novelette, as less satisfactory term
then "novella," 3. *See also*
Terminology
Novella: anthologies, 2–4, 79; arises
in nineteenth century, 17; as better
term than "novelette" or "short

Novella (*continued*)
novel," 3-4 (*see also* Terminology);
character dominance in, 129; compared to novel, 4, 8, 11, 13, 15,
41-42, 64, 75, 101-4, 120, 145,
148, 157; compared to short story,
2-3, 6-8, 10, 11, 12, 13, 14-15,
52-53, 63-64, 157; compared to
sonata, 153; definition of, 9, 11,
15; as distinct genre, 5; distinguished by its several forms, 11-14;
forms of, listed, 11-13; frequency
of learning plot, 130; lack of
formal comedy in, 13-14; lack of
theory of, 2-7; length limits of, 5,
6-7, 8, 9, 10, 12, 13, 15, 137;
plural forms or "qualities" of the,
8-9; problem of defining, 1-10;
rise in nineteenth century, 8, 17;
shapeliness and beauty of, 6-7,
passim; incompatible with naturalism, 80; in translation, formal
problems of, 172-73 n 6; in the
twentieth century, 17
Novelle, 17. *See also* Terminology
"NRACP, The" (Elliott), 89, 92-93
Number: "magic," attached to repetition, 38; seven, 38, 50; seven and
three, 44

O'Brien, Edward, 3-4
O'Connor, Flannery: *The Violent
Bear It Away*, 14; *Wise Blood*, 14
Oedipus Rex (Sophocles), 101, 103
Of This Time, Of That Place (Tril-
ling), 131
Old Man (Faulkner), 37-39, 40, 42,
43, 45, 46; apologue statement of,
70-71
Old Mortality (Porter), 12, 137-42,
148, 149, 153, 155, 157
Olson, Elder, 10, 18, 90, 98, 100
*One Day in the Life of Ivan Denis-
ovitch* (Solzhenitsyn), 57, 59,
65-72, 121, 122, 126, 127; apo-
logue statement of, 56
Open Boat, The (Crane), 38-39, 41,

42, 45-46, 48, 57; apologue state-
ment of, 49-50
Organizing principle, 32, 78
Ortega y Gasset, José, 16
Orwell, George: *Animal Farm*,
92-95; "Why I Write," 93
"Overfurnished" fiction, 134,
174-75 n 5
Overt good, in satire, 97-99
Overt statement, in apologue, 65

Parable, 10, 98; as analogical proof,
169 n 2; distinguished from apologue, 46
Paris Review, 7
Parodic plot, of satire, 81-83
Pater, Walter, 159-60
Pathos: character related to, 129; in
inverse ratio with irony in degenerative tragedy, 110; limited by irony,
111-15; of lonely protagonist, 105;
as power of "tragic" novellas, 101;
as slenderer than tragedy, 115. *See
also* Degenerative tragedy
Paul, Saint, 155
Phaedrus (Plato), 17
Photographs and paintings, as device
of learning and maturing plots,
142, 146, 155
Pilgrim Hawk, The (Wescott), 137
Pilgrim's Progress (Bunyan), 13, 19,
42
Platonic dialogue: as access to truth
about fiction, 16-17; as lacking in
Death in Venice, 105; in *Tonio
Kröger*, 149-55; structure of,
153-55
Playtime (Tati), 91, 96
Pleasure: in allegory, 24; in character
revelation plot, 136; in degenerative
tragedy, 129; in the didactic and
mimetic, 51-53; in example apologue, 71; in recognition of form,
16, 40, 72
Plot: in actions, 25; in apologue, 25,
40, 42-43; character degeneration
as major type of, in tragic novellas,

Plot (*continued*)
102, 106-7, 120, 132; of character
revelation, 129-30, 131, 132;
distinguished from story line,
42, 63; elements of "speech,"
"scene," and "episode," 132; in
example apologue, 71, 121, 127; of
learning, defined, 129-31; of
maturing, defined, 129-30; parodic,
in satire, 81-83; in satire novellas,
78, 81, 83-87, 95; "simple," in degenerative tragedy, 12, 101-2, 120;
situational degeneration as a major
type of, in tragic novellas, 120;
structure of, in *Melanctha*, 118-21;
subordination of expectations in
learning plot, 138; "tyranny" of,
25, 129, 167 n 10
Plotlessness, as signal of apologue,
42-43
Plum for Coco, A (del Castillo), 107
"Pocket of Good" in satire, 77, 83,
87-99; demonstration of the good as
necessity in social protest satires,
92-93; does not violate unity,
95-97
Poetics (Aristotle), 9, 10, 51, 129
Point of view: in actions, 75; in *Daisy
Miller*, 111; in example apologue,
65, 66, 68, 70; in learning plot,
138-39; in *Melanctha*, 123; in *The
Pupil*, 74; in satire, 85; in *The
Virgin and the Gypsy*, 144-45
Pope, Alexander, 77
Portability of literary devices, 120
Porter, Katherine Anne, 7, 11, 52;
Old Mortality, 12, 137-42, 148,
149, 153, 155, 157; *Noon Wine*,
11; *Ship of Fools*, 7, 52
Portrait of a Lady, The (James), 12,
130
*Portrait of the Artist as a Young Man,
A* (Joyce), 157
"Positive heart" of satire, 87-92
Power: achieved best at "likely or
necessary" length, 9; of apologue,

11, 19, 22-53; comic, 13-14, 116;
irony in ratio to the pathetic, 101,
114-15; pathetic, compared to
serious, 136; pathetic, increased by
"education," 116-17; pathetic, as
predominant in "tragic" novellas,
12, 100, 101-2, 105, 106, 109-10
112; or "potential feeling" of fictional forms, 11; of satire, includes
positive purpose, 89, 97-98; serious, 12, 13, 116, 129, 136, 137;
serious defined, 131; tragic, 12, 13,
100, 101-27, 129
Present tense: in apologue, 121; universality of, 43
Pride and Prejudice (Austen), 116
"Prophetic" actions, distinguished
from apologue, 24
Prose fiction, science of, 14
Proust, Marcel, *Remembrance of
Things Past*, 153
Pupil, The (James), 72-76, 107

Questions: as device of learning and
maturing plots, 137-42, 147-48,
156; in *Old Mortality*, 139-41; in
Tonio Kröger, 149, 151-54; in *The
Virgin and the Gypsy*, 148

Rahv, Philip, 30, 80
Rasselas (Johnson), 19, 20, 29
Realism, 169 n 1; in apologue, 35;
functions organically, 55; governed
by form, 80; intrusive narrator
and, 38; is never really real, 80;
in modern fiction, 21; lessened in
contemporary fiction, 80; modern
taste for, 55, 167 n 10; moves across
formal boundaries, 57; paradoxically related to plot, 83-84; related
to ritual elements, 44; in satire, 79,
83, 89; twentieth-century, 44
"Recognition": in tragedy, 112, 120;
in maturing plot, 152-53

Red Leaves (Faulkner), 41

Remembrance of Things Past (Proust), 153

Repetition: as device of apologue, 33; in apologue and degenerative tragedy compared, 120-23; of epithet, 59; in example apologue, 67; may function to reveal change, 62; of numbers in apologue, 38; psychology of, in tragedy, 124-25; related to length, 52, 124-25; of words and images in apologue, 45-46

"Reversal," in tragedy, 120

Rhetoric of character: Aristotle on, 129; in actions, 119-20; in apologue, 19-20, 22, 25-34, 40-42; in character-revelation plot compared to example apologue, 136-37; in degenerative tragedy, 101-9, 115-20; differences of, in apologue and action, 125-27; in example apologue, 65-68, 74-76; in learning plots, 138-48; in maturing plot, 150-53; related to ethical judgments, 97; in satire, 79, 81-83, 85-86, 95-97; two-dimensional character in apologue, 42; in *The Virgin and the Gypsy*, 144-46. *See also* Character

Rhetoric of diction: in character revelation and learning plots, 142; in example apologue, 66-68; in learning plots, 139, 146-47; in satire, 82-83; in degenerative tragedy, 102, 109; in *Melanctha*, 122-25; in recognition of form, 120. *See also* Diction

Rhetoric of narrative manner, 120; in satire, 85-86. *See also* Narrative

Rhetoric of plot: Aristotle on, 129; in character plots, 131-32; in degenerative tragedy, 101-2; in relatively plotted structures of satire, 83-87; in example apologue, 72-73; in *Melanctha*, 118-20; in satire, 78, 79, 81-83, 86-87, 95. *See also* Plot

Rhetorical question: as device of example apologue, 67; in learning plots, 141

Richards, I. A., 125

Ridicule: not the exclusive formal component of satire, 77, 78, 87-99; not invariably humorous, 89

Ritual elements, 26, 30, 48, 59; as apologue device, 44-45, 55; rare in actions, 125

Robertson, D. W., 21

Romain, Jules, 17

Room of One's Own, A (Woolf), 84, 167 n 10

"Rose for Emily, A" (Faulkner), 41, 52-53, 72

Rosenheim, Edward W., Jr., 77

Roth, Philip, 155

Sacks, Sheldon, 10, 18, 19, 22, 23, 24, 46, 70, 88-89, 90, 94, 96-97, 98-99, 104, 171 n 12

Sandbox, The (Albee), 92

Satire: as "allegory in reverse gear," 88; and apologue akin in didactic ends, 98; character in, 79, 85-86; compared with tragedy, 101, 119-20; definitions of, 10, 11, 12, 88, 99, 171 n 8; distinguished from actions, 84, 85, 95; distinguished from apologue, 40, 87-88, 97-99; "good" characters in, 95-97; episodic plot in, 12, 78; humor in, 88-90; journey structure in, 88; length of, 78, 79, 83, 97; in media other than fiction, 91-92; more ironic when less certain, 81; names in, 86; narration in, 85-86; parodic plot in, 81-83; picks up minor objects of ridicule, 78-79, 83; positive purpose in power of, 97-99; prescriptive ruling out of the good in, 88-89; redefinition of, 90-91, 99; with single object of ridicule, 83-84; in social protest novellas, 81, 92-95; Swiftian structures and de-

Satire (*continued*)
  vices of, 80–81; weak links of plot
  and character in, 85
Satiric power, 9
Satirist and didact compared, 97–99
"Scene of suffering" compared in
  tragic action and "tragical" apo-
  logue, 126–27
Scholes, Robert, 24, 52
Schorer, Mark, 5
Science of prose fiction, 14
Secret Sharer, The (Conrad), 131
Seize the Day (Bellow), 152, 157
Selectivity of events in example apo-
  logue, 63, 68, 71
Serious power, 9, 157; available at
  novella length, 137; of character
  plots, 13; defined, 131; as one for-
  mal principle in actions, 10–11; of
  learning plots, 138; natural to
  learning and maturing plots, 131
Seven Who Were Hanged, The
  (Andreyev), 41
Shakespeare, 80, 91; *Hamlet*,
  65–66, 101, 103, 109, 117, 149;
  Troilus and Cressida, 91, 95
Ship of Fools (Porter), 7, 52
Short novel, 17. *See also* Terminology
Short story: allegory in, 55; as apologue, 52–53, 72; attempt to
  define, 3; character delineation in,
  137; compared to novella, 2–3,
  6–8, 10, 12, 13, 14–15, 52–53,
  63–64, 157; as condensation of
  novel, 2; difference in unity between novel and, 5; length of, 2,
  6–7, 10; theory of, 2
Shroder, Maurice, 101
Significant names as signal of apologue, 75
Simple Heart, A (Flaubert), 43, 121;
  apologue statement of, 56
Simple plot in degenerative tragedy,
  12, 100–102, 120, 129
Singer, Isaac Bashevis, 21
Situational degeneration as a major
  plot type in tragic novellas, 109–25

Slaughterhouse Five (Vonnegut),
  78–81, 89, 91
Social protest novella satires, 81,
  92–95
Socrates, 17, 156
Solzhenitsyn, Alexander, 58, 60; *One
  Day in the Life of Ivan Denisovitch*, 57, 59, 65–72, 121, 122, 126,
  127
"Sore thumb" characters, 87, 90,
  95–99
Spenser, Edmund, 57
Spotted Horses (Faulkner), 32–37,
  41, 45–46, 51, 70; apologue statement of, 32
Statement: of apologue confirms
  form, 40; of apologue *made*, distinct from *stated*, 46; apologue, of
  Old Man, 37; apologue, of *Spotted
  Horses*, 32; articulation of, in apologue, 36; difficult to abstract from
  actions, 40; in example apologue,
  56, 127; of apologues may be
  related to author's life and times,
  55; as organizing principle of apologue, 40; overt, in apologue, 46,
  49–50, 65; rhetorical question as,
  50. *See also* Apologue; Example
  apologue
Static character in degenerative tragedy, 124
Stein, Gertrude, 102, 117
Steiner, George, 101, 106
Stevens, Wallace, 136
Story line: distinguished from plot,
  20, 42, 60, 63; as "plot" of apologue and example apologue, 42,
  47, 70; structure of, related to
  novella length, 42
Stranger, The (Camus), 66, 103
Stylized prose, as apologue signal,
  50–51
Subhuman or animal characters, as
  distancing device of apologue, 41
Suspense, in example apologue,
  70–72
Swift, Jonathan, 84, 89; *A Modest*

Proposal, 92, 96; *Gulliver's Travels,* 12, 78-81, 88, 91, 95
Symbolic interpretation: in allegory and apologue, 35; in *Old Man,* 37
Symbols: in degenerative tragedy, 125; not a certain sign of apologue, 39; symbolic names in example apologue, 68; traditional, 35

Tati, Jacques: *Playtime,* 91-92
Technical improvement of fiction, 57, 80
Terminology: of didactic fiction, 23; novella, 2, 3-4, 5-7, 17
Textual comparison of forms, 122, 125-27
Theme: as critical principle, 12-13; in diction of *Maggie,* 61-62; discussion of, inhibits definition of novella, 165 n 3 and 4; distinguished from apologue statement, 23, 37; enlarged to apologue statement, 45-46; as imposition, 32; musical, in *Tonio Kröger,* 153; study of, detracts from attention to character, 12; thematic criticism versus formal criticism, 27
Thibaudet, Albert, 54
Time: gaps in, 43, 52, 72, 74, 121; uncertainty of, in apologue, 43; universality of present tense, 43
Time manipulation: in apologue and degenerative tragedy compared, 120-21; as signal of apologue, 43-44; in degenerative tragedy, 119
Tindall, William York, 27
Tolstoy, Leo, 60, 134; *The Death of Ivan Ilyich,* 2, 41, 43-44, 65, 72, 121; —— apologue statement of, 56
Tom Jones (Fielding), 41, 46, 48, 116
Tonio Kröger (Mann), 12, 82, 105 148-57
Traditional symbolic settings, 46
Tragedy: distinguished from "tragical" apologue, 26, 125-27; "high,"

distinguished from pathetic, 101-2; limited in the novella, 13, 101; as one formal principle of actions, 10-11; plot of, 9, 84; plot and character compared in achievement of, 129; as protest, 101-2; "real" characters in, 15; related to satire by irony, 101; "scene of suffering" in, 126-27; "wildness" in, 101-2; 106. *See also* Degenerative tragedy; Pathos; Tragic power
Tragic power: compared to serious, 131; limited in the novella, 13, 101; minimal definition of, 101. *See also* Degenerative tragedy; Pathos; Tragedy
Translation, of novellas, 172-73 n 6
Trilling, Lionel, 48; *Of This Time, Of That Place,* 131
Tristan (Mann), 81-83, 87, 88, 89, 91, 96
Troilus and Cressida (Shakespeare), 91, 95
Tuve, Rosemond, 60
Twain, Mark, *The Man Who Corrupted Hadleyburg,* 50

Ulysses (Joyce), 72
Unity of structure in example apologue, 60
Universality: of forms, transcends time, 23; in actions, 24; by means of comparison, 38; in diction of example apologue, 66-67; of diction not a certain sign of apologue, 39; in degenerative tragedy and example apologue compared, 123-24; diction of, 127; historical, as apologue device, 37; in *Old Man,* 37; of present tense, 43; in significant names, 41

Violent Bear It Away, The (O'Connor), 14

Virgin and the Gypsy, The (Lawrence), 137, 142–48, 149
Visconti, Luchino, 103
Voltaire, 84; *Candide*, 78–81, 88, 89, 95
Vonnegut, Kurt, Jr., 84, 92; *Cat's Cradle*, 12, 78, 89, 94; *Slaughterhouse Five*, 78–81, 89, 91

Warren, Robert Penn, 17; *The Circus in the Attic*, 41, 43, 51
Washington Square (James), 101, 110, 115, 129, 132
Wasserstrom, William, 113–14
Watt, Ian, 41
Waugh, Evelyn, 78, 81, 84
Weigand, Hermann, 49

Wellek, René, 17
Wescott, Glenway, 137
Wimsatt, W. K., 11
Windows: in character plots, 135–36; in learning plots, 143, 146–48; in maturing plots, 154–57
Wise Blood (O'Connor), 14
Woman Who Rode Away, The (Lawrence), 25–32, 38, 40, 42, 44, 48, 50, 55, 120
Woman's Kingdom, A (Chekov), 117, 120
Woolf, Virginia, *A Room of One's Own*, 25, 84, 167 n 10

"Yellow Book, The," 6
Youth (Conrad), 46